To Philip

A

CW00321801

01

Field Guide
to the
WILDLIFE
of Britain and Europe

LAROUSSE

Field Guide
to the
WILDLIFE
of Britain and Europe

General Editor
MICHAEL CHINERY

LAROUSSE

Artists

Terry Callcut
Martin Camm
Denys Ovenden
Gordon Riley
Bernard Robinson
Rod Sutterby
George Thompson
Norman Weaver
David Wright

Larousse plc
Elsley House, 24–30 Great Titchfield Street,
London W1P 7AD

This edition published by Larousse plc 1996

10 9 8 7 6 5 4 3 2 1

First published by Kingfisher 1987

A CIP record for this book is available from
the British Library

ISBN 0 7523 0042 3

Phototypeset by Southern Positives and
Negatives (SPAN), Lingfield, Surrey
Colour separations by Newsele Litho, Milan
Printed in Portugal

CONTENTS

INTRODUCTION
Michael Chinery
Page 6

CHAPTER ONE
MAMMALS
Iain Bishop
Page 18

CHAPTER TWO
BIRDS
Neil Ardley
Page 60

CHAPTER THREE
REPTILES AND AMPHIBIANS
Michael Chinery
Page 153

CHAPTER FOUR
FISHES
Alwyne Wheeler
Page 169

CHAPTER FIVE
INVERTEBRATES
Michael Chinery
Page 188

INDEX
Page 280

USEFUL ADDRESSES
Page 288

INTRODUCTION

Wherever you go, whether it is simply into your garden or further afield to the forest or seashore, or even into the middle of town, you will find wildlife of some description around you. It is always satisfying to be able to put names to the animals you see and even more satisfying to discover something about their natural history – their reasons for being where they are. This field guide is designed to provide just such information.

The area covered by this book is essentially Western Europe, although a few species from Greece and neighbouring areas are included. With the exception of the little-visited tundra of the far north, all the major habitats of Western Europe are covered – the coniferous forest belt, the deciduous forests of the central region and the dry Mediterranean area with its largely evergreen vegetation. Added to these major life zones are the mountains, lakes and rivers, coastal waters, and the vast expanses of grassland created through human destruction of the original forests during the last few thousand years.

Each of these habitats supports its characteristic animal life. A single book could not possibly cover all the species found in the different habitats, but the great majority of European birds and mammals are included here, as are many of the reptiles, amphibians and fishes you are likely to come across. The invertebrates – the insects and other 'creepy-crawlies' – are much more numerous than the other types of animal life and only a small proportion of the thousands of European species can be covered here. All the major groups are represented, however, and the illustrations will enable you to name most of the larger and more colourful invertebrates that come to your notice.

Classification

Throughout this book the animals are arranged in their natural groupings, the largest of which are the phyla (singular: phylum). All the backboned animals (vertebrates) belong to the phylum Chordata, and the mammals, birds, reptiles, amphibians and fishes fall into different classes of this phylum. The phyla to which the invertebrates (animals without backbones) belong are similarly divided into classes (see page 188). The classes are split into orders and the orders into families – whose names always end in -idae. The members of a family have much in common and often look quite similar. They are arranged in a number of smaller groups called genera (singular: genus), each of which contains one or more individual species or kinds of animal. The members of a genus are all very closely related.

All the animals in this book are assigned to their families, and where several members of a family appear there is usually a short paragraph giving the main characteristics of that family. If no family name appears under a species it may be assumed that the animal belongs to the same family as the preceding species.

Most species in the book are given both an English name and a scientific name, the latter consisting of two parts and conventionally printed in italics. The first part is the generic name (the name of the genus) and may be shared by several closely related species, while the second part is the specific name. Together, the two parts of the scientific name positively identify one particular kind or species of animal. Scientific names are understood all over the world but they are not entirely stable so you may find that an animal is given different names in different books – especially if you compare new publications with less recent ones. Such changes are brought about when biologists make new discoveries about the relationships of various species. Names also change when biologists discover that experts in different countries have given different names to the same creature: the oldest name must then be adopted as the correct one. It might also happen that the same name is given to two different animals, and then one of them obviously has to be given a new name.

Many small invertebrates have no individual English names so they are given just their scientific names, as are many non-British creatures which have failed to acquire English names. In order to achieve uniformity of appearance, these names are not printed in italics in this book.

Measurements and Distribution

Size can be an important clue to the identification of animals, although rarely the most important one. With many colourful birds and insects, for example, it is the colour and pattern that you notice. Most people would describe the male Golden Oriole (page 118) as a bright yellow bird with black wings and would make no reference to its size. Similarly, the Peacock butterfly (page 232) might be described simply as a dark red butterfly with a large 'eye' on each wing. Size tends to be noticed and recorded only when there is no conspicuous pattern. The Common Blue butterfly (page 244), for example, might be described as a bright blue butterfly about 30 mm across and the Garden Warbler (page 133) as a light-brown bird about the size of a robin.

Sizes are given for all the animals in this book, though they serve only as a guide since animals vary in size considerably even when mature. Unless otherwise stated, the measurements given are normal averages for mature specimens, but a range of sizes is given for species that are particularly variable or in which males and females are markedly different. Most measurements are lengths, but wingspans are quoted for many insects. The form of measurement employed is indicated at the beginning of each chapter. Where males and females differ significantly in appearance the illustrations are labelled with the appropriate sex.

Distribution maps are given for the birds, which have been particularly well studied. Do not, however, expect to find the birds everywhere within their indicated ranges: each species has its preferred habitat and you will not find skylarks in the forests or grebes scratching about in the hedgerow. Knowing the habitats of the birds can aid in their identification and also help you to decide where to look for certain species. As far as the other animals in the book are concerned, it may be assumed that, unless otherwise stated, they occur in all suitable habitats throughout Western Europe. For the purposes of this book, southern Europe includes all areas south of the main alpine chain (south of 45°N); central Europe stretches north from the Alps to southern Denmark (from 45°N to 55°N) and includes Britain; and northern Europe covers most of Denmark and the whole of Scandinavia (north of 55°N).

Many animals, especially insects and other terrestrial invertebrates, are mature only at certain times of the year, and the dates given in the descriptions are those during which the adults are normally found. It should be remembered, however, that many of these creatures have longer seasons in southern Europe than they do in the cooler regions. Many butterflies have two or even three broods in the south and can be seen throughout the summer, while further north the same species may have only one brood and be on the wing for just a couple of weeks. If no dates are given in the descriptions it may be assumed that the animals can be found at all times of the year, although many species go into hibernation for the colder months.

Watching Wildlife

Many animals, especially birds and butterflies, are easy to see because they are active by day and quite happy to come into the open. Others are very shy and you will need a lot of patience if you want to watch them. This is particularly true of mammals. It is important to get to know the habitats the animals occupy if you want to see particular species, and then learn to recognize the signs they leave behind to show where they spend most of their time. As far as the mammals are concerned, footprints are some of the most common signs. It is usually quite easy to pick out the footprints or slots of deer on muddy paths or around pools and puddles in the woods. Each print is clearly cleft into two, showing the outlines of the two toes. Badgers and foxes also leave quite clear footprints in soft ground, but the smaller mammals rarely leave obvious marks unless the ground is really soft. Bird footprints, especially those of the larger species like coots and moorhens, are common in the mud at the edge of ponds.

Deer

Fox

Badger

Hedgehog

Footprints of many of the larger mammals are quite easy to spot in soft ground, especially around woodland puddles. (Not to scale)

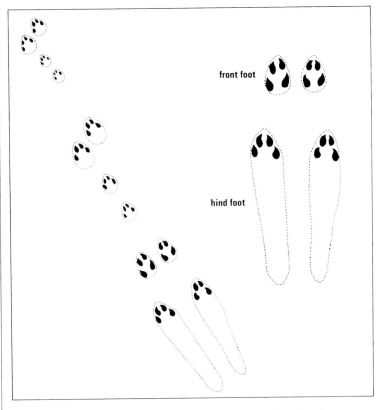

These tracks show where a rabbit has crossed a snowy field, and also where it sat to rest for a moment, leaving the long imprints of its hind feet and round prints of its front feet.

When there is snow on the ground you can easily see where animals have been. Although the details of the footprints are usually lost, the relative positions of the prints can tell you what animals have been around. Bird footprints are often quite clear in the snow, and you may also find prints of the wing feathers, showing where the birds landed or took off.

Several good books containing pictures and descriptions of animal tracks are available, but the best way to learn exactly how to relate animals to their tracks is to try to watch the animals yourself and then to examine the ground where they have walked.

As well as looking for footprints, keep your eyes open for the remains of the animals' meals and for tell-tale hairs showing where they squeeze under fences or through hedges. Piles of chewed pine cones or empty hazel nuts will tell you where to watch for squirrels and mice. Look also for animal droppings, often of quite characteristic shape, to tell you where the animals spend some of their time. Even caterpillars give themselves away by the little droppings that fall onto the leaves below them. You can make quite a collection of caterpillars by looking for such clues – although the caterpillars themselves might still be rather hard to spot because many are extremely well camouflaged.

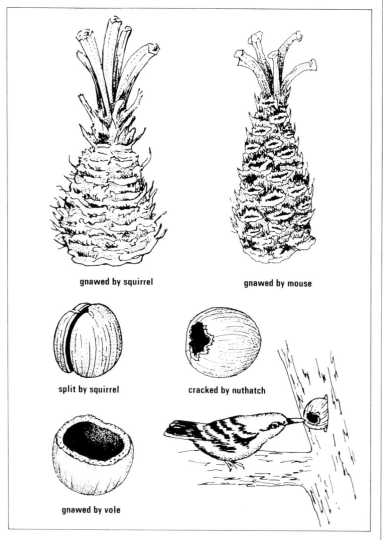

gnawed by squirrel   gnawed by mouse

split by squirrel   cracked by nuthatch

gnawed by vole

The remains of meals will often show you where to look for wild mammals, for they often return to eat at the same place each day. Squirrels and mice both strip pine cones to get at the seeds, although mice make a neater job of it. Squirrels split hazel nuts cleanly in half, while mice and voles gnaw holes in them. Nuthatches (see page 123) wedge the nuts in bark crevices and hammer them open, and so do woodpeckers.

Deer dig their lower teeth into the bark of young trees and pull upwards, tearing the bark away and leaving frayed edges at the top (left). In winter they tend merely to gnaw small patches of bark (right).

Badgers leave tell-tale scratch marks where they sharpen their claws on tree trunks.

When you have decided on the best place to watch, you will be ready to settle down and wait. Make sure you are not conspicuous – do not wear bright clothing and do not make a noise. If you are hoping to watch mammals, make sure that you are down-wind of them so that they do not catch your scent. Have your field guide and notebook ready.

Wear sensible clothes for birdwatching – warm and waterproof and with no bright colours to warn the birds that you are about. Keep your binocular straps around your neck and then you won't drop your binoculars or leave them behind.

brown back

Short black bill

Cream with
black spots

pink legs

Most birds can be sketched quite successfully with the aid of two ovals – one for the head and a larger one for the body.

You will be able to identify some animals immediately, but others will be less easy: you might get only a fleeting glance, so you must look for prominent features that will help you when going through your field guide later. Spotting such features is very much a matter of practice. It is not easy to make notes on the spot, especially when there is not much light – dawn and dusk are some of the best times for watching mammals – but you should try to get your observations on paper with little delay because it is very easy to forget small details. Sketches are often better than notes and you do not have to be a good artist to make useful sketches. Many birdwatchers base their sketches on just two ovals, one for the head and a larger one for the body, and simply add the important details as they watch. It is a good plan to have a number of blank ovals ready in your notebook before you go out.

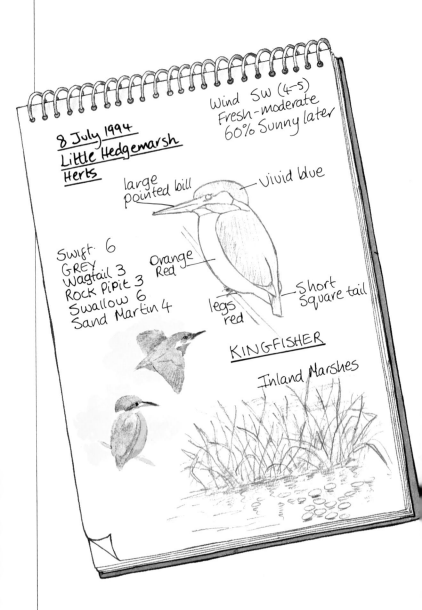

8 July 1994
Little Hedgemarsh
Herts

Wind SW (4-5)
Fresh-moderate
60% Sunny later

large pointed bill — Vivid blue

Swift 6
GREY
Wagtail 3   Orange Red
Rock Pipit 3
Swallow 6
Sand Martin 4   legs red

Short square tail

KINGFISHER

Inland Marshes

Always keep your notebook and pencil handy for making notes and sketches of the animals you see.

You can also use blank butterfly shapes in the same way: they can all be the same size and you simply fill in any striking colours and patterns. Of course, it will help if you can give some idea of the size as well – perhaps merely saying larger than or smaller than a Meadow Brown – but, as we have already seen, size is not necessarily important.

Insects and many other small creatures are quite easy to catch and examine and compare with your field guide pictures at close quarters. You can then be pretty sure of your identifications – but remember to release the animals in the place that you found them (see page 16).

Choosing Binoculars

Binoculars are essential for any serious study of birds and mammals because you usually have to watch these animals from a distance and it is impossible to pick out their details with the naked eye. You will also find binoculars useful for insect-watching, especially if you are interested in dragonflies which always seem to rest on plants which are just out of reach in the water. There are many models of binoculars on the market to choose from but it is important to choose a pair that suits your particular purpose.

If you look at a pair of binoculars you will see two numbers marked on them: 8 × 30 is a typical example, indicating that the binoculars magnify eight times and that the objective lenses – those further from your eyes – are 30 mm in diameter. The size of the objective lenses has nothing to do with the power of the binoculars, but it does control the amount of light passing through them. Small objectives allow less light to pass through than larger ones and are thus not very good in dim light. If you expect to do much watching at dusk or at night you should choose a pair with relatively large objectives. Large objectives also give a wider field of view and are better for picking up birds in flight.

Binocular magnifications generally range from about × 6 – the smallest to be of any real use – to about × 12. You might think that the most powerful are the best, but this is true only if you are particularly interested in sea birds or mountain animals, which are usually a long way away. Powerful binoculars cannot be focused on nearby objects and you might not be able to use them to study the birds on your bird-table. They are certainly no good for watching insects that are just out of reach. Until recently, powerful binoculars were also very heavy and tiring to carry for long. Improvements in design have overcome this problem, but powerful lightweight binoculars are still rather expensive. 8 × 40 is a good specification for general use, but before going out to buy a pair it is worth talking to other naturalists and trying out their binoculars to see which ones suit you. Buy the best you can afford within the size you need, but make sure that you try them before handing over your money. Do they feel comfortable at your eyes? Do they focus smoothly and quickly – very important for birdwatching. Take them outside the shop and focus on buildings at different distances. Is everything sharp and clear?

For studying the smaller plants and animals, and to make detailed investigations of flowers, you will certainly need some kind of magnifying glass. The most convenient for use in the countryside is the folding pocket lens; a magnification of × 10 is ideal for most purposes. Tie the lens to a piece of string and hang it round your neck: it will then always be handy and won't get left behind!

Remember the Rules

Large areas of our countryside are disappearing every year as a result of house-building, road-building and other human activity, and wildlife is declining as the available habitats shrink. The one bright side to these changes is the increased area of gardens, which are playing an ever more significant role as reservoirs of wildlife, but the protection of our wildlife must at all times be uppermost in our minds when watching or photographing in the countryside.

Small insects usually have to be caught and examined at close quarters if they are to be identified accurately, but they should be released again as soon as possible. Always try to take your field guide to the insects and not vice versa. Many of our rarer animals are legally protected and must not be caught or harmed in any way. In many areas, including nature reserves, it is not permissible to capture or interfere with any of the wildlife. Remember also that it is illegal to interfere with nesting birds in any way. Even photography can endanger the animals by exposing them to enemies. The trampled area where a thoughtless photographer has been working has often led unscrupulous egg-collectors and plant-hunters to rarities which they might not otherwise have found.

Botanists, ornithologists, entomologists and many other people concerned about our countryside have drawn up a number of Codes of Conduct designed to help us all get the best from the countryside without doing it any harm. These codes can be summed up as follows:

- Always ask permission if you want to visit private land.
- Leave the area as you found it. This means replacing logs and stones that have been turned over in the search for small animals, and also 'combing' the vegetation to cover up your tracks.
- Collect no more specimens than are absolutely necessary for identification.
- Follow the Country Code and give no one cause to regret your visit.
- The welfare of the subject is more important than any photograph.

A sensible attitude to the wildlife around us will ensure that it will still be there for the enjoyment of future generations.

The Country Code

1. Leave no litter.
2. Fasten all gates.
3. Avoid damaging fences, hedges and walls.
4. Guard against all fire risk.
5. Keep dogs under control.
6. Keep to paths across farm-land.
7. Safeguard all water sup-plies.
8. Protect all forms of wildlife.
9. Go carefully on country roads.
10. Respect the life of the countryside.

CHAPTER ONE
MAMMALS

The mammals are backboned animals belonging to the class Mammalia. They are distinguished from all other animals by the fact that the females feed their young with milk. This is produced in the females' mammary glands, which give the class its name. The mammals are warm-blooded like the birds, but are readily distinguished from them and from all other vertebrates by the possession of hair; only some of the whales are completely devoid of hair.

There are about 3,500 living species of mammals, of which about 170 – belonging to 9 of the 16 living orders – are native to Europe. A further 23 introduced species, including an Australian wallaby, now run wild in Europe, as do a few feral species. The latter are domesticated species, including goats, ferrets and cats, which have escaped and become established in the wild.

There is an enormous range of size within the mammals – from the tiny Etruscan Shrew, a mere 40 mm long, to the giant Blue Whale which can reach 30 m in length and weigh over 100 tonnes. The mammals eat a wide variety of plant and animal material and their teeth are correspondingly varied. Meat-eaters usually have sharp, stabbing canines and sharp-edged cheek teeth (molars and premolars) for slicing meat. Grazing mammals have broad, flat surfaces to their cheek teeth, ideal for grinding plant matter. Canine teeth are normally absent in rodents and other vegetarians. It is thus usually quite simple to identify mammalian groups just from their jaws and teeth, and often easy to identify individual species as well. In fact, detailed examination of the teeth is sometimes the only way to differentiate between some of the shrews with certainty.

All the native European mammals belong to the group known as placentals, in which the young are retained in the mother's body for a time and nourished through a special organ known as the placenta. They are born at various stages of development. Mice and rabbits, for example, are born blind, naked and utterly helpless. Cats and other carnivores are also born with their eyes closed; although they usually have a good coating of fur, they need plenty of parental care. Young carnivores tend to stay with their parents longer than many other mammals because they have to learn how to hunt. Hooved mammals, such as horses and deer, are born in a very advanced state and many can walk within an hour of birth. Within a day or two, they can usually run with the herds – an absolute necessity if they are to escape from predators in the open.

Mammals in all Habitats

Mammals are found all over the world, their fur coats and their ability to regulate their body temperature enabling them to survive in some of the coldest and some of the hottest places on earth. Although they are essentially terrestrial animals walking on four legs, they exhibit many modifications of body and limbs associated with their many different modes of life. There are runners, jumpers, burrowers, and climbers; bats which have evolved wings and become the only truly aerial mammals; and several species which spend all or most of their lives in water. The whales and seals, for example, have evolved streamlined bodies with limbs converted into paddles for efficient swimming. This ability to adapt to different environments makes the mammals an extremely successful group of animals.

Finding and Watching Mammals

Deer and other grazing mammals are quite easy to watch by day, but the carnivores and most of the smaller mammals tend to be solitary and nocturnal and thus less easily observed. Footprints and other signs will indicate their favoured haunts; baits can then be used to tempt them into suitable viewing places, though a great deal of patience will be needed. Binoculars are essential, even for viewing the small animals on your doorstep: 8 × 40 is a good size for general use – fairly powerful and with sufficient light-gathering ability for use at dawn and dusk, when many mammals are most active.

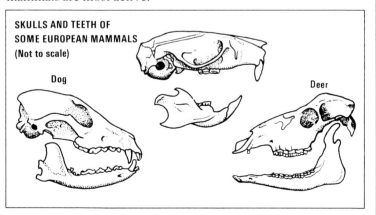

SKULLS AND TEETH OF SOME EUROPEAN MAMMALS
(Not to scale)

Dog

Deer

Insectivores

This widely distributed and rather ancient group (Order Insectivora) includes some 300 species, most of which exhibit various primitive features. Many, for example, possess 44 teeth, which was the full complement for the earliest placental mammals. Most other mammals have lost some of their teeth during their evolution. There are 8 families of insectivores, of which just 3 occur in Europe—the hedgehogs (Erinaceidae), the moles and desmans (Talpidae), and the shrews (Soricidae). All are small, long-snouted, short-legged animals with sharp-cusped teeth and 5 clawed digits on each limb —another primitive feature. Although the name means 'insect-eaters', the insectivores actually eat a wide variety of small animals and some take vegetable food as well. They are extremely common animals and play an important role in the ecology of many habitats.

WESTERN HEDGEHOG
Erinaceus europaeus Family Erinaceidae

Head and body 18–27cm: tail 2–3cm. Back and sides clothed with spines about 2cm long. Spines are modified hairs, dark brown or black with white tips. There is a narrow parting on the back of the head. Face, underside and limbs are clothed with soft hair.
Food and habits: eats slugs, worms, and a wide range of insects, together with fallen fruit and fungi. Almost entirely nocturnal, and very noisy when foraging. It can roll into a tight ball when disturbed. Sleeps by day among dead leaves and other rubbish in hedge bottoms and similar places. Hibernates October–April in a nest of dry leaves, but often active until well into winter. Swims and climbs well: can also burrow. Western and northern Europe. The Eastern hedgehog (*E. concolor*) of eastern Europe is very similar but has a white breast. The Algerian hedgehog (*E. algirus*) of the western Mediterranean region is paler all over, with a wide parting on the head.

NORTHERN MOLE
Talpa europaea Family Talpidae

Head and body 12–15cm: tail about 4cm. Front feet greatly enlarged and spade-like for digging. The animal lives almost entirely underground in an extensive tunnel system. Mole hills are the piles of soil excavated from the tunnels and periodically pushed up to the surface. The velvety black or dark grey fur can lie in any direction, allowing the animal to move backwards and forwards in its tunnels with equal ease. It feeds almost entirely on earthworms. The eyes are very small, although it is not completely blind. Active day and night, sometimes emerging to rummage in leaf litter.

Habitat and range: mostly in grassland and deciduous woodland, even where quite wet (the mole can swim well). Most of Europe apart from Ireland and the far north.

PYRENEAN DESMAN
Galemys pyrenaicus

Head and body 11–13·5cm, tail 13–15cm. Muzzle long, flat and broad; tail flattened from side to side and fringed with stiff hairs; hind feet large and webbed for swimming.

Range and habitat: mountain streams and canals in the Pyrenees and northern Spain and Portugal.

Food: small aquatic invertebrates.

SHREWS Family Soricidae

This large family contains some 200 species. Shrews are small, short-legged animals with long pointed noses. Their fur is short and usually brown or grey, they have very small eyes and their senses of hearing and smell are very well developed. Most species are terrestrial, active day and night and solitary. They are usually carnivorous or insectivorous, though a little plant food is eaten. Because the many species are very similar, a detailed examination of teeth and skulls is often necessary for accurate identification. The 15 European species can be split into 2 main groups: the red-toothed shrews (*Sorex* and *Neomys*), in which the teeth have red tips, and the white-toothed shrews (*Suncus* and *Crocidura*).

COMMON SHREW
Sorex araneus

Head and body 70–85mm, tail 45mm, hind foot 12–13mm. The teeth are red-tipped. The silky fur on the back is dark brown, the underside pale, and along the sides there is a distinct band of an intermediate colour.
Range and habitat: Britain, Scandinavia and eastern Europe, wherever the ground cover is sufficient. Abundant in grassland, woods and hedgerows. The very similar Millet's shrew (*S. coronatus*) inhabits most of western Europe.
Food and habits: eats mainly insects, worms and spiders; will also eat carrion.

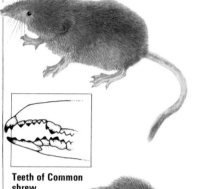

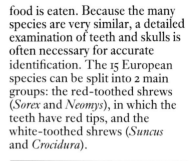

Teeth of Common shrew

PYGMY SHREW
Sorex minutus

Head and body 45–60mm, tail 40mm long. Distinctly smaller than the Common shrew and no band of intermediate colour is present on the flanks.
Range: widespread in Europe, but only at high altitude in the south.

GREATER WHITE-TOOTHED SHREW
Crocidura russula

Head and body 65–85mm, tail 35–50mm, hind foot 12–13mm. Has whiskers on the tail, and is greyish-brown above, fading to yellowish-grey below.
Range and habitat: dry grassland, woodland and hedges in southern and central Europe.

Teeth of Greater White-toothed shrew

BICOLOURED WHITE-TOOTHED SHREW
Crocidura leucodon

Head and body 64–87mm, tail 28–39mm, hind foot 12–13mm. The dark grey upper side contrasts sharply with the yellowish-white below. Tail whiskered and clearly bicoloured.
Range and habitat: often found on the edges of woods in central Europe and on the steppes of eastern Europe.

PYGMY WHITE-TOOTHED SHREW or ETRUSCAN SHREW
Suncus etruscus

Head and body 36–50mm, tail 24–29mm, hind foot 7–8mm. The smallest mammal in the world. Usually weighing less than 2g. Long hairs form whiskers on the tail. Reddish-grey above, dull grey below.
Range and habitat: widespread in grassland and often found in arable farmland and gardens. Southern Europe.

WATER SHREW
Neomys fodiens

Head and body 70–90mm, hind foot 17–20mm. A large, dark shrew, nearly black above, with underside colour varying from silver-grey to black. Stiff hairs on the underside of the tail and on the hind feet assist swimming.
Range and habitat: found throughout Europe, except Ireland, in dense vegetation near fresh water.
Food and habits: insect larvae and other water invertebrates. Also uses its poisonous saliva to kill small fishes, frogs and even small mammals.

Teeth of Water shrew

Bats

The bats, which belong to the order Chiroptera, are the only mammals that fly, though other kinds of mammals can glide from tree to tree. The bat's wings are skin membranes and they are supported by fingers, fore and hind limbs and tail. Bats are distributed throughout the world, with the exception of the polar regions, but most species are tropical or subtropical. There are about 1,000 known species, of which about 30 – all insect eaters – occur in Europe. Bats usually fly at night using high-pitched sound pulses to navigate and find food. They spend the daylight hours in a torpid state in dark, sheltered cavities in trees, caves, attics or cellars. In temperate regions most bats hibernate in winter. Correct identification of some European bats is difficult and may depend upon minute details of structure of the skull or teeth, but many can be identified by looking at the face and ears and the membrane surrounding the tail, and also by measuring the length of the forearm (from elbow to thumb). Many bats have a prominent lobe of skin, called the tragus, standing up at the base of the ear, and the shape of this is a good guide to identification. All bats have a thin spur of cartilage, known as the calcar, attached to the ankle. It usually lies inconspicuously along the edge of the tail membrane, but in some bats the membrane extends as a small lobe beyond the calcar. Three families of bats occur in Europe. The Horse-shoe bats (Rhinolophidae) are represented by five species, all with horseshoe-shaped flaps of skin around the nose. Free-tailed bats (Molossidae), in which the tail extends well beyond the membrane, have a single repesentative in Europe. Most European bats belong to the Vespertilionidae, whose members can all be recognized by the possession of a tragus.

GREATER HORSE-SHOE BAT
Rhinolophus ferrumequinum
Family Rhinolophidae

The largest Horse-shoe bat in Europe. Head and body about 70mm, forearm 50–60mm. The thick fur is grey above, pale buff below. Ears large and broad with curved pointed tips. Flight is relatively slow, rather like that of a butterfly, and usually within a metre or so of the ground.
Range: south and central Europe; s.w. Britain only. Mainly wooded country.

FREE-TAILED BAT
Tadarida teniotis Family Molossidae

Head and body up to 85mm, forearm 58–64mm; tail up to 55mm, of which about half is free of the membrane. The only bat in Europe with the tail extend- ing more than 2 vertebrae beyond the membrane. It often lives in rocky areas and flies high and fast.

Range: Mediterranean area: often active throughout the year, with little or no hibernation.

VESPERTILIONID BATS Family Vespertilionidae

This family of small bats includes about 280 species, of which 26 are European. The family is widely distributed in tropical and temperate areas. The nose has no complex lobes, and the tail never projects beyond the membrane by more than one or two vertebrae. Three groups can be recognized within the European members of the family: the Myotis bats, which are mostly small, with a long, slender, pointed tragus in the ear; the larger noctules and serotines, with a short, kidney-shaped tragus; and the small pipistrelles, with a short, blunt tragus. The pipistrelles, noctules and serotines have a lobe of tail membrane extending outside the calcar which is absent in Myotis bats.

COMMON PIPISTRELLE
Pipistrellus pipistrellus

The smallest European bat; head and body 38–50mm, forearm 27–32mm. Ear short, broad and triangular, tragus short and blunt. Fur variable in colour from dark brown to light reddish, but uniform.

Habitat: both wooded and open country. Forms large colonies in trees and buildings, sheltering in caves in winter. All of Europe except the far north.

WHISKERED BAT
Myotis mystacinus

Another small species; head and body about 50mm, forearm 32–37mm.
Dark grey fur makes this an easily recognizable species. Flight is rather slow and fluttery.
Range and habitat: inhabits wooded areas in most parts of Europe.

COMMON LONG-EARED BAT
Plecotus auritus

Head and body about 50mm, forearm 34–41mm. Distinguished by extremely long ears, the bases of which meet on top of the head. Tragus long and narrow.

Brown or greyish-brown above; yellowish below. Can hover to take insects off tree leaves.
Range and habitat: most of Europe apart from Iberia and far north, roosting on trees and buildings.

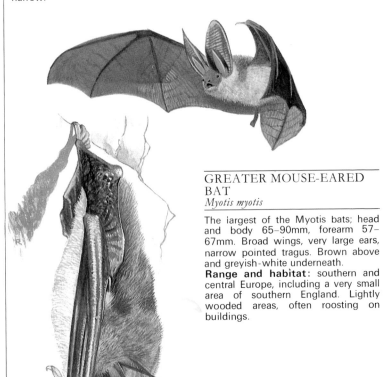

GREATER MOUSE-EARED BAT
Myotis myotis

The largest of the Myotis bats; head and body 65–90mm, forearm 57–67mm. Broad wings, very large ears, narrow pointed tragus. Brown above and greyish-white underneath.
Range and habitat: southern and central Europe, including a very small area of southern England. Lightly wooded areas, often roosting on buildings.

DAUBENTON'S BAT
Myotis daubentoni

A small bat; head and body 50mm, forearm about 35mm. Very large feet more than half the length of the shin. The tragus is straight and slender. Greyish-red above, dull white below. The ears and muzzle pinkish-brown.
Habitat: lives in wooded country often near water, roosting in trees and buildings in summer, but sheltering in caves in winter to hibernate. Most of Europe except the far north and the south-east.

NATTERER'S BAT
Myotis nattereri

Head and body 40–50mm; forearm about 40mm. Greyish-brown above and white below. There is a fringe of hair on the membrane near the tail. Tragus very long and pointed.
Range and habitat: one of the most widely distributed European bats, although absent from much of Scandinavia. Open country with woodland, often near water.

NOCTULE
Nyctalus noctula

Large; head and body about 82mm, forearm 46–55mm. Fur rich golden brown above and below. Noctules are colonial bats roosting in trees, seldom in caves. They fly high in search of insects and may migrate over considerable distances.
Tragus short and kidney-shaped.
Range and habitat: most of Europe except Ireland and far north. Prefers wooded habitats.

Rabbits and Hares

These animals, easily recognizable by their long ears, long hind legs, and short furry tails, belong to the order Lagomorpha. They have some superficial resemblances to the rodents, but they differ in having two pairs of upper incisor teeth—one large pair and a smaller pair tucked in behind them. Rabbits and hares all belong to the family Leporidae. Hares are larger and faster, but the main differences lie in their breeding habits. Rabbits give birth to blind, naked young in burrows, while hares give birth above ground and their babies are sighted and well-furred.

RABBIT
Oryctolagus cuniculus

Head and body up to 40cm, hind foot 7·5–9·5cm. Differs from the hare in its small size, shorter ears and legs. Colour very variable from brown to sandy, and black specimens are common in some areas. White underside of tail always visible as animal runs away.

Range and habitat: widespread in grassland and scrubby places, including sand dunes, heathland, hedgerows and open woodland. Absent from most of Scandinavia.

Food and habits: lives in colonies in underground warrens. Active mainly at night. Feeds mainly on grass, but can destroy cereal crops, roots and young trees. Prey of weasels, foxes, cats, dogs and birds of prey.

MOUNTAIN HARE
Lepus timidus

Head and body 50–60cm, hind foot 12–15cm. More heavily built than Brown hare, with shorter ears and longer legs. Tail white above and below. Summer coat brown with a blue tinge. Often turns white in winter except for ear tips. In far north may remain white all year round, but in some localities, such as Ireland, it never turns white.

Habitat: lives in mountainous areas above tree line in grassland and moorland; also in lowlands in Ireland and the north.

Food and habits: feeds on grasses and shrubs such as heather. Prey of fox, wild cat and eagle.

winter coat

summer coat

BROWN HARE
Lepus capensis

Head and body 50–60cm, hind foot 12–15cm. Yellowish-brown above, white on belly. Has long ears with black tips, and black and white tail.
Habitat: mainly a lowland species, found especially on farmland. Absent from most of Scandinavia.
Food and habits: feeds on bark, grain and other vegetation, and often becomes a pest of agriculture and forestry. Solitary, active mainly at night. Prey of fox, wild cat and eagle. Courtship involves spectacular leaping, chasing and boxing.

Rodents

These are the gnawing animals – the rats and mice and their relatives – and they form the order Rodentia. This is the largest order of mammals, with about 1,500 species distributed throughout the world. About 60 species are represented in Europe. They occupy all the available habitats, and have evolved a variety of life styles, including burrowing, tree climbing, gliding and swimming.

All rodents have four sharp, chisel-shaped, continuously growing incisor teeth for gnawing. The incisors are kept sharp because the hard enamel surface at the front wears less rapidly than the softer dentine behind. Nearly all species are small. Some, such as the rats, are omnivorous, but the rodents are essentially herbivores and several are major pests. The majority are nocturnal.

SQUIRRELS Family Sciuridae

This family includes not only the familiar tree squirrels but also the ground squirrels and some 'flying' (gliding) squirrels. There are about 350 species, but only 7 of them occur in Europe.

Most species are diurnal, but the flying squirrels are nocturnal. Only one flying squirrel (*Pteromys volans*) occurs in Europe, but it does not get further west than Finland.

FLYING SQUIRREL
Pteromys volans

Head and body 16cm, tail 12cm. Upper parts grey or grey-brown, underside white. Large eyes, small ears. It glides by using a furred membrane extended between the fore and hind limbs.
Range and habitat: lives in the forests of northern Russia and Finland.
Food and habits: eats seeds and also fruit and small birds. Climbs up trees then glides for up to 50m. Nocturnal. Hibernates.

GREY SQUIRREL
Sciurus carolinensis

Head and body 26cm, tail 21cm. Winter coat grey with yellowish-brown mid-dorsal stripe. In summer, coat has reddish tinge, especially on the sides. Tail has light-coloured fringes, and ear tufts are lacking.
Range and habitat: originating in North America, it is now widespread in deciduous woodlands of the British Isles: also common in parks and gardens.
Food: can kill trees by stripping bark for food, but main diet is nuts, particularly acorns, and a wide range of roots, bulbs and even some insects, eggs, and small birds. Does not hibernate.

RED SQUIRREL
Sciurus vulgaris

Head and body 22cm, tail 18cm. The only native tree squirrel in Europe. Colour very variable from red to black. Summer coat usually a rich red with a darker mid-back area; winter coat greyish. During the winter, dark ear tufts are prominent, but these are lost in spring.
Range and habitat: lives throughout the wooded areas of Europe, especially in coniferous forest.
Food and habits: feeds mainly on seeds and nuts, but also eats young tree shoots. Does not hibernate, but may sleep for long periods in winter.

ALPINE MARMOT
Marmota marmota

Head and body 50-60cm: tail 14–19cm. One of the ground squirrels, this is a burrowing rodent of the Alps and other European mountains—usually between 2,000 and 3,000 metres up. Diurnal, it is often seen scampering rapidly over the grassy slopes. It feeds on grasses and other low-growing vegetation. Hibernates in deep, hay-filled burrows.

DORMICE Family Gliridae

A small family of about 10 species in Europe, Asia, and Africa. Five species live in Europe. Most dormice have bushy tails and resemble small squirrels. They also have large eyes, rounded ears, and short legs. They are climbing animals, living mainly in trees and bushes and feeding mainly on buds and fruit, including nuts. They are nocturnal and secretive and can be pests in orchards. They sleep through the winter in snug nests of leaves, usually on or under the ground or in hollow logs.

COMMON DORMOUSE
Muscardinus avellanarius

Head and body 7cm, tail 7cm. A small dormouse, light tawny above, yellow-ish-white below. Throat and chest white. Tail thickly haired.
Range and habitat: deciduous forest with shrubs; copses and thick hedgerows. The summer nest is usually built in dense bushes. Most of Europe to southern Scandinavia.
Food and habits: eats nuts, seeds and some insects. Sleeps from October to April rolled in a ball.

GARDEN DORMOUSE
Eliomys quercinus

Head and body 15cm, tail 9cm. The long slender tail has a flattened, black and white tuft at the tip. Body greyish-brown above, white below. Black mask on the face.
Range and habitat: Most of Europe, but not Britain or Scandinavia. Mainly in woodland, but also gardens, orchards and rocky areas.
Food and habits: spends much of its time on the ground. Eats a wide variety of food including insects, snails, birds' eggs and nestling small mammals and birds, as well as fruit and nuts. Becomes dormant in autumn after the summer fattening period. It is nocturnal, hiding in a hole during day.

FAT DORMOUSE
Glis glis

Head and body 14–19cm, tail 13cm. The largest dormouse. Grey-brown above, somewhat lighter below. Dark stripes on outside of legs, dark ring round eyes. Long bushy tail.

Range and habitat: Most of southern and central Europe: introduced to Britain in 1902 and now well established in Chiltern area. Mature woodlands and orchards.

Food and habits: eats nuts, seeds, fruit and insects. Can be pest of fruit and forestry crops. Becomes very fat in autumn and dormant October–April. Nocturnal. In Roman times fattened for the table and considered a delicacy.

EUROPEAN BEAVER
Castor fiber Family Castoridae

Head and body 90cm, tail 35cm. The largest of the European rodents. Coat brown with very dense underfur and a sleek covering of guard hairs. Blunt-nosed, heavily built. Tail broad and flat with prominent scales. Short legs with webbed hind feet.

Range and habitat: exploited for fur and, although once widespread in northern Europe, it is now found only rarely in the Rhône and Elbe valleys, parts of Scandinavia, and Russia. Lives in rivers and lakes in wooded country.

Food and habits: feeds on a variety of aquatic vegetation and tree bark (aspen and willow are preferred). Will fell trees to reach tender shoots. The beaver is mainly nocturnal and spends much time in water. It lives in family groups of up to 12 animals in burrows in river banks or *lodges* built in the water. The burrows have several entrances, some under water, and are now more common than lodges, which are built of mud and sticks with a central chamber above water level. The very similar Canadian beaver (*Castor canadensis*) has been introduced to Finland, where it is now well established.

COYPU
Myocastor coypus Family Capromyidae

Head and body 60cm, tail 40cm, thick and scaly. Head large with short ears. Hind feet webbed. An aquatic animal native to southern South America but kept in captivity for fur farming in many parts of the world.

Range and habitat: escapes have populated several localities in Europe where there is dense marshland vegetation.
Food and habits: water plants and shellfish. Mainly nocturnal. A good swimmer.

NORTH AFRICAN CRESTED PORCUPINE
Hystrix cristata Family Hystricidae

Head and body 70cm, tail 10cm. A large brownish-black rodent with white band under neck. Head and neck with crest of long white and brown bristles. Body quills of two types, long and slender or short and stout, banded black and white. On rump, quills mainly black; on tail white. The quills are not barbed and may reach 40cm in length. They can be rattled to warn off enemies. When attacked, the porcupine can rush backwards to stick the quills into the enemy's skin.

Range and habitat: probably introduced to southern Europe from North Africa. Lives in rocky hill country with cover.
Food and habits: roots, leaves, and bark. Nocturnal. Pest of root crops and forestry.

HAMSTERS, VOLES, RATS AND MICE
Family Muridae

This is the largest rodent family, containing over 1,000 species of rats, mice, voles, hamsters and their allies. Usually small, fast-breeding, short-lived animals, they are found in almost every corner of the world. All have 3 molar or cheek teeth in each jaw, but the shapes of these teeth vary a good deal. The family is divided into several distinct groups or sub-families. Many species are pests of agriculture and of stored products, and several carry diseases. Over 40 species are found in Europe many of which are difficult to identify without close examination.

HAMSTERS AND ALLIES Sub-family Cricetinae

A widely distributed sub-family with 3 representatives in Europe. They are mostly small, terrestrial animals with simple grinding surfaces on the molars.

COMMON HAMSTER
Cricetus cricetus

Head and body 22–32cm, tail 3–6cm. Broad feet and large cheek pouches.
Habitat: grassland, meadows and cultivated land usually near water.

Mainly in Eastern Europe.
Food and habits: feeds mainly on seeds and grain, but also eats roots and insects. Makes extensive burrow systems with many chambers. Mainly nocturnal. Hibernates.

MOLE-RATS Sub-family Spalacinae

A small group consisting of only 3 highly specialized rodents, 2 of which are found in Europe. They are adapted for burrowing and spend nearly all their life underground, although young animals may be found on the surface when dispersing to find new territories. They dig with their teeth, pushing loosened earth behind them with their feet. The jaw muscles are particularly strong, and the jaw is more mobile than in most rodent species.

GREATER MOLE-RAT
Spalax micropthalmus

Head and body 24–30cm. Soft velvety fur and clear white markings on head.
Range and habitat: grassland and cultivated land of eastern Europe.
Food and habits: feeds mainly on roots, bulbs and tubers and may pull whole plants down into burrow. Builds complex tunnel system with separate chambers for food, rest and latrine. The Lesser mole-rat (*S. leucodon*) of south-east Europe is smaller and darker.

LEMMINGS AND VOLES Sub-family Microtinae

Some 25 species of this sub-family are found in Europe. They are characterized by their shortish tail, short legs and blunt muzzles, and by the complex patterns of enamel and dentine on the molar teeth. They are the predominant small grazing animals of European grasslands. Their numbers tend to fluctuate, periodically reaching plague levels.

MUSKRAT
Ondatra zibethicus

Head and body 30–40cm, tail 19–27cm. A North American species introduced to Europe by escapes from fur farms. Much larger than all native voles and with a tail which is flattened from side to side. Dark brown above, dirty white below. Lives close to water and swims well, but feet not webbed.
Habitat: found mainly near slow-moving streams, canals and lakes in north and central Europe; absent from Britain.
Food and habits: eats river-side vegetation, but will take roots and crops when available. Nocturnal. Burrows in banks and may cause considerable damage to waterways.

WOOD LEMMING
Myopus schisticolor

Head and body 85–95mm, tail 16–18mm. Similar to a short-tailed vole. Grey with a reddish tinge above, grey below.
Habitat: northern coniferous forest.
Food: mainly mosses, liverworts and lichens.

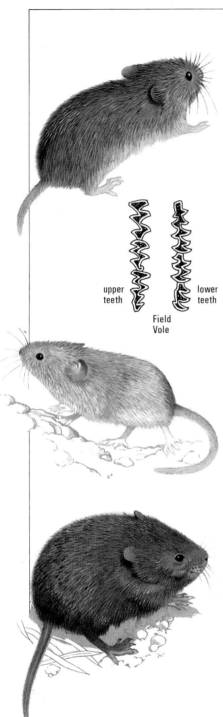

upper teeth   lower teeth

Field Vole

FIELD VOLE
Microtus agrestis

Head and body 90–130mm, tail 30–45mm. Colour variable, yellow-brown to dark brown above, greyish-white below. Blunt head with short round hairy ears. Tail dark above, light below. **Range and habitat:** an abundant and widespread species in grassland, meadows and marshland where ground cover is thick.

Food and habits: eats stems and leaves of grasses, reeds and sedges, and will take some animal food. May strip bark from trees in winter. Makes shallow burrows and a network of tunnels under vegetation on surface. Can cause extensive damage to crops and grassland pastures. Active day and night.

The voles are often confused with the mice (page 39), but the short ears and rounded snouts of the voles readily distinguish them.

BANK VOLE
Clethrionomys glareolus

Head and body 85–100mm, tail 40–65mm. Above, bright chestnut or reddish; below, yellowish, buff or grey-white. Patterns of enamel on cheek teeth are important for identification of this and allied forms.

Habitat: scrub, deciduous woodland and hedgerows.

Food and habits: eats a wide range of vegetable matter and some insects. Active day and night in short bursts, often climbing amongst bushes.

NORTHERN WATER VOLE
Arvicola terrestris

Head and body 16–19cm, tail 8–10cm. Like a large Field vole, but with a relatively long tail. Long, thick, glossy fur, blackish-grey or red-brown above, yellowish-grey below. Smaller and paler in southern part of range.

Habitat: edges of lakes and slow-moving rivers with good cover of vegetation on the banks, but can also be found in drier grassland. Most of Europe, but replaced by Southern Water Vole (*A. sapidus*) in south-west. Absent from Ireland.

Food and habits: eats mostly green vegetation, reeds, grass and some nuts and roots. Swims well, but is not pronouncedly adapted to aquatic habit. Burrows in river banks and makes a large grass-lined nest chamber. Some activity both day and night.

RATS AND MICE Sub-family Murinae

The rats and mice form the large sub-family Murinae and can be distinguished from the voles by their long tails, large ears, and more pointed snouts. There are 3 molar teeth in each jaw, but they have rounded cusps quite unlike the flat grinding surfaces of the vole molars. Most of the rats and mice are of tropical origin, but 12 species occur in Europe. The animals are very adaptable, occupying a wide range of habitats including many man-made situations. The genera *Mus* and *Rattus* are almost world-wide as a result of their close association with man. Most of the species feed on seeds, but other plant materials are included in their varied diets, and some species, especially those associated with man, are distinctly omnivorous. Many species are pests of agriculture and stored products, and some are carriers of disease.

BLACK RAT or SHIP RAT
Rattus rattus

Head and body 16–23cm, tail 18–25cm, hind foot 30–40mm. Distinguished from Common rat by its relatively long tail and short hind foot, and also by its larger, rounded ears. Three colour forms are commonly found: dark grey or black all over, brown above with grey below, and brown above with white below.

Range and habitat: introduced from Asia at about the time of the Crusades, probably overland. More common in southern Europe than the Common rat. Closely associated with man and is the familiar rat of ships and seaports.
Food and habits: omnivorous. Climbs more than the Common rat. A considerable pest of stored produce and a carrier of many diseases. Often nests in roofs and other places above ground.

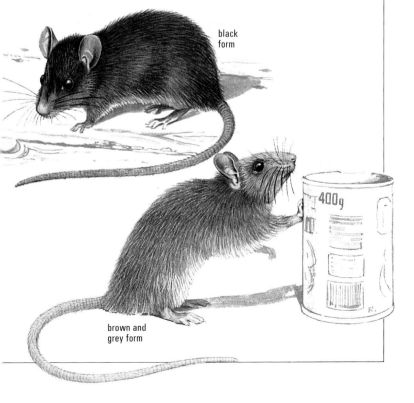

black
form

brown and
grey form

400g

COMMON OR NORWAY RAT
Rattus norvegicus

Head and body 20–26cm, tail 17–23cm, hind foot 40–45mm. Usually brown, occasionally black above, grey below. Albino forms are used in research laboratories, and other colour forms have been bred for research and the pet trade.

Range and habitat: introduced to Europe from Asia in about AD 1500. Prefers habitats modified by man. Mainly terrestrial, but can swim well. Abundant in sewers, on rubbish dumps, and on farms: also on river banks and along estuaries.

Food and habits: eats grain and seeds when available, but will eat almost anything. A devastating pest of stored produce, often polluting far more than it eats and causing a vast amount of damage. Implicated in the spread of many diseases, including plague. Mostly nocturnal, spending the day in an extensive system of tunnels.

YELLOW-NECKED FIELD MOUSE
Apodemus flavicollis

Head and body 90–120mm, tail 90–135mm. Slightly larger and more brightly coloured than the Wood mouse. White below, and with the yellow chest spot large and usually extended sideways to form a collar.

Habitat: woodland, orchards and gardens, and often enters houses. Absent from far north and most of south-west.

Habits: similar to the Wood mouse.

WOOD MOUSE
Apodemus sylvaticus

Head and body 80–110mm, tail 70–110mm. Yellowish-brown above, silvery grey below. Usually has a small yellow patch on the chest which may extend to a streak. Eyes and ears large.

Habitat: very common in woodland, but frequently found in gardens and hedgerows, and often enters buildings. Absent from far north.

Food and habits: eats mainly seeds, especially acorns, beech mast and hazel nuts, but also takes some insects and other invertebrate food. An agile climber. Nocturnal. A major source of food for owls.

HARVEST MOUSE
Micromys minutus

Head and body 60–75mm, tail 50–70mm. A small rodent with thick, soft fur, brown above with a yellowish or russet tone; white below. Bicolored tail, partly prehensile, and used to assist climbing.

Habitat: hedgerows, tall grass and reed beds. The mice remain in thick cover and are difficult to observe. Modern farming methods may be causing some reduction in numbers through the removal of hedgerows, while combine harvesters now make life difficult in the grain fields, but the mice are still common in marshland. Absent from most of Scandinavia.

Food and habits: eats mainly seeds, fruits, and bulbs, but takes some insect food, particularly in summer. Stores seed for winter below ground. Active day and night, and does not hibernate, but spends much more time under the ground in the winter. The summer nest is a spherical ball of woven grass attached to stems well above ground.

HOUSE MOUSE
Mus musculus

Head and body 70–95mm, tail 70–95mm. Size varies with habitat, and island forms often large. Soft brown-grey fur, slightly lighter below, but colour variable. Large eyes. Characteristic musty smell.

Range: origin probably central Asia, now worldwide associated with man.

Food and habits: eats almost anything, but prefers grain when available. A major pest of stored food and a carrier of several diseases. Mainly nocturnal.

STRIPED FIELD MOUSE
Apodemus agrarius

Head and body 90–115mm, tail 70–85mm. Very similar to the Wood mouse, but with a prominent dark stripe from nape of neck to base of tail. Reddish-brown above, white below.
Habitat: lives in scrub, grassland, hedgerows and woodland margins, but not found in dense woodland. More terrestrial than Wood mouse and less strictly nocturnal. Eastern Europe, as far west as Italy and Denmark. Could be confused with Birch mouse, but latter has much longer tail.

BIRCH MICE Family Zapodidae

A family of some 11 species, widely distributed in the northern hemisphere. Two species occur in Europe. Birch mice have exceptionally long prehensile tails and a dark stripe along the back. The upper jaw has an extra grinding tooth.

NORTHERN BIRCH MOUSE
Sicista betulina

Head and body 50–70mm, tail 75–100mm. Russet above, white below, but with a prominent dark stripe along the back from neck to base of tail.
Range and habitat: distributed patchily in northern and central Europe, but usually found in damp birch woodland with dense undergrowth.
Food and habits: feeds mainly on small invertebrates, but also eats seeds and bulbs. Nocturnal. Agile, and an especially good climber aided by the prehensile tail. Hibernates from October to April. The Southern Birch mouse (*S. subtilis*) of the steppes is very similar.

Carnivores

About 250 species of carnivores (Order Carnivora) are scattered around the world, although they were not present in Australia or New Zealand until introduced by man. About 25 species occur in Europe. The range of size in the group is enormous, from the tiny weasel to the polar bear. The name Carnivora means flesh-eater and, although the diets vary, most species are adapted for eating meat, with stabbing eye teeth and sharp-edged cheek teeth which shear cleanly through the flesh.

BEARS Family Ursidae

There are about 10 species of bears distributed around the northern hemisphere and in northern South America. Bears are heavily-built animals with small ears and eyes. They have 5 digits in each foot and strong claws. They walk with the feet flat on the ground. The molars are not noticeably modified for shearing.

BROWN BEAR
Ursus arctos

Head and body up to 2m, tail vestigial. Colour of shaggy coat varying shades of brown. Weighs up to 250kg.
Range and habitat: wild, wooded country, often in mountains. Population in forests of western Europe heavily persecuted and the remaining specimens are smaller than their eastern and northern counterparts.
Food and habits: a very varied diet, mostly vegetarian with roots, bulbs, tubers, berries and grain. Also eats small mammals, eggs, and fish. Can open bees' nests for the honey. Solitary and mostly nocturnal.

DOGS AND ALLIES Family Canidae

This family contains about 35 species, including the wolves and jackals. There are 5 species in Europe. Most members are long- legged, deep-chested animals with plenty of stamina for the chase. The claws are blunt and not retractable.

WOLF
Canis lupus

Head and body up to 140cm, tail 40cm. The size is variable, with animals in the south being smaller. A dog-like animal with broad head and chest; long, bushy, drooping tail; and pointed ears. Colour variable, but usually a brownish- or yellowish-grey brindled with black. **Range and habitat:** the original European population is now much re- duced and the animals are found in the more remote forests, mountains and tundra. **Food and habits:** feeds on deer, but will also take smaller prey. In summer lives in small family groups in specific territory, but in winter several groups may join together to form a large pack for hunting.

ARCTIC FOX
Alopex lagopus

Head and body up to 67cm, tail to 42cm. Colour variable, but summer coat usually greyish-brown, turning white in winter. A small percentage of animals are a smoky-grey colour throughout the year and are known as the Blue fox. Muzzle and ears are shorter than in Red fox. **Range and habitat:** the Arctic tundra and the mountains of Scandinavia. **Food and habits:** feeds mainly on voles and lemmings, birds, carrion and shellfish.

RED FOX
Vulpes vulpes

Head and body about 60 cm, tail about
40cm. Fur sandy to brownish-red
above, greyish-white below. Has black
markings on front of limbs and back of
ears. Tail bushy, usually with a white
tip.
Habitat: preferred habitat is woodland, but very adaptable and significant
numbers are found in towns.
Food and habits: mainly small mammals, squirrels and rabbits, but also eats
insects, small birds, eggs, grass, fruit
and carrion. Mostly nocturnal.

RACCOON-DOG
Nyctereutes procyonoides

Head and body 50–55cm, tail 13–
18cm. General colour yellowish-brown,
with hairs on shoulder, back and tail
tipped with black.
Range and habitat: a native of
eastern Siberia and Asia, the Raccoon-
dog has been brought to Europe for
fur-farming and has now spread as far
west as Germany. Lives mainly in
river valleys, grassy plains and forests.
Food and habits: varied diet includes
rodents, fish and fruit. Spends worst
of winter in hibernation, the only
member of the family to do so.

JACKAL
Canis aureus

Head and body up to 75cm, tail up to
36cm. Smaller and more lightly built
than the wolf, the jackal can also be
recognized by the reddish-brown
colouring on the side of the neck.
Colour a dirty yellow mixed with black
and brown hairs. Tail reddish with
black tip.
Habitat: lives in steppe and scrub
vegetation of south-eastern Europe.
Food and habits: feeds on small
mammals, birds, eggs, fish and fruit.
More nocturnal than the wolf.

WEASELS AND ALLIES Family Mustelidae

This family of carnivores is widely distributed around the world and includes about 70 species of short-legged, sinuous, long-bodied animals such as weasels, polecats, badgers, otters, mink, and their allies. Most species produce a strong-smelling odour from anal glands.

They are meat-eaters with prominent canines and well-developed shearing teeth. Many species are hunted for their fur; some have been persecuted because they sometimes kill game birds and poultry; others have been farmed and domesticated. They are mainly nocturnal.

WEASEL
Mustela nivalis

Head and body about 20cm, tail 6cm. Female smaller than male. The smallest European carnivore. Weasels of southern Europe are larger than those from the north. Smaller than the stoat, with relatively short tail with no black on tip. Reddish-brown above, white below, often with brownish markings. May turn white in north of range (Russia and Scandinavia). Musky smell from anal glands.
Habitat: found in nearly all habitats, even in towns. Active day and night, preying on mice and voles, other small rodents, birds and eggs. They are slender enough to chase small rodents in their burrows. As with stoat, numbers fluctuate according to population of prey, especially voles.

MARBLED POLECAT
Vormela peregusna

Head and body 30–38cm, tail 15–20cm. Similar to the other polecats in shape, but with distinctly mottled coat of dark brown and cream. Dark brown below.
Habitat: lives in open areas with scrub and trees, and is also found in farmland. South-east Europe.
Food: eats small mammals, birds, lizards and reptiles and some invertebrates.

WESTERN POLECAT
Mustela putorius

Head and body 30–44cm, tail 13–18cm. Coarse, dark brown hair above with yellowish underfur showing through. Black below. White on muzzle and between eyes and ears. The musky scent from the anal glands is particularly strong in this species, which is also known as the foulmart. Often killed as pest of game and poultry, and formerly for its fur. Once almost extinct in Britain, but recovering slowly.
Habitat: lives mainly in woodland and near water, although it rarely climbs or swims. Makes a den among rocks or tree roots, or sometimes in old rabbit holes.
The domestic ferret (*M. fero*), kept for hunting and controlling rabbits, is often thought to have originated from the Western polecat, although its skull shows some similarities with that of the Steppe polecat. It is the size of the Western polecat, but in captivity it is usually very pale and often albino. Feral populations, occurring in many areas, tend to resemble the polecat in colour and habits and interbreed with them when the opportunity arises.

STEPPE POLECAT
Mustela eversmanni

Head and body 30–44cm, tail 13–18cm. Very similar to the Western polecat, but paler in colour above.
Habitat: lives mainly in grassland, scrub and cultivated land of Eastern Europe.

Food and habits: grassland animals such as susliks and hamsters are prominent in diet. More active in daylight hours than western species. Habits otherwise similar, except that it usually lives in an underground burrow, often excavating for itself.

STOAT
Mustela erminea

Head and body 22–32cm, tail 8–12cm. Males considerably larger than females. Body long and slim with short legs. Reddish-brown above, white tinged with yellow below. Tip of tail black. In northern part of range winter coat is white, but tail tip remains black. Fur is known as *ermine*. This is harvested mainly in Russia, but supplies are declining. Musky odour produced by anal glands.

Habitat: lives mainly in woodland, but adaptable and found in hedgerows rough grassland and moorland.

Food and habits: diet almost entirely meat, especially rodents, rabbits, fish, birds and eggs. Mainly nocturnal, but may hunt by day. Numbers fluctuate with abundance of prey species. Regarded as pest of poultry and game birds, and much persecuted.

winter coat

summer coat

PINE MARTEN
Martes martes

Head and body 40–55cm, tail 22–27cm. Colour varies from brown to nearly black above and below. Conspicuous throat patch yellowish to orange, but never pure white. Sharp muzzle, prominent ears, long bushy tail.

Habitat: lives in woodlands, especially the pine woods of northern Europe; being a good climber, is often seen in trees. The Pine marten is trapped intensively for fur, and has become rare in many parts of range; also trapped to protect game birds.

Food and habits: feeds on small birds, squirrels and other small rodents, rabbits and eggs, but will also take honey and berries. Mainly nocturnal.

BEECH MARTEN
Martes foina

Head and body 40–48cm, tail 22–26cm. Similar to Pine marten, but with a pure-white throat patch, which is often divided by a dark streak. In Crete the throat patch is much reduced and may be absent.
Habitat: lives in deciduous woodland and rocky areas, and is often found near houses. Less often seen in trees than Pine marten. Absent from British Isles and Scandinavia.
Food and habits: preys on mice, shrews, birds, frogs and lizards; also eats some fruit and berries. Habits similar to those of Pine marten, but will make den in houses and barns and readily enters towns.

Cretan form

EUROPEAN MINK
Mustela lutreola

Head and body 35–40cm, tail 13–14cm. Male larger than female. A large weasel-like species. Dark brown all over, except for white markings above and below the mouth. No white around eye. Feet partially webbed; swims and dives well.
Habitat: lives in marsh lands and on the banks of lakes and rivers mainly in eastern and northern Europe.
Food and habits: eats water voles, rodents, birds, frogs and fish. Nocturnal and solitary. Sleeps by day in a hole or burrow or in a hollow tree.
The American mink (*M. vison*), introduced to fur farms in Europe, has escaped and become established in Britain and elsewhere. It can be distinguished from the European mink because it has no white on upper jaw.

OTTER
Lutra lutra

Head and body 60–80cm, tail 35–45cm. Fur rich brown above, paler below, especially on throat. Thick underfur grey, mixed with long, glossy guard hairs. Long body with long tapering tail, short legs, webbed feet. Ears very small.

Habitat: lives by lakes and rivers and also inhabits coastal areas in wilder parts of its range. Widely distributed.

Food and habits: feeds mainly on fish of many kinds, although eels are often preferred. Also eats crayfish and other invertebrates, and water birds. On land will take voles, rabbits and other small mammals. Usually nocturnal. Spends much time in the water. Hunted for fur, sport and to protect fishing interests, the otter is becoming scarce in some parts of its range. Habitat destruction is also an important factor in its decrease, as is water pollution.

WOLVERINE
Gulo gulo

Head and body 70–80cm, tail 16–25cm. Often known as the Glutton. Largest of the weasel family. Dense, shaggy coat of thick fur, dark brown above, with band of paler colour on side and dark below. Thick body with short, strong legs.

Range and habitat: lives in evergreen forests in colder parts of northern Europe and on the tundra. Persecuted by man for its fur and as a pest of domestic animals, but is still common in many parts of its range.

Food and habits: eats mostly rodents, birds, eggs, and invertebrates in summer, but mainly carrion in winter. Can attack sickly animals of larger size and may eat deer. Its particularly strong jaws are used to tear carrion. Hunts alone or in pairs. Nocturnal and relatively slow-moving.

BADGER
Meles meles

Head and body 70–80cm, tail 12–19cm. Stout, squat body; head with long tapered snout. The rough coat is grey above, and black below and on limbs. Head white, with conspicuous black stripe on each side running through the eye to the small ears, which are tipped with white.

Habitat: lives mainly in woods and copses in extensive burrow systems called *sets*, which can be recognized by the great mounds of excavated earth surrounding the entrances. May also live in fields and hedgerows.

Food and habits: feeds on a wide range of animals and plants, including earthworms, small mammals, carrion, fruit, nuts and bulbs. Lives in family groups. Nocturnal.

MONGOOSES AND GENETS Family Viverridae

A family of small- to medium-sized carnivores, including about 75 species of civets, genets, and mongooses widely distributed throughout both Asia and Africa. Ecologically, they are the tropical equivalents of the weasels and martens, which occur mainly in the cooler regions of the world. Three species occur in southern Europe. The family includes a number of species with striped and spotted coats, sinuous bodies and long bushy tails. Scent-gland secretions, known as *civet*, are taken from several species and used in the perfume and pharmaceutical industries. Unlike those of the mustelids, the secretions are not usually unpleasant and are not used for defence.

GENET
Genetta genetta

Head and body 50–60cm, tail 40–50cm. Similar to a small, lightly built cat. Coat spotted dark brown on pale ground colour; tail banded light and dark. Short legs, large ears and pointed muzzle.

Range and habitat: range includes most of Africa and Arabia, together with Iberia and much of France. Lives in bush and scrub country.

Food and habits: eats mainly small mammals, birds and insects. Nocturnal, usually solitary.

EGYPTIAN MONGOOSE
Herpestes ichneumon

Head and body 50–55cm, tail 35–45cm. Long sinuous body, grizzled grey all over. Tail tipped with black, tapering to a point.
Range and habitat: found in southern Spain and Portugal, probably as an introduction from Africa, where it is common from Egypt to the Cape. Lives in scrub and open woodland.
Food and habits: feeds on rodents, birds, eggs and reptiles. Known for ability to kill snakes by agility and speed of attack. Nocturnal, but sometimes active by day. Usually solitary, but sometimes found in small family groups.
The Indian Grey Mongoose (*H. edwardsi*) is slightly smaller and has a lighter tip to the tail, which is about the same length (45cm) as the head and body. It has been introduced to southern Italy from Asia.

RACCOONS Family Procyonidae

A small family of about 18 species, including raccoons and kinkajous. Some scientists include the Lesser and Giant pandas of Asia in this family, but otherwise the family is confined to the Americas. Most species are small- to medium-sized carnivores with long tails, and generally rather flat, non-slicing cheek teeth. One species has been introduced to Europe.

RACCOON
Procyon lotor

Head and body 50–60cm, tail 30–40cm. About the size of a cat, but easily identified by its black mask contrasting with white face markings, and by its distinctly banded tail. General colour greyish-brown.

Range and habitat: widespread in the Americas, and now established in Germany, the Netherlands and Luxembourg. Lives mainly in woodland often close to water. Nocturnal.
Food and habits: feeds mainly on aquatic animals, especially crayfish, fish and insects in the water, and rodents and a little plant food on land.

CATS Family Felidae

A family of about 36 species of carnivores widely distributed around the world. Although differing greatly in size and coat pattern—many are beautifully striped or spotted—all are unmistakably cat-like in appearance, with supple, muscular bodies, rounded heads and short jaws, eyes with pupils that contract to vertical slits, and well-developed whiskers. They have fewer teeth than other carnivores, but the cheek teeth are superbly suited to shearing through flesh and the canines are large and dagger-like. The claws can be retracted as a rule, and the animals walk on their toes like dogs—not on the soles of their feet like bears. There are nocturnal and diurnal species, and some which hunt by night and day. Most species hunt by creeping stealthily towards their prey and then pouncing or rushing the last few metres. There are 2 native species in Europe.

LYNX
Felis lynx

Head and body 80–130cm, tail 11–25cm. A medium-sized cat with long legs, markedly tufted ears and a ruff round the face. Tail short, black towards the tip. Coat reddish with dark spots which vary in number and are often indistinct, especially in the north of the range. Some scientists consider the Spanish lynx to be a separate species, as it is smaller and more heavily spotted.

Range and habitat: formerly widespread in Europe. Now very scarce in most of range and protected in many areas. Lives mainly in coniferous forest and mountainous country—mainly in Scandinavia and Spain.

Food and habits: feeds on hares, rodents and young deer. Nocturnal.

WILD CAT
Felis sylvestris

Head and body 50–65cm, tail 30cm. About the size of a large domestic cat, but somewhat more robust. Can be distinguished from domestic cats by its short bushy tail, which is marked with clear, separate dark rings; the coat, which is usually clearly striped; and the pale paws.

Habitat: lives in dense woodland and on rocky hills. Southern Europe, Alps and Scotland.

Food and habits: eats mostly small mammals, hares and rabbits, but may also kill small deer and lambs, birds, fish and some insects. Nocturnal.

Hooved Mammals

The hooved mammals, or ungulates, are mostly large grazing and browsing animals which walk on tip-toe and have tough hooves to protect their toes. Walking on tip-toe increases the effective length of the leg, and therefore the stride, and enables the animals to run faster—an important factor for animals living, as most ungulates do, on open grasslands. Batteries of grinding cheek teeth crush the the food, and most species employ armies of intestinal bacteria to digest the cellulose. There are two distinct orders which are not closely related. The Perisso-dactyla, represented by the horses and asses, the tapirs, and the rhinoceroses, are known as odd-toed ungulates because the feet normally have 1 or 3 toes. The weight is all borne on the central toe. The Artiodactyla contain the even-toed ungulates, or cloven-hooved mammals, which have 2 or 4 toes on each foot and support their weight on the two middle toes. They include pigs, sheep, deer, antelopes, cattle and camels—in fact, almost all the world's large herbivores. Many are ruminants—cud-chewing animals with complex stomachs.

WILD BOAR
Sus scrofa Family Suidae

Head and body 1·8m, tail 30cm. Size very variable, larger in eastern part of range. Has a dense, bristly coat of grey to black colour and a long, mobile snout. Canine teeth well developed, giving tusks up to 30cm long in large males. Young has yellow stripes along the body. Ancestor of the domestic pig.

Habitat: lives mainly in deciduous woodland. Not in Britain or Scandinavia.

Food: diet mostly vegetable (roots, bulbs, acorns and beech mast), but also takes animal food. Can be pest by digging up root crops.

HORSE
Equus caballus Family Equidae

The many breeds of domestic horse are descendants of a wild horse known as the Tarpan (*E. ferus*), which roamed the steppes of Asia and eastern Europe until about 200 years ago. No truly wild horses are found in Europe today, although relatively unimproved breeds survive in several areas, some almost wild. New Forest ponies and Exmoor ponies in Britain and the Camargue horses in France are examples. The Przewalski horse of China and Mongolia most closely resembles truly wild stock and many herds are kept in captivity.

Horses are distributed worldwide as a result of introduction by man. Colour and size vary enormously, but all have the characteristic long heads and long, maned necks.

CATTLE, SHEEP, GOATS AND ALLIES
Family Bovidae

There are more than 100 species in this widely distributed family, ranging from graceful antelopes to huge bison and buffalo. All have complex stomachs and all chew the cud. Most species have unbranched horns with a bony core fixed permanently to the bones of the skull and covered with a sheath of horny material. Horns are found in both sexes in most species. Many species are gregarious and form large herds. Most live in open country and many are mountain animals.

DOMESTIC GOAT
Capra hircus

Size very variable: colour ranges from white to black, often piebald. Horns long and divergent in male, often turning up at the tips: shorter in female. Adult males are bearded.

Habitat: feral herds, usually with rather shaggy coats, live in many parts of Europe, roaming on rocky hillsides and scrub.

Food and habits: browses on shrubs and trees, often standing on hind legs to reach branches. Also grazes. Domestic goats are descended from the true Wild Goat (*C. aegagrus*), which is probably extinct, although feral herds on Crete are thought to resemble the original stock very closely. Their horns diverge little and sweep back in a smooth curve.

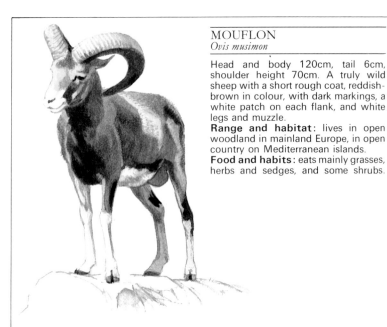

MOUFLON
Ovis musimon

Head and body 120cm, tail 6cm, shoulder height 70cm. A truly wild sheep with a short rough coat, reddish-brown in colour, with dark markings, a white patch on each flank, and white legs and muzzle.
Range and habitat: lives in open woodland in mainland Europe, in open country on Mediterranean islands.
Food and habits: eats mainly grasses, herbs and sedges, and some shrubs.

CHAMOIS
Rupicapra rupicapra

Head and body 90–130cm, tail 3–4cm, shoulder height 75–80cm. Goat-like, with stiff coarse hair, which is tawny brown in summer, changing to a longer, nearly black coat in winter. Lighter in colour below, with white throat patch. Horns up to 20cm long, bent sharply back like a hook at tip.
Habitat: lives on wooded slopes and above the tree line in mountainous areas. Moves down to lower slopes in winter.
Food and habits: mainly herbs in summer, lichens and mosses in winter, but will eat young tree shoots. Gregarious, and forms large herds in winter.

DEER Family Cervidae

A family of about 53 species widely distributed in the Americas and Eurasia, including tropical areas. Ten species live in Europe, of which half are introduced. Nearly all species have antlers. These are solid bony appendages of the skull, developed each year and shed after the *rut*, or breeding season. Growing antlers are covered in blood-rich skin called velvet. With the exception of the reindeer, only males carry antlers. Like the cattle and antelopes, deer are cud-chewing animals. Males are usually larger than females.

RED DEER
Cervus elaphus

Shoulder height up to 140cm. A large species with a reddish-brown summer coat changing to a thicker brown-grey coat in winter. Whitish below; patch around tail buff-coloured.
Habitat: lives in dense deciduous forest, but in some areas has adapted to moorland and open woodland.
Food and habits: mainly browsing animals, eating young shoots and leaves of deciduous trees and shrubs, but will also eat nuts and fruits.

female

ROE DEER
Capreolus capreolus

Shoulder height 75cm, female smaller. A small, slender deer. Summer coat smooth and red-brown in colour; winter coat long and grey. Underparts white. Tail almost invisible. Small, up-right antlers with characteristic knobbed base (the *coronet*) and only 3 points.
Range and habitat: abundant in woodlands of northern Europe, less common in south. Prefers open wood-land, but may be found in any region with enough cover.
Food: mainly a browser eating leaves of trees and shrubs, but will also take grasses, nuts, fungi and herbs. In winter eats shoots and may bark trees.

MUNTJAC
Muntiacus reevesi

Shoulder height 40cm. A tiny deer with a dark red coat marked with white on chin, throat and rump. Coat lighter in female. Tail longish and bushy. Male carries simple antlers pointing backwards. Females carry tufts of hair in place of antlers.

Range and habitat: from southern China, and introduced to parks and estates in England and France, where escaped animals are now established. Lives in woodland with cover, and grazes in clearings.

Food and habits: both grazes and browses, eating shrubs, shoots, grass and fruit. May strip bark and cause crop damage.

REINDEER
Rangifer tarandus

Shoulder height 110–120cm. Coat thick, and variable in colour, but often a dark grey-brown in summer and paler in winter. Ears small, tail short. Hooves particularly broad and deeply cleft. Both sexes carry complex antlers.

Range and habitat: lives on the tundra and taiga of northern Europe. Domesticated in parts of northern Europe especially Lapland. Domestic animals small and very variable in colour.

Food and habits: grasses and sedges in summer; lichens and young shoots in winter. Wild herds are migratory, and strong swimmers.

female, summer

male, summer

ELK
Alces alces

Shoulder height 1·8–2m. The largest deer. Colour grey-brown to black above, lighter on snout and legs. Broad muzzle. Males carry large palmate antlers with numerous branches.
Range and habitat: Scandinavia. Once close to extinction, but herds are now expanding in many areas. Lives in marshlands in summer, moving to drier land, often woodland, in winter.
Food and habits: eats leaves and young shoots, particularly birch and willow, and aquatic plants in summer. In winter subsists on bark and shoots. Spends much time in or near water, and can swim well.

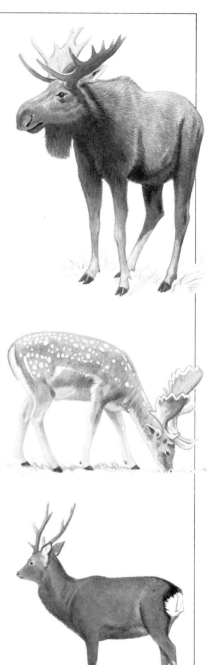

FALLOW DEER
Cervus dama

Shoulder height about 100cm. Many colour varieties, but usually reddish-yellow above, with white spots; yellowish-white below. Greyer with less conspicuous spotting in winter. Rump with a bold black-and-white pattern and a black stripe down the long tail. Antlers have a palmate (flattened) blade.
Range and habitat: deciduous and mixed forests with scrub and clearings. A very common deer in parks, from which many have escaped. Probably Mediterranean in origin.
Food and habits: mainly grasses or herbs and berries. In winter may eat bark of young trees.

SIKA DEER
Cervus nippon

Shoulder height 80–90cm. Colour buff-brown with faint spots in summer and a grey head; in winter a darker brown. Short white tail; rump patch white with a dark edge.
Range and habitat: originally broad-leaved woodland in eastern Asia; introduced to many parks in Europe, where escapes have given rise to herds in several countries.
Food and habits: grazes and browses on young tree and shrub shoots. May strip bark.

Marine Mammals

Although the mammals are basically 4-footed land animals, several groups have reverted to an aquatic existence and 3 orders are almost entirely marine. Two of these orders are found in European waters.

The Order Pinnipedia contains about 30 species of seals, walruses, and sea-lions. These are carnivorous mammals living mainly near the coasts, mostly in temperate and cold regions where there is an abundance of fish for them to eat. They have streamlined bodies (when in the water) and all the limbs are in the form of flippers. Though they spend most of their lives in the sea, the pinnipeds must come ashore to breed. They also bask on rocky shores and sand banks at low tide, often in large numbers.

A few species live in fresh water, although not in Europe. The three species described here are the only ones likely to be seen south of the Baltic, although several others occur around the shores of Scandinavia.

The Order Cetacea contains the whales, dolphins and porpoises – about 90 species in all and even more completely adapted for aquatic life than the seals. They never come ashore, even to breed, although they still have their lungs and have to come to the surface for air. Their bodies are beautifully streamlined, with the front limbs in the form of flippers and no hind limbs. The tail has horizontal flukes which provide the forward thrust.

head profile

COMMON SEAL
Phoca vitulina Family Phocidae

Length 2m, females smaller. Colour variable, grey-yellow to dark brown, usually marked with dark spots. Nostrils form a distinct v when seen from the front.
Food and habits: feeds mainly on fish, molluscs and crustaceans. Inhabits shallow coastal waters and estuaries of north-west Europe.

pup

GREY SEAL
Halichoerus grypus

Length 3·8m, females very much smaller. Muzzle long; nostrils widely separated. Colour dark brown or black with lighter spots or blotches. Females paler.
Food and habits: feeds mainly on fish and squid. Prefers rocky coasts and more exposed places than Common seal. North-west Europe.

pup

head profile

MONK SEAL
Monachus monachus

Length 2·7m. Colour is a uniform brown on back, greyer below and usually with a white patch on belly. Pups black.
Range: Mediterranean and Black Sea, but now rare.

CHAPTER TWO

BIRDS

The birds make up the class Aves – one of the major divisions of the backboned or vertebrate animals. There exist about 9,000 species, found in all kinds of habitats: from the open oceans to the deserts and from the polar ice-caps to the equatorial forests. About 470 species breed in Europe, including the numerous migrants that fly in from Africa for the summer.

There is enormous variation in the shape and size of birds, with the European species ranging from the mighty Mute Swan to the tiny Goldcrest. Behaviour is equally varied, but no one ever has any difficulty in recognizing a bird as such because of its characteristic coating of feathers. No other kind of animal possesses feathers. Other features which are characteristic of birds include the beak, or bill, and the conversion of the front limbs into wings – although not all birds can actually fly.

Beaks and Feet
Just as the teeth of mammals tell us about their feeding habits, so the beaks of birds provide information about their diets. Birds' beaks normally have to catch or pick up food, and then crush or tear it, so their shape is very much related to diet. Whole families, such as the ducks, can sometimes be recognized from the shape of the beak alone. Seed-eating birds have fairly short, stout beaks for crushing hard seeds; insect-eaters have either very slender beaks for picking up small creatures or wide-gaping beaks for scooping up their prey in mid-air; the flesh-eaters have sharp, hooked beaks for tearing up food.

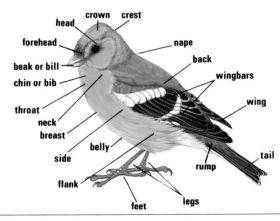

A male chaffinch in breeding plumage, showing the main areas used when describing a bird.

Feet also very often reveal a good deal about a bird's habitat and mode of life. Marsh-loving birds, for example, usually have long legs and long, spreading toes, while swimmers generally have webbed feet. The perching birds which include all the common garden birds, have three forward-pointing toes and one backward-pointing toe on each foot – admirably arranged for grasping branches and other perches.

Identifying Birds

Size and colour are clearly the main features to look for when trying to identify a bird; in the following pages the description of each species begins with the size, from the tip of the beak to the end of the tail, and the diagnostic points of that species. The diagram shown here indicates the major regions of the body used in the bird descriptions. The position of stripes, if any, on the head is of particular value in identifying many small birds. Wing and tail shapes are very useful clues, especially when birds are seen only as silhouettes in flight. Beak shapes can also help if you can get close enough to see them. Attention should also be paid to birds' habits, for many species have characteristic movements and attitudes both on the ground and in the air.

Songs will enable you to identify birds even before you see them, although it takes time to learn to recognize the songs of even the most common birds. The best way to become familiar with them is to listen to the good recordings now available or to go bird-watching with an expert and learn to recognize the songs as you watch the birds. The distribution maps and the habitat information given in this chapter may also help to determine the identity of certain birds.

Binoculars are indispensable for watching and identifying birds: 8 × 30 is a very good size for general bird-watching, but if you can afford a lightweight pair, you will find 10 × 24 slightly more powerful and yet lighter to carry

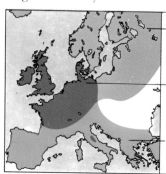

The maps on the following pages show in which parts of Europe a bird is likely to be found and at which times of the year. Many birds, such as swallows and most of the warblers, visit Europe only for the summer and have no blue on their maps because they spend the winter in Africa. A bird is unlikely to be found in a white area unless migrating to or from its breeding grounds.

pink
breeding range, can be seen in summer only.

purple
breeding range, can be seen throughout the year.

blue
can be seen in winter only.

Divers

Divers are really at home underwater, where they catch fish and crustaceans. They either dive suddenly from the surface or sink slowly in to the water. On land, divers walk clumsily and they normally come ashore only to breed. In winter, all divers become greyish above and white below. They can then best be told apart by their size and bill shape. Divers belong to the order Gaviiformes, of which there is just one family – the Gaviidae.

GREAT NORTHERN DIVER
Gavia immer

76 cm. Heavy bill. Summer: all-black head; chequered back. Winter: grey-brown back. Breeds on lakes in Iceland. Found at coast at other times.

RED-THROATED DIVER
Gavia stellata

56 cm. Thin, upturned bill. Summer: red throat patch; plain grey back. Winter: grey-brown back, speckled with white. Breeds by coast and on lakes, flying daily to the sea to feed. May be seen on reservoirs and lakes as well as at coast during autumn and winter.

BLACK-THROATED DIVER
Gavia arctica

63 cm. Intermediate bill. Summer: black throat patch; dark spotted back. Winter: blackish back. Breeds at remote lakes or lochs, usually on rocky islands. Seen at coasts in autumn and winter, often in small flocks.

Grebes

Grebes are elegant water birds with colourful breeding plumage in spring and summer. The boldly patterned heads and necks, with their ear tufts and frills, clearly mark them out from other birds. In winter, grebes lose their colour and adornments, becoming grey-brown above and white below. Then they look like divers, but are smaller and have wedge-shaped heads.

Grebes feed by diving for fish and other water animals. Although agile in the water, they are not good fliers and may escape danger by partly submerging themselves until only the head remains above water.

Grebes build nests of water plants among reeds at the edges of lakes and rivers, and lay about four eggs. The eggs may be covered with vegetation. Before building the nest, the birds perform extraordinary courtship dances in which they rush to and fro over the water and freeze in absurd postures. The chicks are often carried on the parents' backs, even during dives.

Grebes spread to the coast and open water in autumn and winter. They belong to the Podicipitidae, the only family in the order Podicipediformes.

GREAT CRESTED GREBE
Podiceps cristatus

46 cm. Long white neck and pink bill. Summer: large ear tufts and frill. Found on inland waters in summer and winter, also at coast in winter. Once hunted for its plumage, it came near to extinction in Britain in 1800s. Recovery mainly due to protection, though building of reservoirs has enabled it to expand.

RED-NECKED GREBE
Podiceps grisegena

43 cm. Medium-sized neck and black and yellow bill. Summer: red neck and pale grey cheeks but no frill. Found on inland waters in summer: usually at coast in winter.

SLAVONIAN GREBE or HORNED GREBE
Podiceps auritus

36 cm. Blue-grey bill. Summer: golden ear tufts and chestnut neck. Winter: white cheeks. Found on inland waters in summer and at estuaries in winter.

BLACK-NECKED GREBE
Podiceps nigricollis

30 cm. Slightly upturned bill. Summer: black neck and chestnut ear tufts. Winter: dusky neck and cheeks. Often seen in small flocks on inland waters in summer and on estuaries and inland in winter.

LITTLE GREBE or DABCHICK
Tachybaptus ruficollis

25 cm. Duck-like shape with almost no tail. Summer: rust-coloured neck. Found on inland waters in summer and winter, also at coast in winter.

Gannets, Pelicans and Cormorants

Gannets (family Sulidae), pelicans (family Pelecanidae) and cormorants (family Phalacrocoracidae) are the largest European sea birds. Although they all have webbed feet, they are not habitual swimmers. They all have different and interesting methods of fishing. All belong to the order Pelecaniformes.

GANNET
Sula bassana

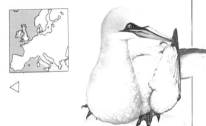

91 cm. White body with pointed tail; black wingtips; yellow head with blue eye-ring. Breeds in summer in vast colonies on cliffs, mainly on rocky islands. Winters at sea, but may be seen offshore. May follow ships. Makes spectacular dive into the water to catch fish.

CORMORANT
Phalacrocorax carbo

91 cm. Atlantic form: all black with white chin. Continental form: black with white head and neck in summer. Found at seashores and on inland waters. Flies low over water but settles on surface before diving for fish. Often perches with wings outspread, probably to dry them. Atlantic form is found in Britain, Norway and Iceland and breeds on rocky cliffs. Continental form is found in mainland Europe and nests in trees and bushes.

Atlantic form

Continental form

SHAG
Phalacrocorax aristotelis

76 cm. Green-black; yellow base of bill. Identical to cormorant in behaviour, but smaller in size and rarely seen inland at any season. Breeds on rocky cliffs at coast.

PYGMY CORMORANT
Phalacrocorax pygmaeus

48 cm. Breeding: dark spotted plumage; rust-coloured head. Non-breeding: unspotted plumage, white throat, rust-coloured breast. Usually found on inland waters. Nests in trees and bushes.

WHITE PELICAN
Pelecanus onocrotalus

168 cm. Underside of wings white at front, dark at rear; flesh-coloured feet. Breeds in swamps and marshes in eastern Mediterranean. May also be seen at coast in winter. Uses pouch beneath bill as net to catch fish. Rare.

DALMATIAN PELICAN
Pelecanus crispus

168 cm. Underside of wings all white except for dark wingtips; grey feet. Same habitat and behaviour as white pelican and inhabits same areas. Rare.

Fulmars, Petrels and Shearwaters

The fulmar and shearwaters (family Procellariidae) and petrels (family Hydrobatidae) form the order Procellariiformes. They are ocean birds that normally come ashore only to breed. They may then be seen in colonies on coastal cliffs and islands. Some shearwaters are southern birds that visit European waters when migrating.

light phase

FULMAR
Fulmarus glacialis

46 cm. Thick neck; stubby bill; light grey with white head and underparts (light phase) or smoky grey all over (dark phase). Often follows ships, but may come ashore and occupy buildings. Nests in colonies on cliffs. Parents protect the young by ejecting a foul-smelling oily liquid at intruders.

CORY'S SHEARWATER
Calonectris diomedea

46 cm. Light brown head; yellow bill. Breeds on Mediterranean islands and ventures into Atlantic in autumn. Does not follow ships.

MANX SHEARWATER
Puffinus puffinus

36 cm. Dark upperparts and white underparts; small size. Breeds in colonies in burrows on islands and cliff-tops. Does not follow ships. Commonest European shearwater.

GREAT SHEARWATER
Puffinus gravis

46 cm. Black cap and white throat; white at base of tail. Breeds in south Atlantic in winter and visits open north Atlantic in summer and autumn. Sometimes seen offshore.

SOOTY SHEARWATER
Puffinus griseus

41 cm. Dark all over; narrow wings. Breeds in south Atlantic in winter and visits north Atlantic in summer and autumn. May be seen offshore.

STORM PETREL
Hydrobates pelagicus

15 cm. Square tail; flitting and pattering flight. Nests in crevices in rocks or stone walls on islands. Can be seen following ships, flitting over the waves summer and autumn. May be seen offshore.

LEACH'S PETREL
Oceanodroma leucorhoa

20 cm. Shallow fork in tail, erratic flight. Breeds in burrows on islands. Flight is more erratic than storm petrel, and does not follow ships or patter over waves.

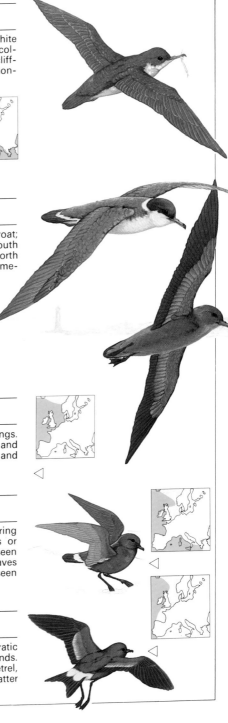

Herons and Allies

These birds are elegant long-legged waders belonging to the order Ciconiiformes. They feed mainly in shallow water, lowering their long necks and bills to catch aquatic animals. Some herons spread their wings while fishing, perhaps to cut out the reflection of the sky. Herons and bitterns (family Ardeidae) and storks (family Ciconiidae) all have straight bills. They can easily be identified in flight because herons and bitterns draw back their heads whereas storks fly with necks outstretched.

PURPLE HERON
Ardea purpurea

79 cm. Long S-shaped chestnut neck with black stripe; reddish underparts. Found in swamps and marshes, where it breeds in colonies.

NIGHT HERON
Nycticorax nycticorax

61 cm. Stocky with rather short legs, black back, white breast; black cap. Usually seen feeding at dusk in pools and marshes, or roosting in bushes and trees during the day.

SQUACCO HERON
Ardeola ralloides

46 cm. Thick neck and stocky shape; buff body with white wings, but looks white in flight. Found in marshes and swamps and at small stretches of water, where it nests among reeds or in bushes or trees. It is like a bittern in shape but is much less shy.

GREY HERON
Ardea cinerea

91 cm. Pale grey and white with black crest; black wing edges. The most common and largest European heron. Found on inland water and at seashore, where it stands motionless in or near water then suddenly darts head down after prey. Also perches in trees, where it usually nests in colonies.

GREAT WHITE EGRET
Egretta alba

89 cm. Black feet; no summer crest. Found by shallow water; nests in reed-beds. Resembles little egret but is much larger and less common.

LITTLE EGRET
Egretta garzetta

58 cm. Yellow feet. May be found at shallow water of any kind. Usually nests near water. In summer develops a long white crest of hanging plumes, for which it was once hunted.

summer

winter

LITTLE BITTERN
Ixobrychus minutus

36 cm. Black wings with buff patch, black back (male) or brown back (female). Hides away and nests among dense reeds and thickets near water. May escape detection by freezing stock-still.

BITTERN
Botaurus stellaris

76 cm. Large stocky shape. Same habitat and behaviour as little bittern, but much larger size. Freezes with bill pointing upwards. Foghorn-like booming call may be heard at a great distance.

WHITE STORK
Ciconia ciconia

102 cm. White neck and upperparts; red bill and legs. Found in marshes, farmland and open country. Nests on buildings, often on special platforms, or in trees near farms and villages. Walks slowly over ground as it searches for insects and other small animals to eat.

GREATER FLAMINGO
Phoenicopterus ruber

125 cm. Large bent bill; very long neck and legs; pink and black wings (in flight). Found in flocks only in the nature reserves of the Camargue region in southern France, where it breeds, and of the Coto de Doñana in southern Spain, where breeding is rare. Single birds seen in the wild have probably escaped from collections. Wades in shallow water, dipping its bill to strain tiny creatures from the water, and nests on mudflats or on heaps of mud in water.

Waterfowl or Wildfowl

This group of birds consists of ducks, geese and swans. They are all water birds, and use their webbed feet to swim strongly. The young are born with feathers and can walk and swim soon after hatching. Many species can be seen on lakes in parks. All belong to the Anatidae, the only family in the order Anseriformes.

DUCKS Family Anatidae

Ducks are usually smaller in size and have shorter necks than geese and swans. The two sexes have different plumage, although in late summer the drakes (males) moult and for a time resemble the ducks (females). Ducks nest on the ground or in holes. There are three main groups of ducks. *Surface-feeding* or *dabbling ducks* live in shallow water, where they feed on water plants by up-ending. They leap into the air to get airborne, and have a brightly coloured patch of glossy wing feathers called a *speculum* The colour of the speculum is important in identifying the females. *Diving ducks* dive from the surface for water plants and animals. Their legs are set farther back so that they can swim underwater, and they run along the surface to take wing. The third group of ducks, the *sawbills*, are also divers.

male

female

MALLARD
Anas platyrhynchos

58 cm. Male: dark green head; chestnut breast. Female: blue-purple speculum. Dabbling duck, very common on all kinds of inland waters and at coasts and estuaries. Often seen in flocks. Most domestic ducks, though different in colour, are descended from wild mallards.

TEAL
Anas crecca

36 cm. Male: brown and green head. Female: small size, green speculum. Dabbling duck. Smallest European duck. Prefers secluded inland waters in summer, spreads to open waters and coasts in winter.

female

male

GADWALL
Anas strepera

51 cm. Male: grey body with black rear; brown wing panel; black and white speculum. Female: white belly, black and white speculum. Dabbling duck. Prefers inland waters.

GARGANEY
Anas querquedula

38 cm. Male: white stripe on head. Female: blue-grey forewing; indistinct speculum. Dabbling duck. Prefers inland waters, seldom seen on coast.

WIGEON
Anas penelope

46 cm. Male: chestnut head with light crown; white forewing. Female: black and green speculum; white belly. Dabbling duck. Prefers inland waters in summer, spreads to coast in winter, when it may be seen in flocks. May graze on land.

PINTAIL
Anas acuta

63 cm. Large but slim build. Male: long pointed tail; white neck stripe. Female: Long neck, long tail. Dabbling duck. Prefers inland waters in summer, but coasts in winter. Breeds on moors, marshes.

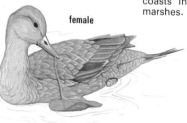

SHOVELER
Anas clypeata

51 cm. Spoon-shaped bill. Male: green head, white breast and chestnut flanks. Female: blue forewing with dark green speculum. Dabbling duck. Usually found on ponds and in marshes. The odd-shaped bill, unlike that of all other ducks, is used to strain tiny plants and animals from the water.

female male

EIDER
Somateria mollissima

61 cm. Male: white back and black belly. Female: brown plumage closely barred with black. Diving duck. Most marine of all ducks, seldom found inland. Breeds at seashore, lining nest with soft breast feathers known as eider down.

male female

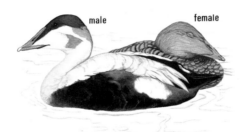

SHELDUCK
Tadorna tadorna

61 cm. Male: green-black head and white body with broad chestnut band; red knob over bill. Female: as male but no red knob. Large goose-like duck. Nests in hollow trees and burrows or among bushes. Winters mainly at coasts, often on mudflats.

male female

female

male

female

male

female

male

FERRUGINOUS DUCK
Aythya nyroca

41 cm. Male: rich brown head, neck and breast; white eye; white patch under tail; bold white wingbar. Female: as male but dull brown and brown eye; white patch under tail and white wingbar. Diving duck. Breeds among reeds on inland waters; winters at open inland waters, rarely at coast.

GOLDENEYE
Bucephala clangula

46 cm. Male: round white patch before eye. Female: brown head with white collar. Diving duck. Nests in tree holes and burrows near fresh water; winters on lakes, rivers and coastal waters. Drakes raise bill in courting display in early spring. Wings whistle in flight.

POCHARD
Aythya ferina

46 cm. Male: dark chestnut head and neck with pale grey back; black breast. Female: brown head with light stripe through eye; blue band on bill; grey wing band. Diving duck. Breeds among reeds on inland waters, otherwise seen mainly on lakes and at estuaries.

SCAUP
Aythya marila

46 cm. Male: as tufted duck, but no crest and with grey back. Female: as

tufted duck, but no crest and with larger white face patch. Diving duck. Breeds inland, but otherwise seen at coast and on estuaries.

male

female

TUFTED DUCK
Aythya fuligula

43 cm. Male: drooping crest; dark head and neck, black back and tail with white belly. Female: small crest; small white patch at base of bill, white wingbar. Diving duck. Often seen on lakes and ponds; also at seashore and estuaries in winter.

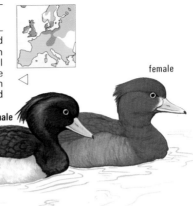

RED-BREASTED MERGANSER
Mergus serrator

56 cm. Male: green-black head with double crest, white collar and chestnut breast band. Female: chestnut head with double crest. Sawbill. Breeds near fresh or salt water, hiding nest among rocks or vegetation. Mainly found at coasts in winter.

GOOSANDER
Mergus merganser

66 cm. Male: dark green head with long thin red bill, pinkish-white breast and flanks. Female: as female red-breasted merganser, but with single crest and striking white throat. Sawbill. Nests in tree cavities and burrows near fresh water. Usually remains inland in winter.

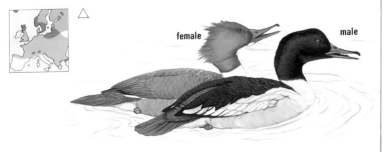

GEESE Family Anatidae

Geese are between ducks and swans in size. They graze mainly on land, and the legs are set forward so that they can walk easily. The sexes are alike. There are two groups of geese. Geese of the genus *Anser* are grey-brown and those of the genus *Branta* are black and white.

BARNACLE GOOSE
Branta leucopsis

63 cm. White face, black neck and breast. Winter visitor from Arctic to salt marshes and estuaries and surrounding fields. The odd name comes from a medieval belief that the birds hatch from goose barnacles instead of eggs.

CANADA GOOSE
Branta canadensis

97 cm. Long black neck, black head with white throat, light breast. Largest European goose. Introduced from North America to parks. Escaped birds now breed in Britain and Sweden, and may move further south for the winter. Wild birds nest on islands in lakes and graze in marshes and fields by lakes and rivers.

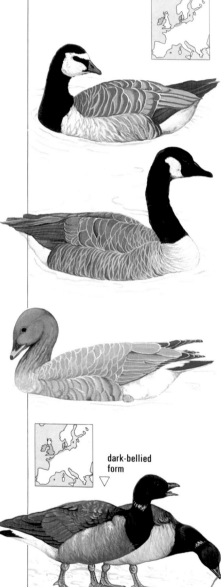

dark-bellied form

PINK-FOOTED GOOSE
Anser brachyrhynchus

68 cm. As bean goose, but pink feet and legs and pink and black bill. Breeds in Arctic; similar winter habitat to bean goose.

BRENT GOOSE
Branta bernicla

58 cm. Black head and neck with small white neck mark. Winter visitor to coasts and estuaries. Feeds mainly on eel grasses in water, and feeding times depend on tides. There are two subspecies. The light-bellied form (*B.b. hrota*) breeds in Greenland and Spitsbergen, and the dark-bellied form (*B.b. bernicla*) in northern Russia.

WHITE-FRONTED GOOSE
Anser albifrons

71 cm. White patch at base of bill; irregular black bars on belly, pink bill (main race) or yellow or orange bill (Greenland race). Found in same habitat as greylag goose in winter, but breeds in far north. The Greenland race (*A.a. flavirostris*) migrates from Greenland to winter in Ireland and western Scotland. The main, or typical, race (*A.a. albifrons*) breeds in northern Russia and winters in the rest of mainland Europe and in Britain.

Greenland race

Main race

BEAN GOOSE
Anser fabalis

76 cm. Orange-yellow feet and legs; dark head and neck; black and orange-yellow bill. Breeds in northern woods and tundra; winters inland in fields near water.

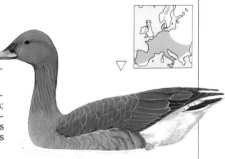

GREYLAG GOOSE
Anser anser

84 cm. Pink feet and legs with head and neck no darker than body, orange bill (Western Europe) or pink bill (Eastern Europe). Very common. Breeds on moors, marshes, reedy lakes, and offshore islands. Winters in fields, inland and coastal marshes and at estuaries. There are two subspecies, or races. The western race (*A.a. anser*) is found in Iceland, Britain and western Europe; the eastern race (*A. a. rubrirostris*) inhabits eastern Europe.

Eastern race

Western race

SWANS Family Anatidae

Swans are the largest waterfowl and immediately recognised by their long elegant necks, which they lower into the water or to the ground to pull up plants. The sexes are alike. The black swan seen in parks has been introduced from Australia. The birds should be approached with caution, especially when breeding. Juveniles of all European species are brown, with indistinct bill patterns.

BEWICK'S SWAN
Cygnus columbianus

122 cm. Black bill with yellow base; neck usually straight. Winter visitor from Arctic. Similar habitat to whooper swan, though prefers larger areas of water in more open country.

WHOOPER SWAN
Cygnus cygnus

152 cm. Yellow bill with black tip; neck usually straight. Nests in swamps and by lakes in far north; winters further south along coasts and on lakes and rivers. Its name refers to whooping sound of call.

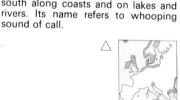

MUTE SWAN
Cygnus olor

152 cm. Orange bill with black knob, neck usually curved. Very common. Often found in tame state on park lakes and village ponds and along rivers. Usually nests at banks of rivers and lakes; winters on open waters and at coast.

Birds of Prey

The birds of prey hunt other animals. They usually catch them alive – on the ground, in the air or in the water – but sometimes they eat dead animals. Some other birds, such as kingfishers and crows, may take similar prey, but the true birds of prey, often called raptors, have sharp talons with which they catch their victims.

Their hooked beaks then tear the flesh. Eagles, falcons and vultures are all birds of prey and all are included in the order Falconiformes. The owls also have sharp talons and hooked beaks, but they hunt mainly by night and, although they are birds of prey, they are placed in a separate order (pages 107–9).

VULTURES, EAGLES, BUZZARDS, HAWKS, KITES AND HARRIERS Family Accipitridae

Most of these birds of prey soar through the air, keeping a sharp lookout for prey below and then dropping on an unsuspecting victim. However, vultures land on the ground to feed on carrion (dead animals) and on refuse. Eagles mainly seek live prey as they soar. Buzzards and kites also soar and look rather like small

eagles, though buzzards may also be seen perching and kites can be told by their long forked tails. Hawks and harriers fly near the ground, hawks dashing rapidly through the air and harriers gliding gently.

GRIFFON VULTURE
Gyps fulvus

100 cm. White neck and head with white ruff. Usually found in mountains. Unlike eagles, has head and tail that appear very small in flight.

EGYPTIAN VULTURE
Neophron percnopterus

63 cm. Long thin bill with bare yellow skin on face; white plumage with black wingtips. Usually seen in mountains, but comes to rubbish dumps in villages. In Africa, it is well known for its habit of dropping stones on ostrich eggs to break them open.

MONK VULTURE
Aegypius monachus

102 cm. Dark patches on head and long bare neck with dark ruff. Usually found in mountains and plains, but rare. If all three vultures arrive at a carcass together, the monk vulture feeds first, then the griffon vulture and finally the Egyptian vulture.

LAMMERGEIER
Gypaetus barbatus

110 cm. Long narrow wings and long diamond-shaped tail; orange breast. Found in mountains; does not join other vultures to feed. Well known for unusual habit of dropping bones on to rocks to break them open.

BONELLI'S EAGLE
Hieraaetus fasciatus

71 cm. White underparts; wings dark above or white with dark band beneath. Usually found in mountains, but may also be seen in more open country in winter. Dashes rapidly through the air, hunting for small mammals and birds. Nests in trees and on rock ledges.

SHORT-TOED EAGLE
Circaetus gallicus

66 cm. White underparts with white underwings and often dark breast and head. Head plumage may be light or dark, dark being more common. Found in mountains and gorges, plains and woods and at coasts. Often hovers, seeking snakes, lizards and frogs. Nests in trees.

GOLDEN EAGLE
Aquila chrysaetos

84 cm. Dark brown all over with golden feathers on head. Usually seen soaring above mountain slopes, though may hunt near the ground. May also be found at coasts and in woods and fields. Nests in trees or on rock ledges.

IMPERIAL EAGLE
Aquila heliaca

81 cm. White shoulders; white wing patches (Spanish form only). Found in low-lying forests, woods, plains and marshes. Nests in tall trees.

Spanish form

dark form

BOOTED EAGLE
Hieraaetus pennatus

51 cm. Small size like buzzard but long narrow tail. Plumage varies from light to dark, but light birds are more common than dark birds. Usually found in forests or woods, hunting in clearings. Nests in trees.

light form

HONEY-BUZZARD
Pernis apivorus

53 cm. Like buzzards, but longer tail with black bands. Colour varies from cream to dark brown. Usually found in clearings and at edges of forests and woods. Gets its name from its habit of feeding at the nests of bees and wasps, though for grubs and not for honey. Nests in trees.

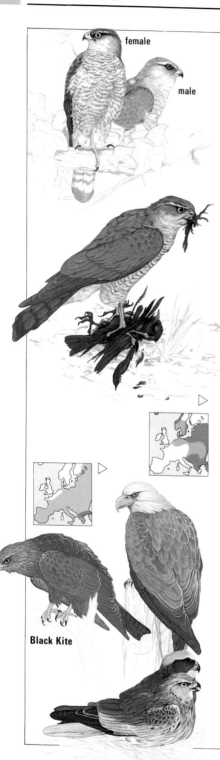

female

male

SPARROWHAWK
Accipiter nisus

33 cm. Broad rounded wings with long tail; closely barred underparts. Usually seen in forests and woods, but also among scattered trees and bushes. Dashes through trees and hops over hedges, hunting small birds. Female is much larger than male. Nests in trees and bushes.

GOSHAWK
Accipiter gentilis

53 cm. Both sexes similar to sparrowhawk but larger size. Female is larger than male. Usually seen in woods and forests, dashing through trees in pursuit of birds. Nests mainly in fir trees.

WHITE-TAILED EAGLE or SEA EAGLE
Haliaeetus albicilla

81 cm. White tail with brown body. Found at coasts and remote lakes. Takes fish from surface of water or plunges; also hunts mammals and birds. Nests in trees and on rock ledges.

BLACK KITE
Milvus migrans

53 cm. As red kite, but dark plumage and shallow forked tail. Usually seen near lakes and rivers surrounded by trees. In southern Europe, also found in more open country and searching for refuse in towns and villages. Nests in trees.

Black Kite

MARSH HARRIER
Circus aeruginosus

51 cm. Male: grey wing patch and tail. Female: pale crown and throat. Usually seen flying low over swamps and marshes and nearby fields. Nests in reed-beds.

MONTAGU'S HARRIER
Circus pygargus

43 cm. Male: as male hen harrier but black wingbar, grey rump and streaky underside. Female: very similar to female hen harrier. Found in same places and has similar flight and nesting habits to hen harrier.

male

female

HEN HARRIER
Circus cyaneus

46 cm. Male: grey with white rump and underside. Female: streaky brown with white rump (very like Montagu's harrier). Hunts while flying low over moors, heaths, fields, marshes and swamps. Makes its nest on the ground.

female

male

BUZZARD
Buteo buteo

53 cm. Like small golden eagle but broad rounded tail. Plumage varies from cream to dark brown. Found in woods, fields and plains, at coasts and on mountain slopes and hillsides. Often soars, but hunts near the ground. Nests in trees and on rock ledges.

Buzzard

ROUGH-LEGGED BUZZARD
Buteo lagopus

56 cm. Dark belly; white tail with black band at tip. Found in winter on moors and in marshes and fields, in summer among mountains. Nests on cliff ledges or on ground in Arctic. Often hovers before swooping on small mammals; also hunts birds.

Rough-legged Buzzard

RED KITE
Milvus milvus

63 cm. Like buzzard, but reddish colour and deeply forked tail. Usually found in woods, but also among scattered trees. Nests in trees.

FALCONS Family Falconidae

Falcons are generally smaller than other birds of prey, and have long, pointed wings and long tails. They are ferocious hunters, diving on or chasing their prey at great speed. Falconers train falcons to hunt and bring their prey back to them.

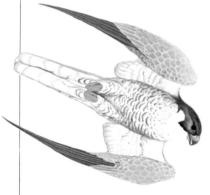

PEREGRINE FALCON
Falco peregrinus

43 cm. Light underside with bars and dark grey back; black moustache marking. Found among cliffs and crags, on which it nests, and also on flat coasts and marshes in winter; sometimes seen in forests and towns. Hunts by diving steeply at great speed, wings drawn back, mainly after birds, especially pigeons. Has become rare, suffering badly from effects of pesticides and raids by egg collectors.

HOBBY
Falco subbuteo

33 cm. Streaky underside and chestnut 'trousers'. Lives in light woodland and among scattered trees, streaking through the air in pursuit of small birds such as larks, swallows and swifts, as well as flying insects. Nests in trees.

KESTREL
Falco tinnunculus

33 cm. Male: grey-blue head and nape, reddish back and wings with dark spots, grey-blue tail with black band. Female: as male but brown head and nape, bars on back and wings, and brown tail with black bands. Very common bird of prey. Found in all kinds of places, including cities and towns; often spotted alongside motorways. Usually seen hovering 5-15 metres above the ground, flapping wings quickly, and then diving down in pursuit of rodents and insects. The Lesser Kestrel of southern Europe is very similar but male back is unspotted. It seldom hovers.

Lesser Kestrel

female

male

Kestrel

MERLIN
Falco columbarius

30 cm. Male: blue-grey back with red-brown streaky underside. Female: as male but brown back. Found in open country, on hills and moors in summer and also at coast in winter. Nests on ground or in trees. Darts through the air close to the ground, chasing small birds. May be seen hovering and perching.

male

female

OSPREY Family Pandionidae

The osprey is placed in a family by itself because it differs in several ways from the other birds of prey. In particular, the osprey has a reversible outer toe, which is used in catching and holding slippery fishes, and it can also close its nostrils – a useful feature for a bird which plunges into the water.

OSPREY
Pandion haliaetus

56 cm. Dark above and white below, with white head crossed by dark line. Found on lakes and rivers and at coast, where it hunts fish by soaring or hovering high over the water and then plunging in feet-first. Carries fish back to perch near water.

Game Birds

These birds are plump in shape, rather like chickens. They rarely fly very far or high and prefer to run or hide from danger, only taking to the air at the last moment. They spend most of their time on the ground rooting for seeds and insects, and they also nest on the ground. The game birds all belong to the order Galliformes, of which two families occur in the wild in Europe.

GROUSE
Family Tetraonidae

These birds live in cold places, and their legs and sometimes their feet are covered with feathers for warmth.

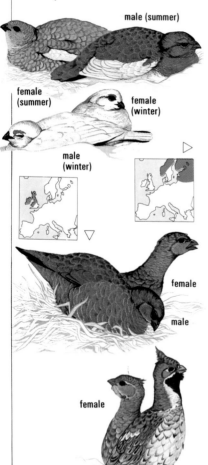

male (summer)

female (summer)

female (winter)

male (winter)

female

male

female

male

WILLOW GROUSE
Lagopus lagopus

38 cm. Male: in summer, red-brown body with white wings and belly; in winter, pure white with black tail (but exactly like female ptarmigan). Female: in summer, as male, but body less red and more barred; in winter, as male. Found on moors, often living among heather and scattered bushes. Plumage changes from white in winter to brown and white in summer, helping to hide the bird among both winter snow and summer vegetation.

RED GROUSE
Lagopus lagopus scoticus

38 cm. Male: red-brown body with dark wings and tail edges. Female: as male, but body less red and more barred. A variety of willow grouse found only in the British Isles. No colour change takes place because snow does not always fall in winter. Lives among heather on moors, but also found in fields in winter.

HAZEL GROUSE
Bonasa bonasia

36 cm. Male: black throat and grey tail with black band. Female: as male but whitish throat. Lives in woods, usually hiding among bushes and thickets.

PTARMIGAN
Lagopus mutus

36 cm. Male: as willow grouse, but greyer body in summer and autumn, and black face patch in winter. Female: very like female willow grouse. Found on high mountain slopes, usually above tree level. Plumage changes from brown and white in summer to grey and white in autumn and pure white in winter.

female (summer)

female (winter)

male (winter)

autumn

male (summer)

BLACK GROUSE
Tetrao tetrix

53 cm. Male: glossy black with lyre-shaped tail. Female: grey-brown with slightly forked tail, 41cm. Found on moors, in woods, among scattered trees and in fields. In spring, groups gather at courting grounds and the males display themselves before the females, spreading their wings and raising their tail feathers in a fan.

male

female

male

CAPERCAILLIE
Tetrao urogallus

Male: 86 cm. Dark grey with broad fan-shaped tail; brownish wings. Female: 61 cm. As female black grouse, but with fan-shaped tail and reddish breast patch. Lives among fir trees on hills and mountains. Male raises tail in a fan when courting female.

female

PARTRIDGES AND PHEASANTS Family Phasianidae

Unlike grouse, these birds have bare legs and feet and are not found in cold places. Brightly coloured pheasants from other parts of the world are seen in parks. Some now live in the wild.

Pheasants make their nests on the ground and produce large numbers of young birds. Partridges too nest on the ground and are difficult to see. Quail are small shy birds prized as a delicacy.

male   female

PARTRIDGE
Perdix perdix

30 cm. Grey legs; orange-brown face and throat; dark belly patch (male only). Seen mainly in fields, but also on moors and heaths and in marshes, sand dunes and low treeless hills.

ROCK PARTRIDGE
Alectoris graeca

33 cm. Red legs; white throat patch surrounded by solid black band. Found on rocky ground and among trees, usually in hills. Looks very like red-legged partridge, but lives in different countries.

PHEASANT
Phasianus colchicus

Male: 84 cm. Very long tail with green head and red eye patch. Female: 58 cm. Mottled brown body with long pointed tail. Often seen in fields, especially in winter, also in woods and marshes. Pattern of male varies; for example some have white neck-ring while others do not. Introduced from Asia, probably in ancient times. Most pheasants are semi-domesticated, being protected during the breeding season by gamekeepers to raise numbers for hunting later. Some are truly wild.

male

female

RED-LEGGED PARTRIDGE
Alectoris rufa

34 cm. Like rock partridge, but with black streaks below breast band. Found on moors and in fields and low treeless hills, often in dry and stony places.

QUAIL
Coturnix coturnix

18 cm. Striped head; dark throat patch (male only). The smallest European game bird, and the only one that migrates. Hides among grass and crops. May be seen in bevies (small flocks) during migration, but is usually a solitary bird.

male

female

Cranes, Rails and Bustards

All these birds have long legs and many of them wade in shallow water. Cranes (family Gruidae) are tall, elegant birds living on dry land and in marshes, whereas rails, crakes, gallinules, moorhens and coots (family Rallidae) are mainly water birds, small to medium in size and chunky in shape. Bustards (family Otididae) are land birds, medium to large in size with long thick necks. These birds all belong to the order Gruiformes.

CRANE
Grus grus

114 cm. Red crown and white cheek stripe; bushy drooping tail. Nests on the ground in swamps and among reeds; in winter moves to rivers, fields and plains. Told from storks and herons by bushy tail. Flies with neck outstretched, migrating in long lines or V-formations. In spring, cranes perform crazy leaping dances before nesting.

CORNCRAKE
Crex crex

25 cm. Buff plumage with reddish wing patches. Hides away and nests among long grass and crops in meadows and fields. Mowing machines and other changes in agriculture have caused a drop in numbers.

WATER RAIL
Rallus aquaticus

28 cm. Long red beak. Usually hides among reeds in marshes and ponds, and nests on concealed platform of reeds built above water. Likely to come into the open during cold weather.

SPOTTED CRAKE
Porzana porzana

23 cm. Dark brown spotted and streaky plumage. Location and behaviour similar to water rail, but even more shy.

BAILLON'S CRAKE
Porzana pusilla

18 cm. Grey underside with bars on flanks; flesh-coloured legs. Same location and behaviour as water rail, and similar appearance but much smaller. Very shy.

LITTLE CRAKE
Porzana parva

19 cm. Male: as Baillon's crake, but no bars on flanks and green legs. Female: as male, but buff underside. Same location and behaviour as water rail but much smaller. Very shy.

female

male

MOORHEN
Gallinula chloropus

33 cm. Black body with red bill and shield above bill and white feathers under the tail. Lives on ponds, lakes and streams, bobbing its head up and down and flicking its tail as it swims to and fro. Sometimes dives for food. Often seen in parks. Nests in reeds, bushes and trees, usually near the water. Often feeds on grassy banks and in nearby fields.

COMMON COOT
Fulica atra

38 cm. Black body with white bill and shield. Found on lakes, reservoirs and rivers, and in parks. Also on coasts and estuaries winter. Prefers larger stretches of water than moorhen, and dives more often. Usually seen in groups, with the birds always quarrelling.

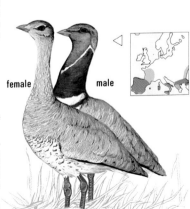

female

male

LITTLE BUSTARD
Tetrax tetrax

43 cm. Male: black and white pattern on neck (summer only). Female and male in winter: streaky brown head and neck. Hides by crouching flat when danger approaches. Grassland.

Waders, Gulls and Auks

This is a huge group of birds with widely differing appearances, although they all belong to the order Charadriiformes. There are many families. The birds are all closely associated with water for at least a part of their lives. Many live by the sea. The waders, which include the plovers and sandpipers and several other groups, are long-legged birds and, as the name suggests, they spend much of their time wading in shallow water where they find their food.

OYSTERCATCHERS Family Haematopodidae

OYSTERCATCHER
Haematopus ostralegus

43 cm. Black and white plumage with long orange beak. The only European member of its family. Seen at seashore, prizing shellfish open with its chisel-like beak. Also probes for food in mud. May also be found inland on moors and by lakes and rivers.

PLOVERS Family Charadriidae

Plovers can be told from almost all other waders by their short beaks. They probe for worms, grubs and shellfish.

NORTHERN LAPWING
Vanellus vanellus

30 cm. Black and white plumage with crest; glossy dark-green back. Very common plover. Found in fields and marshes and on moors; also at coast in winter. Usually in large flocks.

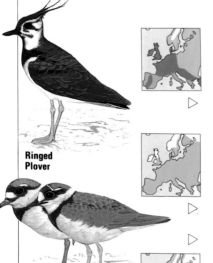

Ringed Plover

Little Ringed Plover

LITTLE RINGED PLOVER
Charadrius dubius

15 cm. As ringed plover but no wing-bar and legs often pink. Lives on sandy or stony shores of lakes and rivers, and in old gravel pits.

GREAT RINGED PLOVER
Charadrius hiaticula

19 cm. Black breast band and orange-yellow legs; white wingbar in flight. Usually found on sandy and stony beaches, sometimes inland.

GREY PLOVER
Pluvialis squatarola

28 cm. Summer: black below and silver-grey above. Winter: white below and grey above. Found on mudflats and sandy beaches.

KENTISH PLOVER
Charadrius alexandrinus

15 cm. As ringed plover, but breast band incomplete and legs black. Found at seashore, on sandy or stony beaches.

EUROPEAN GOLDEN PLOVER
Pluvialis apricaria

28 cm. Summer: black below and golden-brown above. Winter: white below and golden-brown above. nests on moors in summer. In winter, also found in fields and at seashore, usually with lapwings.

DOTTEREL
Charadrius morinellus

23 cm. White eye-stripe and breast band; chestnut belly and dark underparts. Paler in winter. Nests on barren high ground. Found in fields and on the seashore in winter.

TURNSTONE
Arenaria interpres

23 cm. Summer: brown and black patterned wings. Winter: generally paler, but with dark breast band and orange legs. Found at coast, usually on rocky and stony shores. Gets its name from its habit of turning over stones, shells and seaweed when looking for food.

winter

summer

southern form (summer)

winter

northern form (summer)

winter

summer

winter

summer

SANDPIPERS Family Scolopacidae

These are wading birds with long bills. Most also have long legs. They may be found inland at damp places as well as at the seashore, and they usually nest on the ground. Flocks of several different kinds of sandpipers can often be seen feeding together at the shore, poking their bills into the water, mud or sand to find shellfish and worms. The different kinds of birds have bills of various lengths, so that they probe at different depths and live on different kinds of food.

SNIPE
Gallinago gallinago

27 cm. Long straight beak with dark stripes along head. Hides away in marshes, bogs and damp meadows. Flies away with zigzag flight when disturbed. Often dives from sky, making a drumming noise with its tail.

JACK SNIPE
Lymnocryptes minimus

19 cm. As snipe but shorter bill and pointed tail. Found in same places as snipe and behaves in same way, except that when disturbed it flies off with a more direct flight. Its call sounds rather like a distant galloping horse.

WOOD SANDPIPER
Tringa glareola

20 cm. White rump with pale legs; no wingbar. Found in northern forests and in Arctic, where it nests on ground near water and in old nests in trees.

COMMON SANDPIPER
Tringa hypoleucos

20 cm. Dark rump, white wingbar seen in flight; bobs its tail and nods its head as it wades. Nests beside streams, rivers and lakes, usually in hills. In winter, also seen at seashore.

GREEN SANDPIPER
Tringa ochropus

23 cm. White rump with dark legs, no wingbar. Not green. Nests in swamps in woodland. Winters in marshes and on lakes and rivers, seldom at coast.

CURLEW
Numenius arquata

56 cm. Very long down-curving bill and plain head. Nests on moors and in marshes, damp meadows and sand dunes. In winter, also seen on mudflats at seashore.

BLACK-TAILED GODWIT
Limosa limosa

41 cm. Summer: long bill (very slightly upturned) with chestnut breast and white tail with black band at end. Winter: as summer but grey breast. Broad white wing bar clearly seen in flight. Nests in damp meadows and on boggy land. In winter, also seen on mudflats and in marshes.

BAR-TAILED GODWIT
Limosa lapponica

38 cm. As black-tailed godwit, but upturned bill and barred tail and no wing bar. Nests in marshes in Arctic, and migrates to spend winter at seashore.

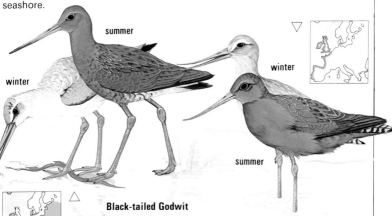

summer

winter

winter

summer

Black-tailed Godwit

Bar-tailed Godwit

WHIMBREL
Numenius phaeopus

41 cm. As curlew, but shorter bill and striped head. Found in same places as curlew, and looks like a small curlew, but told apart by its head pattern.

DUNLIN
Calidris alpina

summer

winter

18 cm. Summer: black patch on underside. Winter: dark above and pale below with down-curving beak. Nests on moors and in marshes, spends winter in flocks on mudflats at or near coast and also inland. Flies in tight groups known as 'wader smoke' from the way the birds twist and turn through the air.

REDSHANK
Tringa totanus

28 cm. White rump with long red legs; white band at back of wing in flight. Nests among grass in meadows and inland and coastal marshes and on moors and heaths. In winter, usually found at seashore.

GREENSHANK
Tringa nebularia

30 cm. White rump with greenish legs; no wingband. Nests on ground on moors or in forests, usually near water.

WOODCOCK
Scolopax rusticola

36 cm. Long beak with dark stripes across head. Stout shape. Hides away among damp woodland. Most likely to be seen at dawn or dusk flying through the trees or in circles above the trees.

winter

summer

SANDERLING
Calidris alba

20 cm. Summer: reddish plumage with white belly. Winter: almost white with black spot at front of wing. Seen in winter at sandy beaches, racing about as if chasing the waves. Migrates to Arctic to breed.

Male displaying
in summer

RUFF
Philomachus pugnax

Male: 30 cm; easily identified by the ruff, or collar, in spring and summer; autumn plumage is brown, heavily mottled with black. Female: as autumn male, but smaller (23 cm). Nests on moors and in marshes and meadows; also found beside rivers and lakes in winter. In late spring and early summer, the males attract the females by raising a beautiful ruff of feathers around the neck. The colour of the ruff varies greatly. The female is also known as a reeve. Has recently recolonized Britain after earlier extinction as a breeding species.

male (winter)

female

AVOCETS AND STILTS Family Recurvirostridae

These birds are the most elegant wading birds. They pick their way through the shallow water on stilt-like legs, snapping up insects from the air or lowering their long thin beaks into the water.

female

male (winter)

male (summer)

AVOCET
Recurvirostra avosetta

43 cm. Long up-turned bill; black and white back. Nests in marshes at or near coast; spends winter at estuaries. Best seen at bird reserves. Beak curves upwards so that the end skims surface of water when feeding.

BLACK-WINGED STILT
Himantopus himantopus

38 cm. Long straight bill; black back and white underside; long pink legs. Found in marshes and lagoons, often wading deeply in large stretches of water.

PHALAROPES Family Phalaropodidae

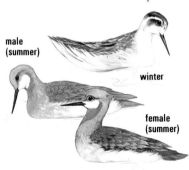

male (summer)

winter

female (summer)

RED-NECKED PHALAROPE
Phalaropus lobatus

18 cm. Female: orange-red neck and white throat in summer. Male: as female but less bright. Both sexes are grey and white in winter, when they can be recognized by the rather slender bill and the large dark eye-patch. Nests in marshes and beside lakes; spends winter out to sea. Often swims, unlike other waders, floating high in the water and sometimes spinning in circles to stir up small animals from the bottom. Phalaropes are unusual birds. The females court the males, and the males build the nests, sit on the eggs and raise the young.

THICK-KNEES Family Burhinidae

STONE CURLEW
Burhinus oedicnemus

41 cm. Large yellow eyes and white wingbar on ground; double white wingbar in flight. Gets its name because it is often found in stony and rocky places, and because its call (usually heard after dark) is like that of a curlew. It likes open treeless country. Runs with its head down when disturbed. Thick-knees got their strange name because their 'knees' (which in fact are their heels) appear to be swollen.

SKUAS Family Stercorariidae

Skuas are fast-flying sea birds with hooked beaks. They are sometimes called the pirates of the skies, for they often chase other sea birds and make them drop a fish they have just captured or even half eaten! The skua then swoops down to catch its stolen meal before it hits the water below.

GREAT SKUA
Stercorarius skua

58 cm. Fan-shaped tail without long protruding feathers. Nests among grass or heather on moors and spends winter out to sea. May be seen at coast on migration in spring and autumn.

ARCTIC SKUA
Stercorarius parasiticus

46 cm. Fan-shaped tail with long protruding central feathers. Lives in similar places to great skua. The neck, breast and underparts may be light, dark or any shade between.

GULLS AND TERNS Family Laridae

These two kinds of sea birds are easy to tell apart. Gulls have broad wings and fan-shaped tails, and their beaks are usually heavy with a hooked tip. They can be seen in flocks at the seashore and at harbours, constantly making mewing cries as they wheel to and fro in the air. To feed, they settle on the water and seize some floating waste or dip their heads under the water to catch a fish. They also follow ships, but not out of sight of land. Gulls also fly inland, especially in winter. They nest in colonies on the ground and on cliffs. Young gulls look brown and white until they are as much as four years old. Terns have slender wings and forked tails, and sharp beaks that often point downwards during flight.

GREAT BLACK-BACKED GULL
Larus marinus

68 cm. Black back and wings, pink legs. Usually seen at rocky coasts and offshore islands; may be seen inland, especially in winter. Often feeds on eggs and young of other sea birds.

Little Gull in winter

summer

LITTLE GULL
Larus minutus

28 cm. Like small black-headed gull but black head (not dark brown) in summer, no black on wingtips and dark beneath wings. Gets its name because it is noticeably smaller than other gulls. Nests in marshes and swamps, but seen at coast and inland at other times. Catches insects in flight.

GLAUCOUS GULL
Larus hyperboreus

71 cm. Silver-grey back and wings; no dark patches at wingtips. Nests in Iceland and in Arctic; seen at coasts and harbours in winter, rarely inland. Preys on eggs and small birds.

BLACK-HEADED GULL
Larus ridibundus

38 cm. Dark-brown head in summer, becoming white with a dark spot behind the eye in winter; white patch on front of wings and black edge on back of wings; red legs. A very common gull, often seen inland. Nests in marshes, on moors, and by lakes and rivers. At other times found at coasts and harbours, and in fields and towns. Eats anything, including fish, worms, flying insects and even garbage.

summer

Black-headed Gull in winter

LESSER BLACK-BACKED GULL
Larus fuscus

53 cm. Grey to dark grey back and wings (British form) or black back and wings (Scandinavian form); legs usually yellow or orange. Often seen at seashore and harbours and also inland.

British form

Scandinavian form

HERRING GULL
Larus argentatus

56 cm. Pale grey back and wings, with black and white wingtips and red spot on yellow bill; legs usually pink. A very common gull, seen both at the coast and inland.

COMMON GULL
Larus canus

41 cm. As herring gull, but yellow-green legs and greenish bill without red spot. Found at coast and inland. In spite of its name, it is not the most numerous gull.

KITTIWAKE
Rissa tridactyla

41 cm. Solid black wingtips and black legs. Nests in colonies on cliff ledges and also on buildings in coastal towns. Usually spends winter far out to sea.

COMMON TERN
Sterna hirundo

36 cm. Orange bill, black tip. Nests on beaches, among sand dunes, in coastal swamps, on offshore islands and by lakes. Often seen flying along seashore and diving for fish.

LITTLE TERN
Sterna albifrons

24 cm. Yellow bill with black tip; white forehead. The smallest European tern. Nests mainly on sandy and stony beaches, but sometimes inland.

ARCTIC TERN
Sterna paradisaea

36 cm. All-red bill, short legs; greyer breast than common tern. Found in same kinds of places as common tern, but less likely inland. May migrate as far south as the Antarctic to spend the winter.

BLACK TERN
Chlidonias niger

24 cm. Black head and body, grey wings and tail. Builds floating nest on lakes and marsh pools; may be seen at coast during migration in spring and autumn. Chases insects in air; rarely dives into water.

WHISKERED TERN
Chlidonias hybridus

24 cm. Grey belly, white cheeks. Found in same places as black tern, but often dives for food.

AUKS Family Alcidae

Auks look and behave very much like penguins. They dive for fish and chase them underwater, using their wings like oars and their feet like a rudder. On land, they sit up and waddle about. Also like penguins, they spend most of the year at sea and only come ashore to breed. However, unlike penguins, they can fly well – although the great auk, which is now extinct, could not. It was a very easy target for hunters, and the last pair of birds was killed in 1844. The great auk was a large bird as big as a goose.

GUILLEMOT
Uria aalge

41 cm. Slender pointed bill. Breeds in large colonies on coastal cliffs and on offshore islands. The guillemot's egg is laid on bare rock and is pear-shaped, so that it rolls in a circle and not over the edge, if knocked. Spends winter out at sea, but may be driven ashore by gales.

summer

winter

BLACK GUILLEMOT
Cepphus grylle

33 cm. Summer: black body with white wing patch. Winter: mottled grey back with white wing patch. Nests in holes and crevices on rocky shore and sea cliffs, but not in large colonies. Stays near shore in winter.

PUFFIN
Fratercula arctica

30 cm. Triangular beak (bright red and yellow in summer). Nests in colonies in burrows in steep slopes by sea. May run down slope to get into the air. Can hold several fish at once in its parrot-like beak. Spends winter far out to sea and is seldom blown ashore.

RAZORBILL
Alca torda

41 cm. Broad dark bill with white marks. Breeds in colonies on cliff ledges at coast, often with guillemots. Spends winter out at sea, although storms may force it back to shore.

LITTLE AUK
Alle alle

20 cm. Small size and short bill distinguish this species. Nests in Arctic and spends winter in northern seas, but may be driven ashore by storms.

Pigeons and Doves

These birds have plump bodies, small heads and short legs. They can all fly very fast, and people raise pigeons for racing.

They belong to the family Columbidae in the order Columbiformes.

STOCK DOVE
Columba oenas

33 cm. Grey rump, no obvious neck mark or wing marks. Found in woods and on farmland; may also be seen in parks and on cliffs and sand dunes along coast. Often found in the company of woodpigeons

TURTLE DOVE
Streptopelia turtur

28 cm. Black tail with white edges; white neck patch with black stripes. Found in spring and summer in light woods and among scattered trees and bushes; also on farmland and in parks and gardens.

WOODPIGEON
Columba palumbus

41 cm. Grey rump, white neck mark, white wingbar. Found in woods and on farmland, and also in parks and gardens. Often seen in flocks containing stock doves and domestic pigeons.

COLLARED DOVE
Streptopelia decaocto

30 cm. Black stripe edged with white at back of neck. Usually found in towns or close to houses and farms. Nests on buildings or in trees nearby. It has spread rapidly through Europe from the Balkans during the last few decades. It first nested in Britain in 1955 and is now found throughout the British Isles.

ROCK DOVE
Columba livia

33 cm. White rump, no neck mark, two black wing stripes. Lives on rocky coasts and on mountains, and nests in caves and on cliff ledges. The pigeons that can be seen in city squares and parks, as well as the pigeons that people raise for racing, are all descended from the wild rock dove. Some of these pigeons still look like their wild ancestor, but many now have different plumage. The pigeons are interbreeding with rock doves, and the truly wild species is slowly disappearing. Because the wild birds are naturally at home on cliffs, pigeons can live and nest on the ledges of buildings. They have long been a companion of man, carrying messages for him as well as providing him with a source of food.

▷

Cuckoos

Cuckoos are famous for laying their eggs in the nests of other birds and leaving the other birds to bring up the young cuckoos. Both of the cuckoos found in Europe breed in this way. They belong to the family Cuculidae in the order Cuculiformes.

red form

grey form

CUCKOO
Cuculus canorus

33 cm. Grey head and breast with bars on white underside; but female sometimes red-brown with bars all over body. Found in woodland, open ground with scattered trees and bushes, and on moors. Only the male makes 'cuckoo' call; female has babbling call. The female cuckoo lays several eggs, one each in the nests of other birds. Small birds are chosen, such as meadow pipits and robins, but each female cuckoo always uses nests of the same species. When it hatches, the young cuckoo pushes out any other eggs and nestlings, but its adopted parents continue to feed it, driven by instinct.

 △

GREAT SPOTTED CUCKOO
Clamator glandarius

41 cm. White spots on wings, grey crest, long white-edged tail. Found in woods and among scattered trees. Does not call 'cuckoo'. Usually lays its eggs in the nests of crows, particularly magpies.

Owls

The owls are mainly nocturnal hunters, feeding mostly on small rodents. Some also eat other birds and insects. They are not closely related to the diurnal birds of prey (pages 79-85) and they are placed in the order Strigiformes. They have powerful talons and a large, hooked beak, although the beak is partly buried in the feathers and does not look very large. The eyes look forward and are extremely efficient. The ears are also very sensitive, allowing the owls to hear their prey on the ground. Feathery edges to the wings allow the owls to fly silently. The barn owl belongs to the family Tytonidae, while all the other owls belong to the Strigidae.

dark-breasted form

light-breasted form

BARN OWL
Tyto alba

36 cm. Heart-shaped face; brown back with white or buff unstreaked breast (may look all white at dusk). Found on farmland and in marshes but also occupies unused buildings, such as barns and church towers, and ruins. Most likely to be seen at dusk. Two forms occur, a white-breasted form (*Tyto alba alba*) in south and west Europe, and a buff-breasted form (*Tyto alba guttata*) in north and east Europe.

LONG-EARED OWL
Asio otus

36 cm. Slender shape and long ear tufts. Sleeps in woods, especially in fir trees, by day and comes out to hunt, often over open ground, at dusk. May be seen sleeping in groups in winter.

SCOPS OWL
Otus scops

19 cm. Small, with short ear tufts. Found among trees, often near buildings, as well as in ruins. Rarely seen in daytime. Like many other owls, has ear tufts that are not ears but merely tufts of head feathers.

PYGMY OWL
Glaucidium passerinum

18 cm. Very small, with round head, no ear tufts; flicks tail up and down when sitting on perch. Usually seen in fir forests. Active day and night, chasing small birds through air. Smallest European owl.

TAWNY OWL
Strix aluco

38 cm. Streaky plumage with black eyes; stocky shape and no ear tufts. A very common owl. Lives in woods and also in parks and gardens. Usually hunts by night, but may be seen sleeping in tree during daytime, when it is sometimes bothered by small birds. Colour varies from brown to grey.

brown form

grey form

LITTLE OWL
Athene noctua

23 cm. Small, with flattened head, no ear tufts. Found among scattered trees in fields and on open ground, often near buildings. May be seen in daytime bobbing its head as it perches on a post or branch.

SHORT-EARED OWL
Asio flammeus

38 cm. Similar to tawny owl but yellow eyes and lighter plumage. Seen hunting over moors, marshes and open ground during daytime and at dusk. Ear tufts are very short, often invisible.

EAGLE OWL
Bubo bubo

68 cm. Huge, with long ear tufts. Largest European owl. Lives in forests, among mountain crags and gorges, and on dry plains. Active at dawn and dusk, when it hunts animals as large as hares. Rare.

Nightjars

The nightjars (family Caprimulgidae) are nocturnal birds with long wings and tail and a very agile, silent flight. The bill is short, but opens very widely to scoop up insects in flight. The name is derived from the penetrating churring song which can be heard at dusk. Two species breed in Europe. The birds belong to the order Caprimulgiformes.

NIGHTJAR
Caprimulgus europaeus

28 cm. Plumage pattern looks like dead leaves from above; fine bars below. Lives in woods, among bracken in clearings and on hillsides, on moors and sand dunes. Unless disturbed, it is very difficult to spot. Sleeps during the day and hunts for insects at night. Lays eggs on the ground.

male

female

Swifts

Swifts are masters of the air and are usually seen in flocks, wheeling high in the sky at great speed. They may spend weeks in the air without coming down, as they catch flying insects for food and can sleep in flight. Swifts have weak feet and if they land on the ground, they cannot walk and find it hard to get back into the air. Instead, they usually cling to vertical surfaces and simply fall off them to become airborne. The small feet are responsible for the family name of Apodidae, which actually means 'footless'. The birds belong to the order Apodiformes, which also includes the hummingbirds.

SWIFT
Apus apus

16 cm. Dark body; shallow forked tail. Nests in holes in trees, crevices in cliffs, and under the eaves of buildings. Often to be seen at dusk, dashing around rooftops in noisy flocks. May be seen with swallows, but can easily be recognized by dark underparts and shallow forked tail.

ALPINE SWIFT
Apus melba

20 cm. White belly and throat with dark breast band; very long wings. Found in mountains, at cliffs and around buildings. Nests in crevices. Has very long wings, unlike similar sand martin.

Kingfishers and Related Birds

Any birds in this mixed group are worth a special effort to see, for they are the most colourful and spectacular birds to be seen in Europe. None is like any other and they all belong to different families. The kingfisher belongs to the family Alcedinidae, and the bee-eater to the family Meropidae. The roller is a member of the family Coraciidae, and the hoopoe of the family Upupidae. All belong to the order Coraciiformes.

KINGFISHER
Alcedo atthis

16 cm. Blue-green back and orange underparts. Seen by rivers and lakes, perching on a branch beside the water or darting down to plunge for a fish. May also be seen at coast in winter.

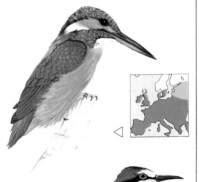

BEE-EATER
Merops apiaster

28 cm. Yellow throat and blue-green breast. Found in open country among scattered trees and bushes, often perching on bushes or telegraph wires. Nests in hole dug in bank of river or pit, or in burrow dug in the ground. Chases flying insects, especially bees and wasps.

ROLLER
Coracias garrulus

30 cm. Blue-green with chestnut back. Found in open country with scattered trees and in woods. Nests in hole in tree or bank. Often seen perching and then swooping down to catch insects and other small animals. Gets its name from the way it rolls over in flight to attract a mate during the spring courtship.

crest up

crest down

HOOPOE
Upupa epops

28 cm. Black-and-white striped wings; large black-tipped crest. Seen among scattered trees and in woods; sometimes in parks and gardens. Nests in hole in tree or wall. Often seen perching, usually with its crest down. Named after its call. Several recent nesting records from Britain (not mapped).

Woodpeckers

Woodpeckers are members of the family Picidae in the order Piciformes. They are often heard before being seen. Their sharp beaks make a loud rat-a-tat as they chisel into the bark of a tree in search of insects. They also dig out holes for nesting.

Woodpeckers grip the trunk or branch with sharp claws and thrust their tails stiffly against the bark to prop themselves up and give a powerful blow with the beak. In the spring, they make a drumming noise by clattering their beaks on a piece of wood; this is part of their courtship.

male

female

BLACK WOODPECKER
Dryocopus martius

46 cm. Black body, with red crown in male (slightly crested) and crimson patch on the back of the head in female. Lives in woods and forests, often in mountains. Largest European woodpecker.

GREY-HEADED WOODPECKER
Picus canus

25 cm. Grey head with thin moustache; only male has red forehead. Found in same places as green woodpecker. Often drums in spring, unlike green woodpecker.

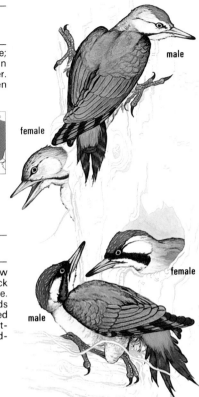

male

female

GREEN WOODPECKER
Picus viridis

30 cm. Greenish back and yellow rump; large red crown. Thick black (female) or red (male) moustache. Dull-green upperparts. Found in woods and forests, usually of broad-leaved trees, and in open country with scattered trees. Also seen on ground, feeding at anthills. Seldom drums.

female

male

THREE-TOED WOODPECKER
Picoides tridactylus

23 cm. White back, black cheeks and striped flanks. Yellow crown (male only). Lives in forests on mountains and in far north.

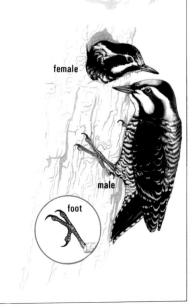

female

male

foot

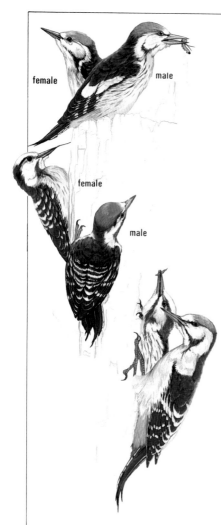

female

male

female

male

MIDDLE SPOTTED WOODPECKER
Dendrocopos medius

20 cm. As great spotted woodpecker but red crown in both sexes and less black on face. Lives in woods and forests, though seldom among fir trees. Usually stays high up in trees.

LESSER SPOTTED WOODPECKER
Dendrocopos minor

15 cm. Black and white stripes on back with no red under tail. Crown red (male) or whitish (female). Lives in same places as middle spotted woodpecker, but may also be found in parks and orchards. Smallest European woodpecker.

WHITE-BACKED WOODPECKER
Dendrocopos leucotos

25 cm. As lesser spotted woodpecker, but larger and with white rump and red under tail. Found in woods and forests, though not often among fir trees.

WRYNECK
Jynx torquilla

16 cm. Long banded tail; small beak. Lives in light woodland, and in open country with scattered trees, bushes and hedges, orchards, parks and gardens. Does not look like a woodpecker and does not chisel into bark. Often feeds on ground and nests in existing holes, including nest-boxes. Gets its name from the way it can turn its head round.

male

female

GREAT SPOTTED WOODPECKER
Dendrocopos major

23 cm. Large white wing patch and black crown (red in young); black stripe across neck; red patch at back of head (male only). Found in woods and forests of all kinds, and also in parks and gardens. Comes to bird tables, being able to hang upside-down to feed as tits do. Also likes to wedge nuts into cracks in bark and hammer them open with bill. Known for its habit of drumming very rapidly on dead branches. The most common and widespread European woodpecker.

Perching Birds and Songbirds

These birds make up the biggest group of birds – the order Passeriformes, which contains more than half of all bird species. There are many families. They are found everywhere. None is very large, and most are fairly small. Their feet have three toes in front and a long one behind, which enables them to perch easily – although, of course, other birds can perch too. Many, but by no means all, can sing well and, in a few cases, the song must be heard to be sure of the bird's identity.

LARKS Family Alaudidae

These birds are most often seen in the air, singing strongly. They make their nests on the ground where, being dull-coloured, they are difficult to spot. However, they may sometimes be seen running along the ground. Some larks look rather like buntings (pages 149-50), but have thin beaks whereas buntings have stout beaks.

CRESTED LARK
Galerida cristata

16 cm. Large crest. In southern Spain, almost identical Thekla lark (*Galerida theklae*) may be seen. Found on stony and sandy ground and in fields; also seen on waste land in towns and villages and beside roads.

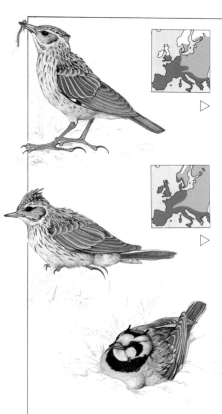

WOOD LARK
Lullula arborea

15 cm. Black and white mark at front of wing; all-brown tail; slight crest. Found in fields and open country, often among scattered trees and bushes and at woodland edges. Often flies in circle while singing; also sings while perched.

SKY LARK
Alauda arvensis

18 cm. White edges to tail; slight crest. Found in all kinds of open country – moors, marshes, fields and sand dunes. Rises straight up into air and may hover while singing.

HORNED LARK
Eremophila alpestris

16 cm. Horns on head (male only); black and yellow face pattern. Nests on rocky ground in far north or high in mountains. Spends winter at beaches, and in marshes and fields along coast.

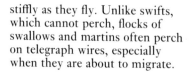

SWALLOWS AND MARTINS Family Hirundinidae

Swallows and martins fly very fast, often near the ground, twisting and turning in the air as they chase flying insects. Swifts (page 110) are similar, but have longer wings that they hold out stiffly as they fly. Unlike swifts, which cannot perch, flocks of swallows and martins often perch on telegraph wires, especially when they are about to migrate.

HOUSE MARTIN
Delichon urbica

13 cm. Deep blue back with white rump, underside completely white. Often seen in towns and villages, but also lives in open country. Builds mud nest with tiny entrance hole beneath eaves of buildings, under bridges, and also on rock faces and cliffs.

BARN SWALLOW
Hirundo rustica

19 cm. Deeply forked tail, red throat, deep blue back. Builds an open nest of mud and straw on beams and ledges in farm buildings and sheds. Hunts for insects in nearby fields, often swooping low in flight over water.

RED-RUMPED SWALLOW
Hirundo daurica

18 cm. As barn swallow but without red throat and with buff (not red) rump. Usually found in rocky country and at coast. Builds mud nest with long narrow entrance on walls of caves, cliffs or rocks, under bridges, or on buildings.

CRAG MARTIN
Ptyonoprogne rupestris

14 cm. Brown back and underside completely pale buff. Lives in mountains and on sea cliffs. Builds cup-shaped mud nest on rock face or cave wall, and sometimes on buildings.

SAND MARTIN
Riparia riparia

13 cm. As crag martin but brown breast band. Lives in open country, especially near ponds, lakes and rivers. Nests in colonies in holes dug in banks of rivers, cuttings and pits, and also in cliffs.

ORIOLES Family Oriolidae

Most orioles are brightly coloured birds of tropical forests.

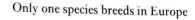

female

male

Only one species breeds in Europe

GOLDEN ORIOLE
Oriolus oriolus

24 cm. Male: bright yellow with black wings. Female: head and body green above and streaky white below. Found in woods and orchards, and among trees in parks. Usually hides among leaves in tops of trees. Has recently colonized small areas of England (not mapped).

CROWS Family Corvidae

Crows are the largest perching birds and they are among the cleverest of all birds. They search boldly for all kinds of food, and will avoid traps and ignore scarecrows that farmers put out to stop them robbing crops. They may also store food for the winter, and open snails by dropping them on to a stone.

ROOK
Corvus frugilegus

46 cm. Like carrion crow, but grey patch at base of beak (making beak look large). Found in fields surrounded by trees or small woods, in which it nests in colonies called rookeries. Also at seashore and open ground in winter. Usually seen in groups.

JACKDAW
Corvus monedula

33 cm. Black body but back of head and neck is grey. Found in fields and open country and at rocky coasts, nesting in holes in trees and rocks. Also seen on farms, and in towns and villages, where it nests in old buildings. Usually seen in flocks, walking jerkily or flying acrobatically.

HOODED CROW
Corvus corone cornix

46 cm. Like carrion crow but grey back and belly. Found in similar habitats and lives in same way as carrion crow. Belongs to same species as carrion crow, and interbreeds with it in places where their ranges overlap, producing birds intermediate in appearance between them.

CARRION CROW
Corvus corone corone

46 cm. Medium size; all-black body with heavy black beak. Found on moors, at coasts, and in fields, parks and gardens. Often seen alone or in pairs, and pairs nest alone in trees or on cliffs. Usually simply called crow rather than carrion crow.

RAVEN
Corvus corax

63 cm. Huge all-black body with massive black beak and wedge-shaped tail. Lives on sea cliffs and crags, in woods and open country, especially in hills and mountains and usually far from towns and villages. Builds huge nest on rock ledge or in tree. Often makes acrobatic display in the air, especially in spring. Hunts animals such as rabbits, hedgehogs and rats, but usually eats dead animals. The largest all-black bird in Europe.

NUTCRACKER
Nucifraga caryocatactes

33 cm. Brown body with white spots; white under tail. Lives in mountain forests, usually among conifer trees. Feeds mainly on conifer seeds but also very fond of hazel nuts, which it may store in the autumn and find months later, even under snow.

CHOUGH
Pyrrhocorax pyrrhocorax

38 cm. Black body with red legs and red curved beak. Lives in mountains and on cliffs by sea; may also be found in quarries. Nests on ledges and in caves and crevices. Often performs acrobatics in flight.

ALPINE CHOUGH
Pyrrhocorax graculus

38 cm. As chough, but yellow beak. Lives on high mountains, right up to the snowy summits. Alpine choughs have even been seen near the top of Mount Everest, higher than any other bird. Comes down to mountain villages in winter to feed on any scraps it can find.

JAY
Garrulus glandarius

36 cm. Blue and white patch on wing; white rump. Found in woods and orchards and sometimes in town parks and gardens. Fond of acorns, which it stores for the winter by burying them in the ground. Can hold as many as six acorns in its mouth. It is a very lively and active bird and often flicks its tail.

MAGPIE
Pica pica

46 cm. Black and white body with very long tail. Found in fields and open country with scattered trees and bushes, in which it builds a large dome-shaped nest. Often seen in town parks and gardens. May steal bright objects, and store them in its nest. It has a characteristic pattern of flight, in which it intermittently glides and then rapidly flaps its wings.

TITS Family Paridae

Tits are mainly woodland birds, but several kinds are frequent visitors to gardens. They can easily be told from other common woodland and garden birds as they have chunky rounded bodies. In woods, they flit through the branches and hang from twigs to get at insects, buds and seeds; they nest in holes in trees, laying at least four or five eggs and sometimes as many as twenty. Tits can easily be attracted to a garden; they are bold birds and show little fear of man. Their agility enables them to feed easily at bird tables and to take food hung from a branch or a gutter. Being hole nesters, they also come readily to nest boxes.

GREAT TIT
Parus major

14 cm. Yellow breast with black central stripe. Very often seen in woods, parks and gardens. Often pecks through milk bottle tops to reach the cream.

CRESTED TIT
Parus cristatus

11 cm. Speckled crest on head. Usually found in woods, especially among coniferous trees. Rarely seen in gardens.

BLUE TIT
Parus caeruleus

11 cm. Blue cap, wings and tail. Very often seen in woods, parks and gardens. Like great tit, it often opens milk bottles. Blue tits also tear strips from wallpaper, books and newspapers, an activity thought to be an extension of their habit of tearing bark from trees to find insects.

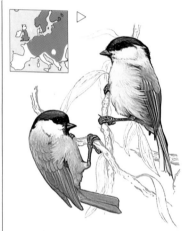

WILLOW TIT
Parus montanus

11cm. As marsh tit, but with light wing markings and a less glossy crown. Common in woods, usually in damp places. Excavates nesting hole in rotten wood.

MARSH TIT
Parus palustris

11 cm. Black crown without white nape of coal tit. Common in woods and often found in gardens. In spite of its name, it does not usually frequent marshes. Nests in existing holes in walls or trees.

COAL TIT
Parus ater

11 cm. White patch at back of head. Common in woods, especially pine woods. Less often seen in gardens than great tit or blue tit.

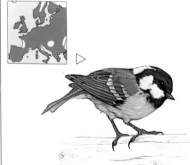

LONG-TAILED TITS Family Aegithalidae

Several families of birds are called tits, which is simply an old word meaning little. If it were not for their tails, which take up more than half their length, long-tailed tits would be among the world's tiniest birds. Only one species is found in Europe.

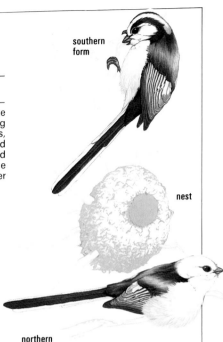

southern form

nest

LONG-TAILED TIT
Aegithalos caudatus

14 cm. Very small black and white body with very long tail. Found among bushes, thickets and hedges in woods, farmland and sometimes parks and gardens. Builds delicate globe-shaped nest with tiny entrance hole. The parent bird has to fold its long tail over its back when it is inside the nest.

northern form

NUTHATCHES AND WALLCREEPERS
Family Sittidae

Nuthatches are very agile tree birds and are to be seen clambering up or running headfirst down trunks and along branches, picking insects from the bark.

Wallcreepers climb over rock faces as well as walls, looking more like treecreepers than nuthatches. They also flutter through the air like butterflies.

NUTHATCH
Sitta europaea

14 cm. Blue-grey back, short tail. Lives in woods, parks and gardens; may visit bird tables. Nests in hole in tree, often plastering up entrance hole with mud. As well as eating insects, it wedges nuts into bark crevices and hammers them open with its beak. There are two distinct colour forms: birds with a white underside in northern Europe (*Sitta europaea europaea*), and birds with a buff underside elsewhere (*Sitta europaea caesia*). In Yugoslavia, Greece and Turkey the very similar rock nuthatch (*Sitta neumayer*) may be seen climbing rock faces.

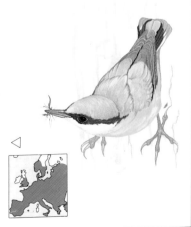

summer

winter

WALLCREEPER
Tichodroma muraria

16 cm. Crimson wing patch. Lives on mountain slopes, among gorges and cliffs; descends to valleys and foothills in winter, when it may be seen on buildings. Nests in rock cavities.

PARROTBILLS Family Paradoxornithidae

This family, so-named because most of its members have strongly-arched bills, has just one European species.

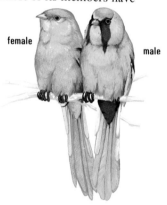

female

male

BEARDED TIT or REEDLING
Panurus biarmicus

16 cm. Tawny body with very long tail; black moustache mark (male only). Lives among reeds, seen in flocks during winter. Gets its name from the large moustache marking of the male bird. Very rare in Britain, the species is also known as Bearded Parrotbill.

DIPPERS Family Cinclidae

Dippers are unusual perching birds because they are water birds. They can swim and dive, and may even walk along the bottom of a stream to look for small freshwater animals. They are called dippers not because they are continually taking a dip, but because they bob up and down as they perch on boulders in the stream. Only one species is found in Europe.

DIPPER
Cinclus cinclus

18 cm. Dark with white breast. Lives by streams in mountains; may also be found by water at lower levels and at seashore in winter. Builds nest in river banks, under bridges or behind water falls.

TREECREEPERS Family Certhiidae

These birds are named after the way they creep up tree trunks, seeking insects in the bark. They nest in holes and crevices in trees and behind ivy.

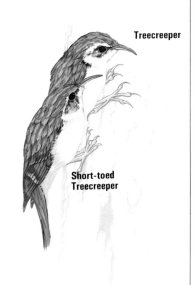

Treecreeper

Short-toed Treecreeper

EURASIAN TREECREEPER
Certhia familiaris

13 cm. Curved beak; streaky brown back and all-white underside. Found in woods, parks and gardens. Often seen with tits in winter.

SHORT-TOED TREECREEPER
Certhia brachydactyla

13 cm. Very similar to eurasian tree-creeper, but may have buff flanks. Lives in same places. In central and southern Europe, this species is usually found at low altitude, whereas the eurasian treecreeper often prefers the mountains here.

WRENS Family Troglodytidae

All but one of the members of the wren family live in America. They are all very small birds.

WREN
Troglodytes troglodytes

10 cm. Small size, upturned tail. Lives among low plants almost anywhere, from mountains, coasts and moors to woods, fields, parks and gardens. Often seen scurrying about in a flower bed or along the bottom of a hedge or wall, seeking insects among the litter on the ground. Nests in hedges and bushes and in holes in walls and trees.

THRUSHES Family Turdidae

This large family contains several birds that are well-known garden visitors. They feed mainly on berries and other fruits and insects, but are often to be seen looking for worms. Thrushes have beautiful songs, which they seem to perform just for the pleasure of singing.

SONG THRUSH
Turdus philomelos

23 cm. Similar to mistle thrush, but smaller size, brown back, breast more lightly spotted, buff underwing and all-brown tail. Often seen in woods and orchards, among scattered bushes and hedges, and in parks and gardens. May be seen on lawns cocking its head to one side, as if listening but in fact looking for a worm. Hammers snails on to a stone (called an anvil) to break open their shells. Nests in trees, bushes and hedges, and also on buildings.

MISTLE THRUSH
Turdus viscivorus

28 cm. Grey-brown back; heavily spotted breast, white underwing, white on outer tail feathers. Found in woods, farmland, parks and gardens; also on moors in winter. Nests in trees.

FIELDFARE
Turdus pilaris

25 cm. Grey head and rump, chestnut back. Breeds in northern Europe, forming colonies in birchwoods and also in parks and gardens, where it builds in trees or on buildings. In winter it moves south in flocks to fields and open country with hedges and scattered trees.

male

female

ROCK THRUSH
Monticola saxatilis

19 cm. Male: blue head, orange breast and tail, white band across back. Female: mottled brown with chestnut tail. Lives and nests on rocky ground and among trees high in mountains in western Europe, but lower down in eastern Europe.

BLUE ROCK THRUSH
Monticola solitarius

20 cm. Male: blue body with dark wings and tail. Female: as female rock thrush but dark brown tail. Lives on rocky and stony ground from the seashore up to mountain tops. May be seen in towns in southern Europe. Nests in holes in rocks or cliffs or on buildings.

male

female

REDWING
Turdus iliacus

20 cm. Reddish flanks and underwing; light stripe over eye. Breeds in northern Europe in woods and in parks and gardens, nesting in trees or on the ground. Moves south for the winter to fields and open country.

RING OUZEL
Turdus torquatus

24 cm. Male: black with white breast band. Female: brown with just a dull white crescent on breast. Lives on moors and mountain slopes, often where there are scattered trees and bushes. Nests among low plants or on rock ledges or walls.

male

female

male

BLACKBIRD
Turdus merula

25 cm. Male: all black with bright yellow beak. Female: dark brown all over. Very often seen in woods, orchards, hedges, parks and gardens; also in fields in winter. Nests in trees, bushes or hedges, on the ground or on buildings. Some blackbirds are albino birds that have white patches or may even be entirely white.

female

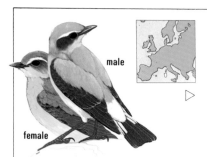

WHEATEAR
Oenanthe oenanthe

15 cm. Male in summer: black patch over eye with grey crown, grey back and rump. Female and male in autumn: white stripe over eye and grey-brown back with white rump. Lives in open country, from high moors and grassy hillsides down to coasts. Nests in holes in ground or in walls and rocks.

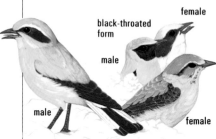

BLACK-EARED WHEATEAR
Oenanthe hispanica

14 cm. Male: black patch over eye with white to chestnut crown, buff back and white rump; black patch may extend to throat. Female: as female wheatear but dark cheek patch and darker wings. Found in rocky and sandy places, often among scattered trees and bushes. Nests in holes in walls and rocks.

BLACK WHEATEAR
Oenanthe leucura

18 cm. Male: black body. Female: dark chocolate-brown body. Both have white rump. Lives in rocky mountains and at sea cliffs. Nests in holes in rocks, often hiding entrance with pile of stones.

REDSTART
Phoenicurus phoenicurus

14 cm. Male: black throat with orange breast; reddish tail. Female: buff breast and reddish tail. Found in woods and among scattered trees; also in parks and gardens and rocky hillsides. Constantly flicks its tail up and down. Nests in holes in trees, walls and rocks.

BLACK REDSTART
Phoenicurus ochruros

14 cm. Male: black with reddish tail. Female: as female redstart but darker and greyer. Found on rocky ground and cliffs; also in towns, especially around factories. Constantly flicks its tail. Nests in holes in rocks and walls, and on buildings.

female

male

STONECHAT
Saxicola torquata

13 cm. Male: black head (brownish in winter) with chestnut breast. Female: as male but much paler. Found on moors, on headlands at coast, and on rough ground with bushes, especially gorse. Often seen perching, flicking its tail up and down. The nest is hidden in a bush or among grass.

male

female

WHINCHAT
Saxicola rubetra

13 cm. Male: dark cheeks with white stripe over eye; white at base of tail. Female: as male but paler. Lives in similar places to stonechat, but also likes grassy areas and fields. Behaves in the same way as stonechat.

female

male

NIGHTINGALE
Luscinia megarhynchos

16 cm. Brown back and chestnut tail with plain breast. Hides away among undergrowth in woods, and in thickets and hedges, sometimes around gardens. Nest concealed near ground. Very difficult to spot, but beautiful, musical song can often be heard, especially at night (though other thrushes may also sing at night).

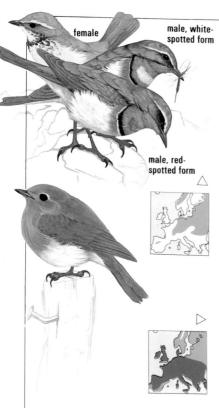

female

male, white-spotted form

male, red-spotted form

BLUETHROAT
Luscinia svecica

14 cm. Male: blue throat with red or white patch in centre. Female: dark breast band and orange patches on tail. Hides away among thickets and hedges, often close to water. Nest concealed near ground. There are two colour forms: the white-spotted blue-throat (*Luscinia svecica cyanecula*) of central and southern Europe, in which the blue throat patch of the male has a white centre; and the red-spotted blue-throat (*L. svecica svecica*) of northern Europe, in which it has a red centre. The blue is obscured during the winter.

ROBIN
Erithacus rubecula

14 cm. Orange-red face and breast. Very often seen in woods, hedges, parks and gardens, hopping over the ground. Nests in holes in trees and walls. In Britain, robins are bold birds and often come to bird tables, but else-where in Europe they are shy. Robins are usually seen alone, or at most in pairs during spring and summer. They are so aggressive towards each other that they will even mistake their own reflection for another bird and attack it.

WARBLERS Family Sylviidae

Warblers are small birds that flit about among trees, bushes and reeds, restlessly searching for insects to eat. They are named after their warbling songs, which vary widely from one species to another. The birds are often shy and difficult to spot. Most have dull colours with no very obvious marks to give away their identity. Recognizing the song of a warbler is therefore helpful in making sure of its identity.

MOUSTACHED WARBLER
Acrocephalus melanopogon

13 cm. Dark streaked back; dark cap with vivid eye-stripe. Song: sweet warble with 'tu-tu-tu' sounds. Lives and nests among reeds and small bushes in swamps and beside streams. Bobs its tail up and down, unlike similar sedge warbler and aquatic warbler.

CETTI'S WARBLER
Cettia cetti

14 cm. Unstreaked red-brown back. Song: repeated 'chewee' in bursts. Hides away and nests among dense thickets and reed-beds beside streams and swamps. Flicks tail.

GRASSHOPPER WARBLER
Locustella naevia

13 cm. Streaked back with faint eye-stripe. The underparts may be white or yellowish. Hides away and nests in dense undergrowth, long grass and reeds in marshes, and in more open country with scattered trees and bushes. Named after the grasshopper-like whirring sound of its song, which is held for a long time.

white form

GREAT REED WARBLER
Acrocephalus arundinaceus

19 cm. Large bird; unstreaked brown back with eye-stripe. Song: loud and strident with harsh sounds. Found among reeds beside lakes and rivers. Builds nest around reed stems. Sings from tops of reeds and may be seen on perch in the open. Largest European warbler.

SAVI'S WARBLER
Locustella luscinoides

14 cm. Plumage like reed warbler but white chin. Song: like grasshopper warbler's, but lower and held for short time. Lives and nests among reeds and bushes in marshes and swamps. May be seen singing while perched on the tip of a reed or top of a bush.

REED WARBLER
Acrocephalus scirpaceus

13 cm. Like great reed warbler, but smaller and with faint eye-stripe. Song: monotonous mixture of sweet and harsh sounds. Lives and nests among reeds and low bushes beside water and sometimes in fields. Perches on reed to sing, and suspends nest among reeds.

MARSH WARBLER
Acrocephalus palustris

13 cm. Like reed warbler, but olive-brown back and pink legs. Song: varied and musical with trills. Lives and nests among low bushes in thickets and swamps and beside ditches and streams; also in cornfields. Sings from low visible perch.

SEDGE WARBLER
Acrocephalus schoenobaenus

13 cm. Like moustached warbler, but paler. Song: varied mixture of sweet and harsh sounds. Lives and nests among reeds, low bushes and hedges, usually near water; also among crops. Sings from perch at top of reed, and also during short flights.

ORPHEAN WARBLER
Sylvia hortensis

15 cm. Black cap extending below straw-coloured eye. Song: warble of repeated phrases. Lives and nests in bushes and trees in woods and orchards.

GARDEN WARBLER
Sylvia borin

14 cm. Light brown above and grey-white beneath, with no obvious markings at all. The plainest of all European birds. Song: musical and liquid, soft but held for a long time. Hides away and nests in the undergrowth in woods and among thickets, hedges and bushes, often in parks and gardens.

ICTERINE WARBLER
Hippolais icterina

13 cm. Like melodious warbler, but blue-grey legs. Song: repeated notes, both sweet and harsh. Lives and nests in similar habitats to the melodious warbler, but less likely to be found near water.

MELODIOUS WARBLER
Hippolais polyglotta

13 cm. Green-grey with yellow underside; brown legs. Song: rapid and varied, but musical. Lives in woods and among bushes along rivers, also in parks and gardens. Nests in bushes and hedges. Very similar to icterine warbler in plumage, but the two species are found together only in a narrow band across the centre of Europe.

OLIVACEOUS WARBLER
Hippolais pallida

13 cm. Grey-brown above and white below, with buffish eye-stripe. Song: like sedge warbler's. Lives and nests in trees, bushes and hedges in light woods, fields, orchards, parks and gardens. Similar to garden warbler, but the two species are usually found in different parts of Europe.

BARRED WARBLER
Sylvia nisoria

15 cm. Bars on underside. Song: musical, but in short bursts interrupted by chatter. Lives and nests in bushes and hedges in woods and fields. Usually shy, but may be seen and heard singing in flight.

BLACKCAP
Sylvia atricapilla

14 cm. Male: black cap, a glossy black crown down to eye level. The sides of the head and the underparts are ash-grey. The female has a red-brown cap and browner underparts. Song: varied warble held for short time. Lives and nests among undergrowth, bushes and hedges in woods, parks and gardens. Usually shy, but may come to bird tables in winter. The blackcap can be distinguished from the orphean and Sardinian warblers by the sharply-defined cap and the lack of white in the tail.

WHITETHROAT
Sylvia communis

14 cm. White throat with plain grey (male) or brown (female) head; red-brown wings. Song: short bursts of chatter. Lives and nests among low bushes, hedges and brambles around woods and in fields, also in gardens. Very active, darting in and out of cover and making short flights, singing in air.

LESSER WHITETHROAT
Sylvia curruca

13 cm. Like whitethroat, but dark patch around eye and grey-brown wings. Song: fast rattle-like sound, often preceded by a short warble. Hides away and nests among bushes and trees in woods, parks and gardens.

CHIFFCHAFF
Phylloscopus collybita

11 cm. Like willow warbler, but legs usually dark. Song: repeated 'chiff-chaff' sounds. Found in same places and as restless as willow warbler, but prefers areas with trees. Nests above ground.

DARTFORD WARBLER
Sylvia undata

13 cm. Red-brown breast, cocked tail. Song: short musical phrases with varying pauses. Lives and nests among low bushes, especially gorse, and heather on dry open ground and hillsides. Very shy, but may sing in flight. Has generally spread its breeding range during the last few years, but could be vulnerable in Britain, partly due to cold winters and heath fires in hot summers.

WILLOW WARBLER
Phylloscopus trochilus

11 cm. Grey-green back. Yellowish underside, white eye-stripe, legs usually pale. Song: liquid warble of descending notes. Found scurrying and flitting about in woods, among scattered trees and bushes, and in parks and gardens. Usually nests on the ground among bushes. Virtually identical to chiffchaff, except for song.

BONELLI'S WARBLER
Phylloscopus bonelli

11 cm. Like willow warbler, but greyer above, whiter beneath and with yellowish rump. Song: short trills. Lives in woods and forests, usually on hills and mountainsides. Nests on the ground, among trees.

WOOD WARBLER
Phylloscopus sibilatrix

13 cm. Yellow throat and breast; yellow eye-stripe. Song: liquid trill followed by a few long notes. Lives and nests among woods and forests. Very active, singing as it moves through the leaves and flies from tree to tree.

FLYCATCHERS Family Muscicapidae

These birds are well named, for they are most likely to be seen sitting watchfully on a perch and then suddenly darting out to capture a fly or some other flying insect or swooping down to the ground to make a catch there. They often return to the same perch to wait for the next meal.

PIED FLYCATCHER
Ficedula hypoleuca

13 cm. Male in summer: black back and white underside with white wing patch. Male in autumn and female: brown back with white wing patch. Found in woods, parks and gardens. Nests in hole in tree or wall, also in nest boxes. Flicks tail, but does not often return to same perch after chasing insects.

female
(and male
in autumn)

male
(summer)

RED-BREASTED FLYCATCHER
Ficedula parva

11 cm. Orange (male) or buff (female) throat; white tail edges. The male looks rather like a small robin, except for the white on its tail. Found in woods and parks, usually feeding among leaves in trees but sometimes chasing insects. Nests in hole in tree or wall and also on tree trunk.

male

female

SPOTTED FLYCATCHER
Muscicapa striata

14 cm. Grey-brown with lightly streaked breast and head. Found at the edges of woods, among scattered trees, and in parks, orchards and gardens. Nests on buildings and tree trunks, often behind creepers. Flicks its tail as it perches. Only young birds are spotted; the adults are lightly streaked instead.

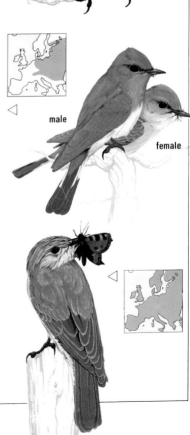

female
(and male
in autumn)

male, western
form (summer)

COLLARED FLYCATCHER
Ficedula albicollis

13 cm. In spring and summer the male's plumage varies. In Italy and central Europe, the western form (*Ficedula albicollis albicollis*), which has a white collar, is found. The eastern form (*F. albicollis semi-torquata*), which is found in eastern Europe, lacks the white collar. Female and male in autumn: very like pied flycatcher. Lives in similar places and behaves in same way as pied flycatcher.

GOLDCRESTS Family Regulidae

Goldcrests are active little birds that flit through bushes and trees, hunting for insects. In the winter, they may join flocks of tits seeking food. Two species are found in Europe and they are the smallest European birds.

female

male

male

female

GOLDCREST
Regulus regulus

9 cm. Tiny; orange (male) or yellow (female) stripe on crown. Found in woods and forests, especially in conifer trees; also in hedges, low bushes and undergrowth in winter. Builds basket-like nest of moss, often hung in conifer tree or among ivy.

FIRECREST
Regulus ignicapillus

9 cm. Like goldcrest, but black and white stripe over eye. Found in same places as goldcrest, but has no preference for conifer trees. Nest may be hung in bushes or creepers as well as in trees.

ACCENTORS Family Prunellidae

Accentors are small birds that root about on the ground or among low plants seeking insects and spiders to eat, and also seeds in winter. Two species are found in Europe.

DUNNOCK or HEDGE SPARROW
Prunella modularis

15 cm. Grey head and breast with brown back. Resembles female house sparrow but is recognized by its narrow bill and dark grey head and underside. Found in woods, bushy countryside, hedges, parks and gardens, where it shuffles through flower beds. Nests in hedges, bushes and low plants.

ALPINE ACCENTOR
Prunella collaris

18 cm. Spotted throat and streaky flanks. Lives on rocky mountain slopes, though may descend for the winter. Nests in holes in rocks.

PIPITS AND WAGTAILS Family Motacillidae

Pipits and wagtails are small birds that spend most of their time on the ground in search of insects. Pipits look like several other streaky brown ground birds, such as buntings and larks, but they can be recognized by their narrow beaks and slender bodies. Wagtails have long tails, which they wag up and down all the time.

TREE PIPIT
Anthus trivialis

15 cm. Breast buff with dark streaks; pink legs. Lives in light woods and clearings and among scattered trees and bushes. Nests among low plants on ground. May be seen and heard singing in short spiral flight rising from a perch.

TAWNY PIPIT
Anthus campestris

16 cm. Sandy unstreaked breast and faintly streaked neck. Lives on dry, open, often sandy ground, also in fields. Nests in low plants on ground.

MEADOW PIPIT
Anthus pratensis

15 cm. Pale breast with dark streaks, brown legs. Found in all kinds of open country – moors, fields, dunes, grassy slopes – and in winter in marshes and along rivers, often at the coast. Makes its nest on the ground hidden among low plants. May be seen and heard singing as it makes short flights rising from and returning to the ground.

winter

summer

WATER PIPIT
Anthus spinoletta

16 cm. Summer unstreaked breast with grey back. Winter: like rock pipit but white eye-stripe. Lives in mountains in spring and summer, nesting in holes in rock. Descends for winter, usually living near water.

ROCK PIPIT
Anthus petrosus

16 cm. Dark and streaky all over; dark legs; grey edges to tail (white in other pipits). Belongs to same species as water pipit, but lives at coast, often among rocks. Nests in rock crevices.

WHITE WAGTAIL
Motacilla alba alba

18 cm. Black and white, with very long tail; grey back. Often found in open country, usually near water, and also on farms and in villages and towns. Nests in holes and on ledges among rocks and on buildings. In winter, large groups sleep on buildings and in trees in cities and towns.

PIED WAGTAIL
Motacilla alba yarrellii

18 cm. As white wagtail, but black back in spring and summer. Form of white wagtail found mainly in the British Isles. Lives and nests in similar places to the white wagtail.

GREY WAGTAIL
Motacilla cinerea

18 cm. Grey back with yellow underside; male has black throat in summer. In spring and summer, found by streams and rivers, mostly in hills and mountains, where it nests in holes in wall or rock beside water. In winter, moves to lowland rivers and lakes, sewage farms and coast.

summer

winter

winter

summer

male (summer)

female

male (winter)

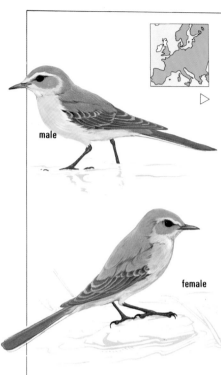

male

female

YELLOW WAGTAIL
Motacilla flava

16 cm. Green-brown back and bright yellow underside (pale in female). Found in marshes and fields, usually near water. Nests on the ground among grass or crops. Several forms with different head patterns and different names live in Europe. They all have their own regions, but where these meet, intermediate forms may be seen. In southern Scandinavia and central Europe, the blue-headed wagtail (*Motacilla flava flava*) – blue-grey crown, white stripe over eye, yellow throat – is found. Britain is the home of the yellow wagtail (*Motacilla flava flavissima*) – olive and yellow head. The Spanish wagtail (*Motacilla flava iberiae*) – grey crown, white stripe starting from eye, white throat – lives in Spain, Portugal and southern France. The ashy-headed wagtail (*Motacilla flava cinereocapilla*) – grey head, no stripe over eye, white throat – lives in Italy and Albania. The black-headed wagtail (*Motacilla flava feldegg*) – black head, no stripe over eye, yellow throat – is found in south-east Europe. Each kind may sometimes stray from its own region.

WAXWINGS Family Bombycillidae

Waxwings are unusual birds because they do not have particular homes. Except when nesting, they continually wander in flocks from place to place, looking for fruits, berries and insects to eat. They may be seen in one place for a short time and then not again for years.

WAXWING
Bombycilla garrulus

18 cm. Large crest; yellow tip on tail and waxy red tips to secondary wing feathers. Found in woods, parks and gardens, busily eating berries and fruits. Nests in Arctic and spreads into Europe in winter in search of food.

SHRIKES Family Laniidae

Shrikes are like small birds of prey. The shrike darts after its prey and snaps it up in its hooked beak. The victim is then usually taken to the shrike's 'larder', a sharp thorn or barbed wire fence where it is impaled so that the shrike can tear it apart – a habit that has earned the shrike its other name of butcherbird. Insects are the main prey, but the larger shrikes also catch lizards, small birds and rodents.

GREAT GREY SHRIKE
Lanius excubitor

24 cm. Black and white with grey back and crown. Found at edges of woods, among scattered trees and bushes and in hedges and orchards. Nests in trees and bushes.

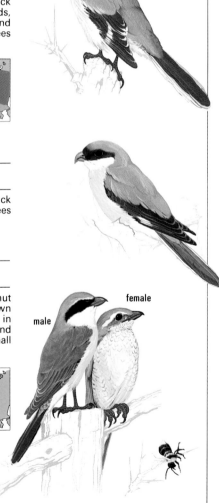

LESSER GREY SHRIKE
Lanius minor

20 cm. As great grey shrike but black forehead. Found among scattered trees and bushes. Nests in trees.

RED-BACKED SHRIKE
Lanius collurio

18 cm. Male: grey crown with chestnut back and wings. Female: plain brown back with bars on breast. Found in bushy places and among brambles and thickets. Nests in bushes and small trees.

female

male

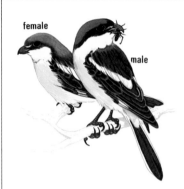

WOODCHAT SHRIKE
Lanius senator

18 cm. Chestnut crown with white wing patch and rump (female paler than male). Found in scattered trees, bushy countryside, orchards and woods. Nests in trees.

FINCHES Family Fringillidae

Like tits, finches are generally among the most well-known and liked of birds, for they often come to gardens and parks, adding a touch of colour with their bright plumage. They are less likely to be seen in the summer when they are nesting. They are primarily seed-eaters and have stout beaks.

GREENFINCH
Carduelis chloris

15 cm. Green-brown with yellow edges to wings and tail (female paler than male). Often seen among scattered trees and bushes, in fields, parks and gardens. Clings to net bags or wire baskets of nuts to feed, like tits. Nests in trees and bushes.

GOLDFINCH
Carduelis carduelis

13 cm. Red patch on face; wide yellow wingbar. Lives and nests in same places as greenfinch, but does not come to feed on nuts. Often seen climbing over thistles or on high perch.

HAWFINCH
Coccothraustes coccothraustes

18 cm. Huge beak above small black bib; wide white wingbar. Lives in woods, orchards, parks and gardens, but may hide away among leaves, especially in Britain. Nests in trees and bushes. Huge beak can crack open hard seeds.

SISKIN
Carduelis spinus

12 cm. Male: yellow-green with black crown and chin. Female: grey-green with streaky breast, yellow tail edges. Found in woods, usually nesting in conifer trees and, in winter, feeding in alder and birch trees. Also seen in parks and gardens.

LINNET
Carduelis cannabina

13 cm. Male: red forehead and breast (pale in winter), grey wing patch. Female: as twite but streaky throat and grey wing patch. Nests in low bushes, thickets and hedges, usually in open country but sometimes in parks and gardens. Roams over fields, rough pastures, and marshes in winter.

male

female

male

female

REDPOLL
Carduelis flammea

13 cm. Red forehead and black bib, pink breast (male only). Usually found in woods, but may be seen in parks and gardens. Nests in trees and bushes, often seen in alder and birch trees in winter together with siskins. Scandinavian redpolls are light in colour.

ARCTIC REDPOLL
Carduelis hornemanni

13 cm. As redpoll but white rump and generally paler plumage. Nests in Arctic. Usually seen in winter in woods, in company with redpolls.

TWITE
Carduelis flavirostris

14 cm. Streaky brown back, head and breast, but unstreaked throat; yellow beak (winter only); pinkish rump (male). Lives on moors and hills in summer, nesting among heather and bushes and in stone walls and rabbit burrows. Descends for winter and roams over open fields, marshes and seashores, where it can often be seen in large flocks.

EUROPEAN SERIN
Serinus serinus

11 cm. As siskin, but no yellow edges to tail and no black crown in male; also yellow rump and yellow (male) or streaky (female) forehead and breast. Found at edges of woods and in orchards, parks and gardens. Nests in trees and bushes.

female

male

BULLFINCH
Pyrrhula pyrrhula

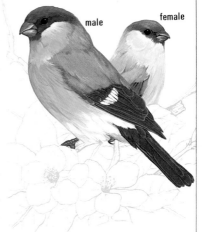

male

female

15 cm. Glossy black crown and bright red (male) or brownish-pink (female) breast. Found in woods, orchards, hedges, parks and gardens, usually in pairs. Nests in trees, bushes and hedges. Raids fruit trees for their buds.

CHAFFINCH
Fringilla coelebs

15 cm. Male: pink breast, grey-blue head (summer only) and green rump; two white wingbars and white edges to tail. Female: yellow-brown with two white wingbars and white tail edges. Often found in woods, among scattered trees and bushes, and in fields, hedges, orchards, parks and gardens. Nests in trees and bushes; spreads to more open country in winter.

female

male
(summer)

male
(winter)

PINE GROSBEAK
Pinicola enucleator

20 cm. Red (male) or green and gold (female) with two white wingbars; heavy hooked bill. Lives and nests in woods, especially among conifers and in birch woods. Largest of all European finches. May be seen in flocks outside the breeding season. Usually rather tame in nature. Named grosbeak for its heavy bill.

CROSSBILL
Loxia curvirostra

16 cm. Crossed bill (not always easy to see); orange-red (male) or green (female) with dark wings and tail. Lives and nests among conifer trees (especially spruce) in woods and forests. The tips of its bill are crossed so that it can lever open the cones to get at the seeds. When cones are scarce, it may spread in search of food, reaching the British Isles, France and Italy in great numbers.

PARROT CROSSBILL
Loxia pytyopsittacus

17 cm. As crossbill but heavier bill and larger head. Lives and nests mainly among pine trees, feeding in the same way as crossbill. Less likely to spread in search of food. Gets its name from the way it holds a cone while opening it, rather as a parrot holds a fruit while eating it (though crossbill performs same action).

BRAMBLING
Fringilla montifringilla

15 cm. Male: orange breast and base of wing; white rump; black (summer) or brown (winter) head and back. Female: as winter male but paler. Nests in trees in woods, and spreads south to fields, parks and gardens in winter, often with chaffinches and other finches. Found especially in beech woods.

female
male (summer)
male (winter)

BUNTINGS Family Emberizidae

Buntings are small seed-eating birds like finches, and have similar stout bills to crack open seeds. Buntings are most likely to be seen feeding on the ground in winter, often in groups, and also singing from a perch in spring and summer.

CORN BUNTING
Miliaria calandra

18 cm. Large, streaky brown. Found in open fields and on rough ground with scattered bushes. Hides its nest in grass or low bushes. May be seen perching on a post, wall or telegraph wires.

CIRL BUNTING
Emberiza cirlus

16 cm. Male: black throat. Female: as female yellowhammer but olive rump. Found among scattered trees and bushes and in hedges, where it nests near ground.

male
female

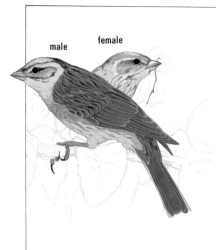

male   female

YELLOWHAMMER
Emberiza citrinella

16 cm. Male: yellow head and under-parts, chestnut rump. Female: streaky pale yellow head and breast, chestnut rump. Found in clearings and at edges of woods, among scattered bushes, and in fields and hedges. Nests on the ground or in a low bush or hedge. Sings throughout spring and summer, repeating its famous phrase that seems to say 'little bit of bread and *no* cheese' – in fact, a group of short notes and a long one.

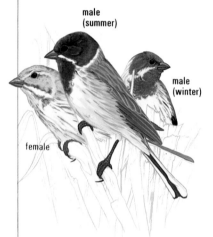

male (summer)

male (winter)

female

REED BUNTING
Emberiza schoeniclus

15 cm. Male: black (summer) or brown (winter) head and throat with white moustache and collar. Female: streaky brown with white moustache. Lives mainly in reed beds and swamps but also among bushes and hedges where it nests on or near the ground. Spreads to fields in winter, and may come to bird tables in gardens.

female   male

ORTOLAN BUNTING
Emberiza hortulana

16 cm. Male: green-grey head with yellow throat. Female: streaky brown with yellow throat. Found among scattered trees and bushes, often in hills; also in fields and gardens. Nests among low plants.

SNOW BUNTING
Plectrophenax nivalis

16 cm. Large white wing patch with white head (male in summer), sandy head (male in winter), or grey-brown head (female). Nests in crevices in rocks, usually high up in mountains. Spreads in winter to open coasts, hills and fields. Usually seen in winter in flocks, known as snowflakes from the way the little white birds dance through the air.

female
male (winter)
male (summer)

SPARROWS Family Ploceidae

No bird is better known than the house sparrow, which lives with man almost everywhere. Sparrows are small streaky brown birds with stout bills, rather like several buntings but having special marks that are easy to recognize.

TREE SPARROW
Passer montanus

14 cm. Chestnut crown with black spot on cheek (both sexes). Found in woods and among scattered trees and bushes, and in fields and gardens. Nests in holes in trees. Also lives and nests in towns and villages like house sparrow, especially in southern and eastern Europe.

HOUSE SPARROW
Passer domesticus

15 cm. Male: grey crown and black bib. Female: streaky back with plain light breast; dull eye-stripe. Found in city centres and squares, parks and gardens, farms and fields, rarely far from human habitation. Nests under eaves, in holes in walls and rocks, and in nest boxes; also builds domed nest in creepers, bushes and trees. In Italy, Corsica and Crete, the Italian sparrow (*Passer domesticus italiae*) is found. It is a form of house sparrow with a chestnut crown and white cheeks.

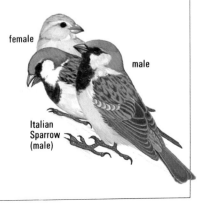

female
male
Italian Sparrow (male)

ROCK SPARROW
Petronia petronia

14 cm. Pale with stripes on head, spots on tail, yellow spot on breast. Found in rocky and stony places, sometimes in gardens and among buildings. Nests in holes in rocks and trees.

SNOW FINCH
Montifringilla nivalis

18 cm. White wings with black tips, grey head and dark chin (female duller than male). Lives on bare mountain slopes and summits, nesting in crevices. Spends winter lower down, often visiting huts and houses. Belongs to sparrow family, in spite of its name and bunting-like appearance.

STARLINGS Family Sturnidae

Starlings like each other's company and live in flocks that in winter may contain thousands of birds. They wander over the ground, busily pecking here and there for food. They chatter constantly, often copying other sounds.

winter

summer

STARLING
Sturnus vulgaris

21 cm. Summer: slightly-speckled glossy black with green-purple sheen. Winter: black with white spots. Found throughout the countryside and also in towns, where flocks sleep on buildings and in trees. Nests in holes in trees or ground, on buildings and in nest boxes. As spring arrives, it loses the white spots of its winter plumage because the white tips of its feathers wear away. Also, the beak, which is dark in winter, turns yellow. Youngsters are dull brown, without spots, and may be confused with female blackbirds, but they have longer beaks than blackbirds.

CHAPTER THREE

REPTILES AND AMPHIBIANS

The reptiles and amphibians are backboned animals belonging to the classes Reptilia and Amphibia respectively. Both groups are cold-blooded: their body temperatures fluctuate with the surrounding air or water instead of remaining more or less constant as in birds and mammals. But reptiles and amphibians are not necessarily cold, and in really hot weather they may actually be warmer than birds and mammals. They are inactive at low temperatures, however, and, with the exception of a few Mediterranean species, European reptiles and amphibians hibernate during the colder months. In the far north this can mean sleeping for as much as eight months of the year.

Reptiles
About 6,000 species of reptiles exist today, of which the great majority are snakes and lizards. Some 330 kinds of turtles and tortoises, 21 species of crocodiles and alligators, and the tuatara of New Zealand make up the rest of the class. Fewer than 90 species occur in Europe. All are air-breathers and the great majority live on land. Most have tough, waterproof skins clothed with horny scales – a feature which readily distinguishes the lizards from the amphibian newts and salamanders. Basically, reptiles have four legs, although these are reduced or absent in several groups of lizards and totally absent in all but a few snakes. With the exception of the tortoises, all European reptiles are carnivorous creatures.

Amphibians
The amphibians include the frogs and toads and the newts and salamanders. Like the reptiles, the majority of the 4,400 or so species live in the tropics. They normally have four legs – all more or less alike in the newts and salamanders. In the frogs and toads, however, the hind legs are much longer than the front legs. The hind legs provide the propulsive force for swimming and for leaping on land. Most amphibians can survive well on land, but they nearly all have to return to the water to breed, for their young are fish-like tadpoles which breathe with gills. They do not occur in the sea, but most freshwater habitats support them. Certain species have managed to adapt themselves to surprisingly dry places.

Lizards

There are about 3,000 species of lizards. Together with the snakes, they form the Order Squamata. They are mostly rather small and very active reptiles, typically with four legs, although these are reduced in the skinks and some other groups and absent altogether in the slow worms. Geckoes have adhesive pads on their toes, enabling them to climb smooth surfaces and even to run across ceilings. The tail is long in most lizards, but easily shed if the animal is caught by it. It can be re-grown, but rarely becomes as long as the original and often has a different scale pattern. Most lizards are active by day, usually only in sunny weather, and they feed mainly on small insects. The lengths given here are from the snout to the back legs.

MOORISH GECKO
Tarentola mauritanica
Family Gekkonidae

Up to 7 cm: tail about the same length. Pads extend all along the toes. A rather flat greyish-brown body with prominent tubercles.

Habitat: mainly nocturnal, but active by day in cooler months. On rocks and walls and in buildings: often lurks near lights to capture insects. Mediterranean: mainly near the coast.

AGAMA
Agama stellio Family Agamidae

Up to 12 cm: tail up to 18 cm. Head sometimes yellowish, especially in males. Body flattened, with a well-defined neck which often raises the head well above the body; head frequently bobs up and down.
Habitat: a sun-loving species found on rocks and tree trunks; often eats flowers and fallen fruit as well as insects. The only member of its family in Europe, it occurs in Greece: often called the Rhodes Dragon.

THREE-TOED SKINK
Chalcides chalcides Family Scincidae

Up to 20 cm: tail about the same. A slender, cylindrical body clothed with large shiny scales. Tiny 3-toed legs. Sandy to brownish-green, with or without longitudinal stripes. Gives birth to active young – up to 23 at a time.
Habitat: damp meadows with dense herbage. Active by day, but secretive: very fast despite short legs. Eats a wide range of invertebrates. Southern Europe, from Italy westwards.

SLOW WORM
Anguis fragilis Family Anguidae

Up to 50 cm in total, over half being tail in complete specimens but difficult to see where body ends and tail begins because there are no legs. Tail very fragile and easily broken and hardly grows again. Very smooth and shiny: grey to coppery colour. Female often has stripe along back: male may have blue spots. Easily distinguished from snakes by the presence of eye-lids. Gives birth to active young.
Habitat: damp places with lush vegetation. Spends much time under stones but ventures out at dusk and after rain; rather slow. Eats slugs. Absent from far north, Ireland, and southern Spain.

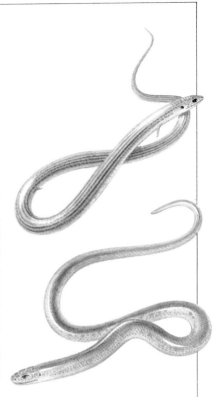

TYPICAL LIZARDS Family Lacertidae

Very active diurnal lizards with slender bodies and well developed legs. Large scales clothe the head, which is larger in males than in females. Most numerous in southern Europe, where they revel in the hot, dry summers. Many of these southern species have very restricted distributions.

COMMON WALL LIZARD
Podarcis muralis

Up to 8 cm, but usually less: tail up to $2\frac{1}{4}$ times body length. A rather flattened body and extremely variable in pattern, especially in southern Europe. In western and central Europe it is basically brown or grey, usually with a thin dark stripe in the middle of the back and often with black and white patches on the sides of the tail.
Habitat: dry rocky places, especially sunny banks. Runs on walls, rocks and tree trunks; is most common lizard around houses. Not in Britain.

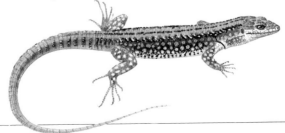

GREEN LIZARD
Lacerta viridis

Up to 13 cm: tail up to twice body length. Male normally all green with black stippling: blue throat when mature. Female may be green or brown, often blotched and frequently with pale stripes. Scales are strongly keeled.
Habitat: dense vegetation, especially with bushes, which it often climbs. Eats some fruit and even birds' eggs as well as insects. Southern and central Europe: not in Britain or southern Spain. Present in Channel Islands.

OCELLATED LIZARD
Lacerta lepida

Up to 25 cm: tail up to 50 cm. This, the largest European lizard, is easily recognized just by its size when mature. The male has a very large head. Body is sometimes grey or brownish and the blue spots are not always present on the sides. The black stippling often forms distinct patterns on the back. The scales are not strongly keeled. Youngsters are dull green with white spots, often ringed with black.
Habitat: dry, scrubby places, including roadside banks, stone walls and vineyards. Food includes insects, fruit, birds' eggs and nestlings, and other lizards. Iberia (where it largely replaces the green lizard) and southern France.

SAND LIZARD
Lacerta agilis

Up to 9 cm, but usually somewhat less: tail about $1\frac{1}{2}$ times body length. A stocky species with relatively short legs and a very deep head, especially in the male. The body colour is extremely variable. The typical male has green sides (very bright in the breeding season) and a brown back with a darker central stripe. Both the back and the sides bear dark blotches, but a pale unmarked stripe runs along the upper part of each side. Some males are entirely green, especially in eastern Europe. Females are grey or brown and only rarely have green on the sides. The dark stripe in the middle of the back is usually fragmented. Both sexes may have a plain chestnut back (not in Britain).

Habitat: mainly dry areas, with shorter and less dense vegetation than required by the Green Lizard: rarely climbs. Roadsides, sand dunes, heathland and rough pasture: often high in mountains in the south. From southern Scandinavia to Alps and Pyrenees: local and rare in Britain: absent from Italy and most of Iberia and Greece.

VIVIPAROUS LIZARD
Lacerta vivipara

Up to 6·5 cm: tail up to twice body length and relatively stout. Body little flattened, with relatively small head and short legs. Grey, brown, or olive green with a variable pattern of streaks and spots. Underside white, yellow, or brick-red. Normally gives birth to active young, which are bronzy-black, but occasionally lays eggs in southern mountains.

Habitat: dense vegetation in fairly humid climates: grassland, heathland, sand dunes, bogs and moorland, and roadsides. Most of Europe, including the Arctic, but absent from most of Iberia and the Mediterranean region. The commonest lizard in most central and northern regions: also known as the Common Lizard in Britain.

male

female

male

female

Snakes

Although they have no legs, the snakes flourish in many terrestrial and aquatic environments.

With a few exceptions, snakes catch live prey, which they find largely by smell. A snake is continually flicking out its tongue to pick up scent from the surroundings. Most snakes simply grab their prey in their jaws and swallow it. Constricting snakes wind their bodies around the prey and kill it by stopping it from breathing. The venomous snakes kill their prey with poison injected by special teeth (fangs). Prey is swallowed whole, and a snake can actually swallow prey of greater diameter than its own body.

Only 27 of the 2,700 known species of snake live in Europe. The measurements given on these pages are total lengths.

SAND BOA
Eryx jaculus Family Boidae

Up to 80 cm. Stout body and blunt tail. Grey to reddish-brown. The only European member of the family. Gives birth to active young.
Habitat: dry and mainly sandy places. Hunts at night, feeding mainly on small rodents which are caught in their burrows or on the surface and killed by constriction. South-eastern Europe.

COLUBRID SNAKES Family Colubridae

A very large family containing most of the European snakes. There are large scales on the top of the head. Most species are non-poisonous and simply grab prey in their jaws. A few species are constrictors. Mainly diurnal.

MONTPELLIER SNAKE
Malpolon monspessulanus

Up to 200 cm. Readily identified by prominent ridges running over the large eyes and on to the snout. Grey, brown, olive, or black: often uniform but may have light or dark spots.
Habitat: dry, rocky and scrubby places mainly. Hunts mainly by sight, feeding mostly on lizards, small mammals, and other snakes. Venomous, but fangs are at the back of the mouth and not dangerous to man. Iberia and Mediterranean.

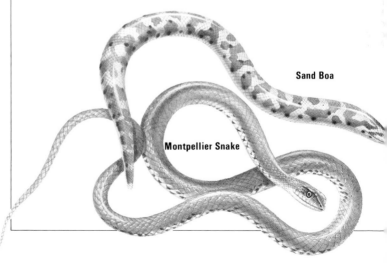

Sand Boa

Montpellier Snake

HORSESHOE WHIP SNAKE
Coluber hippocrepis

Up to 150 cm. Slender, with row of very small scales below eye. Ground colour yellow, greenish or reddish but largely obscured by black pattern. **Habitat**: dry and rocky places: often around houses. Eats mammals, birds and lizards. Iberia and Sardinia only.

WESTERN WHIP SNAKE
Coluber viridiflavus

Up to 150 cm. Slender, with rather blunt snout. Yellowish-green with black markings: sometimes all black above.
Habitat: dry, rocky and scrubby places. Very fast, eating lizards and small mammals. Mainly France and Italy.

Horseshoe Whip Snake

Western Whip Snake

LADDER SNAKE
Elaphe scalaris

Up to 160 cm. Yellowish-grey to brown with 2 darker stripes on back. Named for ladder-like pattern of young.
Habitat: stony and bushy places; climbs well. Feeds mainly on small mammals and nestling birds. Iberia and Mediterranean coast of France.

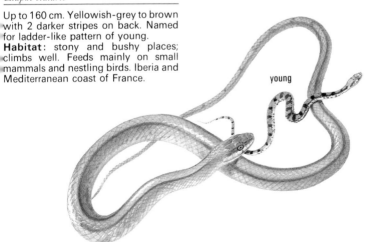

young

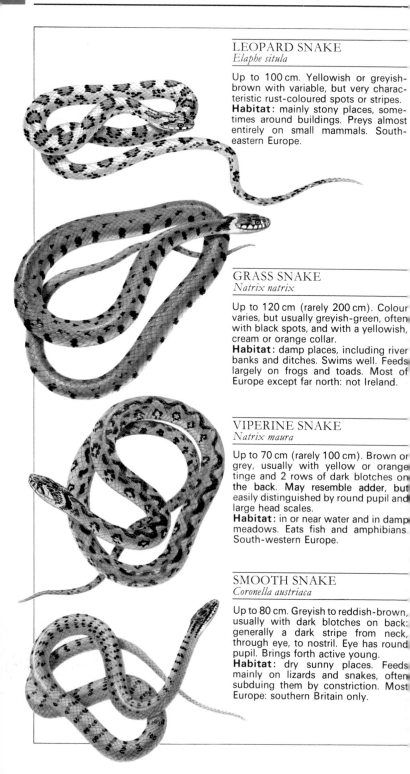

LEOPARD SNAKE
Elaphe situla

Up to 100 cm. Yellowish or greyish-brown with variable, but very characteristic rust-coloured spots or stripes. **Habitat:** mainly stony places, sometimes around buildings. Preys almost entirely on small mammals. South-eastern Europe.

GRASS SNAKE
Natrix natrix

Up to 120 cm (rarely 200 cm). Colour varies, but usually greyish-green, often with black spots, and with a yellowish, cream or orange collar. **Habitat:** damp places, including river banks and ditches. Swims well. Feeds largely on frogs and toads. Most of Europe except far north: not Ireland.

VIPERINE SNAKE
Natrix maura

Up to 70 cm (rarely 100 cm). Brown or grey, usually with yellow or orange tinge and 2 rows of dark blotches on the back. May resemble adder, but easily distinguished by round pupil and large head scales. **Habitat:** in or near water and in damp meadows. Eats fish and amphibians. South-western Europe.

SMOOTH SNAKE
Coronella austriaca

Up to 80 cm. Greyish to reddish-brown, usually with dark blotches on back: generally a dark stripe from neck, through eye, to nostril. Eye has round pupil. Brings forth active young. **Habitat:** dry sunny places. Feeds mainly on lizards and snakes, often subduing them by constriction. Most Europe: southern Britain only.

CAT SNAKE
Telescopus fallax

Up to 80 cm (occasionally over 100 cm). Deep body and broad, flat head. Pupil vertical. Grey or brown, usually with dark collar and blotches on back. **Habitat:** rough and stony places. Hunts mainly at dusk, feeding largely on lizards. Venomous fangs at back of mouth: not dangerous to man. South-eastern Europe.

VIPERS Family Viperidae

Venomous snakes with large, erectile fangs at front of mouth. The only dangerous snakes in Europe. Heavy-bodied and relatively slow-moving. Pupil vertical. Head scales small. Most give birth to active young. There are seven European species.

ADDER
Vipera berus

Up to 70 cm (rarely 90 cm). Also known as the Common viper. Usually a clear dark zig-zag stripe along the back — especially prominent in males, which tend to have pale grey ground colour. Females often brownish and stripe less obvious. Some individuals are black. In Iberia, zig-zag may be replaced by a straight brown stripe with dark spots on each side.
Habitat: very varied, but generally heathland in north and on mountains further south. Mainly diurnal, feeding on small mammals and lizards. Most of Europe, including the Arctic, but not Ireland or Mediterranean.

ASP
Vipera aspis

Up to 75 cm (usually under 60 cm). Similar to Adder in appearance and habits, but distinguished by up-turned snout. More venomous than adder. **Habitat:** very varied, from high mountains to coast. Pyrenees, Alps, Italy and most of France.

LATASTE'S VIPER
Vipera latasti

Up to 60 cm. Similar to last two species but with distinct nose horn. **Habitat:** rocky hillsides and open woods. Iberia only.

Tortoises and Terrapins

The reptiles in this very ancient group (Order Chelonia), which has existed almost unchanged for over 200 million years, are easily recognized by the box-like shells in which they live. The shell is composed largely of bony plates, and there are two main parts – a domed carapace on the top and a flatter plastron underneath. The two parts are normally joined along the middle of each side, with gaps for the head, legs and tail. Head and limbs can be retracted when danger threatens. The carapace is decorated with a number of horny plates (tortoiseshell), whose pattern is characteristic for each species. The name tortoise is usually used for terrestrial forms, while freshwater species are often called terrapins and the marine species are usually called turtles. The tortoises are essentially vegetarians, while the terrapins and turtles are mainly carnivorous. None has any teeth, but a horny beak serves the same function. All species lay eggs. The sexes are much alike, but males have longer tails and slightly concave plastrons, allowing them to mount the females more easily.

HERMANN'S TORTOISE
Testudo hermanni Family Testudinidae

Up to 20 cm long and strongly domed. It differs from the two other European tortoises in having a large scale on the tip of the tail and usually two shell plates immediately above the base of the tail: the others have no scale on the tail and just one plate above it.
Habitat: very varied: dry or moist with dense vegetation. Mediterranean.

EUROPEAN POND TERRAPIN
Emys orbicularis Family Emydidae

Up to 30 cm long. Black or dark brown, usually with yellowish spots and streaks.
Habitat: still and slow-moving water with plenty of submerged and emergent vegetation. Basks at water's edge; dives when disturbed. Eats fishes, amphibians and various invertebrates. South and central Europe: not in Britain.

STRIPED-NECKED TERRAPIN
Mauremys caspica

Up to 20 cm long. Flattened and rather oval like the previous species but with a central keel — at least in hind region. Lighter than previous species, but fewer markings except that the neck bears prominent yellow stripes.
Habitat: like that of *Emys*, but often in larger bodies of water. Both species, which are the only European terrapins, will tolerate brackish waters. Iberia and south-east Europe.

Frogs and Toads

Frogs and toads (Order Anura) are tailless amphibians with squat bodies and long back legs. In common parlance, smooth-skinned species are usually called frogs, while rougher-skinned species are called toads, but many families contain both smooth and warty species and the common names do not necessarily signify any relationship. Tree frogs, for example, are more closely related to the common toad than to the common frog. Toads tend to live in drier places than frogs and they have better-developed lungs. All capture living prey, such as worms, slugs and insects; most catch it with a long, sticky tongue which is fired out at great speed. There are about 25 species in Europe, all with the typical life history involving free-swimming tadpoles. Females are usually larger than males.

PAINTED FROG
Discoglossus pictus
Family Discoglossidae

7 cm. Plump and shiny, rather like common frog but pupil is round or triangular. Colour varies from grey to brick red, usually with pale-edged dark spots.
Habitat: stays mainly in or close to water. Active day and night. Iberia, south-west France, Sicily, Malta.

YELLOW-BELLIED TOAD
Bombina variegata

Up to 5 cm. Rather flattened, with orange or yellow underside which is displayed when alarmed. Pupil round, triangular or heart-shaped.
Habitat: stays mainly in shallow water. Mainly diurnal. South and central Europe: not Iberia or Britain.

eggs

MIDWIFE TOAD
Alytes obstetricans

Family Discoglossidae
Up to 5 cm. Plump; grey, green, or brown. Vertical pupil. Tongue is disc-shaped in this family and cannot be fired out. Male carries string of eggs wrapped round hind legs and enters water when they are ready to hatch.
Habitat: mainly on land, in varied places, including gardens. Mainly nocturnal. Western Europe from Germany southwards: introduced into Britain.

COMMON SPADEFOOT
Pelobates fuscus Family Pelobatidae

Up to 8 cm. Smooth-skinned with large eyes, vertical pupils and a swelling on top of head. A pale projection (the spade) on each hind leg is used for digging burrows. Colour and pattern very variable.
Habitat: sandy ground, including cultivated land. Strictly nocturnal outside breeding season. Central Europe: not in Britain. Western Spadefoot of southwest Europe is similar, but has black spade.

eggs

COMMON TOAD
Bufo bufo Family Bufonidae

Up to 15 cm (usually less). Very warty, usually some shade of brown: pale below. Pupil horizontal.
Habitat: a wide variety of places, often quite dry. Mainly nocturnal. Walks rather than leaps, except when disturbed. As in all members of the family, eggs are laid in long strings. Most of Europe: not in Ireland.

PARSLEY FROG
Pelodytes punctatus Family Pelobatidae

Up to 5 cm. Long-legged and named for bright green decoration on warty grey back. Pupil vertical.
Habitat: shrubby vegetation: agile and climbs well. Nocturnal, resting under stones by day. South-west Europe, from Belgium southwards.

NATTERJACK
Bufo calamita Family Bufonidae

8 cm. Brown, grey or greenish, usually with clear yellow stripe on back. Pupil horizontal.
Habitat: varied, but usually sandy places in north. Often in brackish pools by sea. Nocturnal. South-west and central Europe: rare in Britain.

GREEN TOAD
Bufo viridis

Up to 10 cm. Easily identified by colour pattern. Has shrill, warbling song.
Habitat: varied, often quite dry. Not uncommon around buildings. Mainly eastern Europe, including Italy and Denmark.

COMMON TREE FROG
Hyla arborea Family Hylidae

Up to 5 cm. Usually bright green, but sometimes brownish and may be blotchy. A brown stripe on each side. Toes have suction pads, allowing them to cling to shiny leaves. Male has enormous vocal sac which swells like a balloon under chin when calling.
Habitat: bushes and other dense vegetation near water: very agile and climbs well. Mainly nocturnal. Southern and central Europe: introduced into Britain.

EDIBLE FROG
Rana esculenta Family Ranidae

Up to 12 cm. Green or brown with dark spots, but no dark eye-patch. Vocal sacs bulge from each side of the throat: very noisy.
Habitat: largely aquatic, even out of breeding season. Active day and night. Southern and central Europe but not Iberia: southern Britain only.

tadpole

eggs

COMMON FROG
Rana temporaria

Up to 10 cm. Grey, brown, pink o
yellow with darker blotches. Always a
dark patch enclosing eye and eardrum
although this feature is shared with
several similar species. Horizontal pupi
and clear fold along each side of the
back are typical of the family. Eggs laid
in masses.
Habitat: damp vegetation: rarely in
water outside breeding season. A
Europe except Iberia and Mediterranean.

MARSH FROG
Rana ridibunda

Up to 15 cm. Similar to the previous
species but darker: often brown. Very
noisy, with vocal sacs at side of throat
Habitat: usually in or near water al
year. Active day and night. Southern
and central Europe: introduced in
Britain.

Newts and Salamanders

Newts and salamanders (Order
Caudata) are tailed amphibians.
Some salamanders breed in
water, but the animals are largely
terrestrial and some have
dispensed with the free-living
tadpole stage. They inhabit damp
places and forage for small
invertebrates at night. Outside
the breeding season, the newts
behave much like the salamanders,
but they all return to the water to
breed. Males become very
colourful at this time and display
themselves in front of the females,
who lay their eggs singly on water
plants and wrap the leaves around
them. Unlike the anuran tadpoles
newt tadpoles keep their feathery
gills until they leave the water
and, because the adults have tails,
there is a much less dramatic
change between larval and adult
state. Newt tadpoles are entirely
carnivorous, whereas those of
frogs and toads eat a good deal of
vegetable matter.

There are 20 species in Europe.
the 9 described here all belonging
to the Family Salamandridae.

MARBLED NEWT
Triturus marmoratus

Up to 15 cm. Easily identified by its colour. Female lacks crest, as in all newts, and has a yellow stripe along the back. Male has no crest outside breeding season. Skin velvety on land.
Habitat: breeds in weedy pools but may wander far from water outside breeding season. Iberia and western France.

WARTY NEWT
Triturus cristatus

Up to 14 cm. Breeding male dark grey with black spots and a spiky crest. Female and non-breeding male appear jet black. Yellow or orange below. Coarse, warty skin.
Habitat: may stay in weedy pools all year, but often on land in summer. Most Europe, but not Iberia or Ireland.

SMOOTH NEWT
Triturus vulgaris

Up to 11 cm. Smooth-skinned, dry and velvety on land. Female and non-breeding male pale brown, often with 2 darker stripes on the back. Breeding male heavily spotted on the back and with a large, continuous, wavy crest on back and tail.
Habitat: breeds in still water with plenty of weeds, including garden ponds. Non-breeders roam far from water in a wide variety of habitats. Most Europe except south west and far north.

ALPINE NEWT
Triturus alpestris

Up to 12 cm. Similar to Smooth Newt, but orange or yellow underside is rarely spotted. Breeding male has a yellowish crest, much lower and smoother than in the previous species.
Habitat: aquatic for much of the year in cool, clear pools. Sometimes on land, but rarely far from water. Alps, Pyrenees and much of central Europe (often at low level): not in Britain.

male

female

PALMATE NEWT
Triturus helveticus

Up to 9 cm. Pale brown or sometimes greenish, with or without spots. Female and non-breeding male may be confused with smooth newt, but distinguished by unspotted throat. Breeding male has low, smooth crest on back and a higher one on the tail: latter ends abruptly in a small filament.
Habitat: breeds in still, clear water. Western Europe: not in Ireland.

FIRE SALAMANDER
Salamandra salamandra

Up to 20 cm (rarely 25 cm). A slow-moving species easily recognized by its colour, although spots may be quite small or even run together to form stripes. No other European species has similar coloration. Colours warn of unpleasant skin secretion. Pairs on land in summer, but eggs are kept in female's body until the spring: only then does she go to the water. The eggs have hatched by this time and she dips her hind end into the water to allow the young to swim away. In some areas female retains young in her body until they have turned into miniature adults: she never goes to the water.
Habitat: mainly damp upland woods. Southern and central Europe: not in Britain.

SPECTACLED SALAMANDER
Salamandrina terdigitata

Up to 11 cm. Dull black or brown above with red or yellow patch on head. Undersides of adult legs and tail bright red and exposed if alarmed. Four toes on hind foot (all other European species have five).
Habitat: dense vegetation on wooded mountain slopes, usually near streams. Breeds in water. Confined to Italy.

ALPINE SALAMANDER
Salamandra atra

Up to 16 cm. All black, often with a prominent ribbed appearance.
Habitat: forests and damp meadows, usually between 800 and 2000 metres up in the mountains. Mainly nocturnal, but often about after rain in the daytime. Gives birth to miniature adults and never needs to return to the water. Alps and northern Yugoslavia.

CHAPTER FOUR

FISHES

The general term fishes covers three rather different groups of aquatic animals: the lampreys and hagfishes, the sharks and rays, and the bony fishes. Lampreys have no jaws and are mostly blood-suckers. Their skeletons are made of cartilage. The sharks and rays and the bony fishes are nearly all carnivorous creatures with well-developed jaws. Sharks and rays have skeletons of cartilage. They also have a series of separate gill slits on each side of the body, through which water passes out during breathing movements. Bony fishes have skeletons of bone and their gills are covered by a flap with a single opening at the rear.

Among the fishes' most distinctive features are the fins and scales. Sharks have several fins, always including two pairs at the sides: the pectoral fins behind the head and the pelvic fins on the belly. The fins of bony fishes consist of thin webs of skin supported on bony rays and they are generally more mobile than those of the sharks. Their shape and arrangement, illustrated here, are of great help in identifying fishes.

Many fishes have a line of small pores along each side. This system is known as the lateral line. The pores lead to special sense organs which detect pressure changes in the surrounding water and alert the fishes to nearby movements.

In general, fishes are well organized for life in the water and, with about 20,000 known species, they are the most successful group of vertebrates. Unless otherwise stated, the species described here occur in suitable habitats all over Europe. The sizes given are maximum recorded lengths.

A typical bony fish showing the main external features.

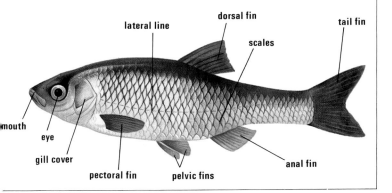

Freshwater Fishes

LAMPREY FAMILY Petromyzonidae

One of the two living groups of jawless vertebrates, with about 30 species, mostly in fresh water. The mouth is a circular suction pad, with teeth in adults. Some species are blood-sucking parasites of other fishes. All feed on minute organisms in the mud when young.

LAMPERN
Lampetra fluviatilis

50 cm. Grey or greeny-brown on back, yellowish or white ventrally. Two dorsal fins.

Habitat: young spend 5 years in muddy river bed, then migrate to sea. Adults move up-river August-November, spawning on shingle beds in April. They attack estuarine and freshwater fishes.

LAMPREY
Petromyzon marinus

91 cm. Olive or yellow, heavily mottled with black on the back; pale underneath. Two dorsal fins.

Habitat: young are blind and spend 5 years in muddy river bed; then migrate to sea. Adults are parasitic on a wide range of sea and estuarine fishes. They spawn May-June on pebble beds in the rivers.

STURGEON FAMILY Acipenseridae

STURGEON
Acipenser sturio

3·5 m for females; males smaller. 5 rows of bony plates on body; upper lobe of tail longer; mouth small and tubular, with 2 pairs of barbels.

Habitat: breeds in large rivers May-June. The young live in fresh water for 3 years and then go to sea. Adults return to the sea after spawning. Feeds on bottom-living animals. Rare in Europe, breeding in only a few southern rivers; more common in the Black Sea.

SALMON FAMILY Salmonidae

Native to the northern hemisphere, these fishes live in the sea and in fresh water, but all breed in fresh water. They have a scaleless head and all have a fleshy adipose fin on the back between the dorsal and tail fins. None of the fin rays is spiny.

SALMON
Salmo salar

1·5 m. Very narrow just in front of tail fin: upper jaw reaches to rear edge of eye. Young fish (parr) have 8-11 dark smudges on each side.

Habitat: eggs are laid in river gravel in mid-winter. Parr live in river for 3 years, then migrate to sea as smolts. After 1-4 years in sea, feeding on fishes and crustaceans, they return to the rivers they were born in to spawn.

BROWN TROUT
Salmo trutta

1·4 m. Body deep just before tail fin: upper jaw reaches beyond eye.
Habitat: eggs are laid in river gravel in winter. Some brown trout live permanently in rivers but others move to lakes or the sea (sea trout).

RAINBOW TROUT
Salmo gairdneri

1 m. Heavily spotted with rainbow stripe along each side.
Habitat: a North American fish introduced to Europe in lakes and rivers.

ARCTIC CHARR
Salvelinus alpinus

1 m. Scales minute; pectoral, pelvic, and anal fins reddish with light margins.
Habitat: mostly mountainous lakes (where rarely over 25 cm long); in rivers and sea in Scandinavia.

POWAN
Coregonus lavaretus Family Coregonidae

70 cm. Blunt-snouted, upper jaw longer than lower.

Habitat: mountain lakes in Britain and the Alps (where no more than 20 cm) and in the Baltic Sea.

VENDACE
Coregonus albula

35 cm. Lower jaw longer than upper.
Habitat: mountain lakes in Britain and Europe, and around the Baltic Sea.

SMELT
Osmerus eperlanus Family Osmeridae

30 cm. With large fragile scales and large, strongly-toothed jaws. Smells strongly of cucumber.
Habitat: northern Europe only. Breeds in spring in rivers on sand or gravel within tidal influence and generally migrates to the sea and estuaries for the winter.

GRAYLING
Thymallus thymallus Family Thymallidae

50 cm. Stout bodied with large scales and a large dorsal fin.
Habitat: cool, clean clear streams,

often in fast-flowing water. Also in large mountain lakes. Spawns in spring in gravelly shallows; the colourful male displays to the female.

PIKE FAMILY Esocidae

PIKE
Esox lucius

1·5 m. Powerful body with a large mouth and big teeth in the lower jaw

only. Dorsal and anal fins near tail.
Habitat: lakes and rivers, usually close to weed beds from which it charges at passing fishes in daytime. Spawns in early spring at the water's edge.

CARP FAMILY Cyprinidae

One of the largest families of fishes, and the dominant fresh-water family in most parts of the world. Mostly scaly fishes with no spines in their fins, scaleless heads, and toothless jaws.

ROACH
Rutilus rutilus

53 cm. Deep-bodied, with dorsal fin origin above the pelvic fin base. Eye and pelvic and anal fins reddish.
Habitat: abundant in lakes and in slow-moving rivers throughout Europe. Feeds on whatever insect larvae, crustaceans or snails are common locally. Spawns April-June; the yellow eggs are shed on plants in shallow water and hatch in 9-12 days.

MODERLIESCHEN
Leucaspius delineatus

12 cm. Slender-bodied, with a small head, large eyes, and a steeply-angled mouth. Scales thin and fragile. Lateral line is incomplete.
Habitat: a small schooling fish living in lakes, ponds and sometimes in slow-flowing rivers. Spawns in summer, the eggs being looped in strands round water plants. Not in Britain.

IDE
Leuciscus idus

1 m. Slender body, with humped back and broad head; scales small.
Habitat: not native to Britain, but widespread in Europe in lower reaches of rivers and large lowland lakes; eats aquatic invertebrates.

DACE
Leuciscus leuciscus

30 cm. Slender bodied with a narrow head; scales moderately large; anal fin concave.
Habitat: widespread in clean small rivers and brooks, in moderate current. Swims in schools, feeding on insect larvae and often taking adults at the surface. Spawns in early spring in gravel shallows.

ASP
Aspius aspius

70 cm. Compressed body with a sharp keel on belly; head pointed, with a prominent lower jaw.

Habitat: lowland rivers and lakes in central Europe, migrating into the Black and Caspian Seas. Eats small fishes and invertebrates.

CHUB
Leuciscus cephalus

61 cm. Slender body, but broad across the head and back; scales large; anal fin rounded.

Habitat: rivers, usually with moderate current; also in large lakes. Eats aquatic invertebrates and small fishes.

NASE
Chondrostoma nasus

50 cm. Slender-bodied, with a small head and protuberant snout; mouth small with hard horny lips.

Habitat: confined to mainland Europe and most abundant in swift-flowing rivers. Forms large schools and feeds on algae growing on rocks and other surfaces, including other plants.

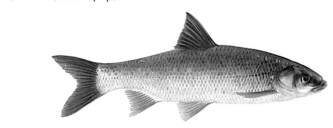

RUDD
Scardinius erythrophthalmus

45 cm. Deep-bodied, with a small head and steeply-angled mouth. Dorsal fin placed behind level of pelvic fins; a sharp keel on the belly. Eye is golden; the pelvic and anal fins blood-red.

Habitat: lakes and backwaters of rivers, swimming in schools near the surface. Feeds on crustaceans and insects, often taking adults at the surface. Spawns April-June, the eggs sticking to plants.

MINNOW
Phoxinus phoxinus

12 cm. Round-bodied with a short, broad head; scales minute. Breeding males have red bellies and black throats.
Habitat: small clean rivers; rarely in large lakes. Forms large schools in shallow water, and spawns in spring over stones. Feeds on insect larvae and crustaceans. Lives in deeper water in winter.

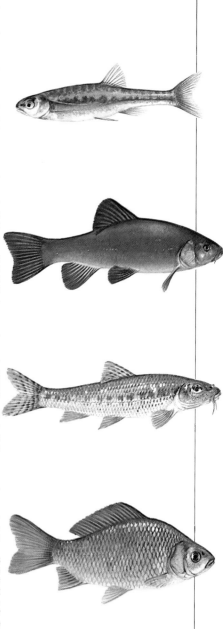

TENCH
Tinca tinca

70 cm. Thickset fish with rounded fins and a deep tail. One pair of barbels at corners of mouth. Scales very small. Body with thick slime layer.
Habitat: slow-flowing rivers, canals and lakes, usually among water plants near the bottom. Buries in mud in winter; can survive high temperatures and low oxygen levels in summer. Feeds on molluscs and insect larvae.

GUDGEON
Gobio gobio

20 cm. Rather round-bodied with a large head; mouth ventral with a pair of barbels. Scales moderately large, 38-44 in lateral line.
Habitat: mainly a river fish of moderately fast currents, but also in slow-moving water and lakes. Lives on the bottom in small schools, and eats various invertebrates.

CRUCIAN CARP
Carassius carassius

51 cm. Deep-bodied; long-based dorsal fin has a convex edge. Head small with no barbels.
Habitat: overgrown pools and lakes and river backwaters; very resistant to low oxygen levels and high and low temperatures. Feeds on plants, insect larvae and water snails. Spawns May-June; the golden eggs stick to water plants; the fry stay attached to the plants for the first few days.

BITTERLING
Rhodeus sericeus

9 cm. Rather deep-bodied with large scales; the lateral line extends only to 5 or 6 scales. Pinkish on the sides, with a metallic blue streak; males are brighter.
Habitat: native only in mainland Europe, but introduced to England. Lives in still and slow-moving water, feeding mainly on planktonic crustaceans. Female uses her long egg-laying tube to deposit a few eggs inside the gill chamber of a freshwater mussel. The eggs develop inside the mussel.

BLEAK
Alburnus alburnus

20 cm. Slender and bright silvery, with compressed sides and a sharp keel on belly; anal fin long-based.
Habitat: very common in rivers, in large schools near the surface. Across Europe, but only in eastern England. Feeds on planktonic animals, especially crustaceans, and insects at the water's surface.

BARBEL
Barbus barbus

90 cm. Round in cross-section although belly is flattened. Mouth ventral, lips fleshy; 2 pairs of long barbels.
Habitat: lowland rivers with moderate currents and a sandy or gravelly bottom; particularly common in weir pools. Feeds on bottom-living invertebrates, particularly insect larvae, worms and molluscs. Breeds on river gravel in late spring.

CARP
Cyprinus carpio

1 m. Heavy-bodied; long-based dorsal fin with a concave edge. Head rather large; 4 barbels on the lips.
Habitat: lowland lakes and slow-moving rivers with much vegetation. Feeds mainly on bottom-living insect larvae and snails, also some plant material. Eggs are attached to water plants in spring. Native to eastern Europe; introduced to Britain and western Europe.

SILVER BREAM
Blicca bjoerkna

35 cm. Moderately deep-bodied with flattened sides. Anal fin long-based, with 22-24 rays. Eyes large. Pelvic fins reddish.
Habitat: slow-flowing lowland rivers, lakes and reservoirs, often among vegetation. Eats plants and bottom-living insect larvae, crustaceans and molluscs. The yellow eggs are attached to plants in summer.

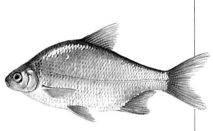

COMMON BREAM
Abramis brama

50 cm. Deep-bodied with a high back, flat sides, and a sharp keel under the belly. Anal fin long-based with 25-31 rays. Eye moderately large.

Habitat: abundant in lakes and slow-flowing lowland rivers. Lives in schools and, in a head-down posture, uses its tubular mouth to pick insect larvae, worms and molluscs out of the mud.

LOACH FAMILY Cobitidae

A family of freshwater fishes, related to the carps. Slender and small, they burrow in the bottom; most have barbels round mouth.

STONE LOACH
Noemacheilus barbatulus

15 cm. 6 barbels; no spine under eye.
Habitat: streams and shallow rivers with stony bottoms and dense weed beds. Active at night and on dull days; feeds on bottom-living crustaceans and worms.

POND LOACH
Misgurnus fossilis

15 cm. 5 pairs of barbels.
Habitat: lowland ponds, marshes, and river backwaters with dense weed and mud; breathes air. Not in Britain.

SPINED LOACH
Cobitis taenia

11 cm. Very compressed sides; head small with very small barbels; sharp spine under each eye.
Habitat: slow-flowing rivers; buries i the mud and weed on the bottom Active mostly at night.

CATFISH FAMILY Siluridae

WELS
Silurus glanis

3 m. Head broad; 2 long barbels on upper lip, 2 pairs under chin.

Habitat: lowland rivers and lakes Native to Europe; introduced to Eng land. Mainly nocturnal; eats fishes amphibians and water birds.

EEL FAMILY Anguillidae

EEL
Anguilla anguilla

1 m. Female larger than male. Lower jaw projecting. Dorsal, tail and anal fins joined.

Habitat: rivers and lakes. Feeds o insect larvae, crustaceans and dead fish; mainly nocturnal. Can wriggl some distance over land.

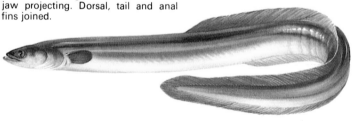

TOOTHCARP FAMILY Cyprinodontidae

female

male

SPANISH TOOTHCARP
Aphanius iberus

5 cm. Dorsal and anal fins opposite.
Habitat: coastal regions of Spain; i ditches and brackish lagoons. Feeds o small crustaceans.

CODFISH FAMILY Gadidae

BURBOT
Lota lota

m. 2 dorsal fins, the second long. ead broad with a chin barbel.

Habitat: lowland rivers and large lakes. Mainly nocturnal. Feeds on fishes, crustaceans and bottom-living insect larvae. Probably extinct in England.

PERCH FAMILY Percidae

Freshwater fishes native to the northern hemisphere. All have 2 dorsal fins, the first with sharp spines, and an anal fin with 2 spines at the front.

PERCH
Perca fluviatilis

51 cm. Dark bars on sides; black spot at rear of first dorsal fin.

Habitat: lowland rivers, lakes, and ponds, usually in small schools close to tree roots or weed beds. Eats crustaceans and insect larvae when young; fishes when older.

ZANDER
Stizostedion lucioperca

1·3 m. Long-bodied; head pointed with several large fangs in jaws.

Habitat: lowland rivers. Native to eastern Europe, introduced to western Europe and England. Hunts in schools, feeding on smaller fishes.

RUFFE
Gymnocephalus cernuus

30 cm. Dorsal fins joined together; first 11-16 rays spiny.
Habitat: native to continental Europe and eastern England. Abundant in low-and lakes and slow-flowing rivers. Feeds close to the bottom, mainly on burrowing insect larvae and worms.

BULLHEAD FAMILY Cottidae

BULLHEAD
Cottus gobio

17 cm. Broad flattened head with short spine on gill cover.
Habitat: streams, small rivers, and lakes with stony beds; usually hides under stones or in dense weed beds. Lays eggs in cavities under stones.

STICKLEBACK FAMILY Gasterosteidae

NINE-SPINED STICKLEBACK
Pungitius pungitius

7 cm. 8-10 short spines on back; tail long and narrow.
Habitat: ponds and rivers with dense vegetation and minimal flow. Nest built in plant stems in early summer.

THREE-SPINED STICKLEBACK
Gasterosteus aculeatus

10 cm. 2-3 long spines on back; tail deep and short.
Habitat: rivers, streams and ponds; the sea in the north. Nest built of plant fibres on the bottom.

Coastal Fishes
CARTILAGINOUS FISHES

LESSER SPOTTED DOGFISH
Scyliorhinus canicula
Family Scyliorhinidae

1 m. Nostrils with large flaps with a small gap in between.
Habitat: sandy or gravel bottoms in shallow water. Lays eggs in long leathery cases attached to seaweed.

PURDOG
qualus acanthias Family Squalidae

·2 m. Long sharp spine before each
orsal fin; no anal fin.

Habitat: common mid-water shark in
depths of 10-200 m. Feeds on small
schooling fishes and hunts in packs.
Gives birth to live young.

THORNBACK RAY
Raja clavata Family Rajidae

85 cm. Large thorns on tail and body.
Habitat: mostly on mud, sand and
shingle in shallow water. Feeds on
crabs and bottom-living fishes.

STING RAY
Dasyatis pastinaca Family Dasyatidae

1·4 m. No dorsal fin; serrated venomous
spine at base of long tail.

Habitat: bottom-living, mainly on
sand or mud. Feeds on crustaceans and
molluscs.

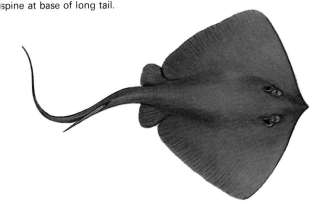

BONY FISHES

ANCHOVY
Engraulis encrasiocolus
Family Engraulidae

20 cm. Rounded snout; large jaws giving an enormous gape.
Habitat: in schools near the surface feeding on planktonic animals. Migratory; a summer visitor in north.

HERRING
Clupea harengus Family Clupeidae

43 cm. Flat-sided with a rounded belly; dorsal fin origin above pelvics.
Habitat: in schools in the surface waters and migrating considerable distances. Feeds on plankton, chiefly crustaceans and fishes.

GARFISH
Belone belone Family Belonidae

93 cm. Long jaws with moderately large teeth.

Habitat: surface-living and migratory inshore summer and autumn. Eats fishes, squid and crustaceans.

CONGER
Conger conger Family Congridae

2·7 m. Upper jaw longer; pectoral fins pointed.
Habitat: among rocks on shore and in wrecks and pier pilings; hidden in crevices and hunting mainly by night. Feeds on crabs and other crustaceans, octopus and fishes. Breeds in deep water in tropical Atlantic. Young are thin and transparent and drift at the surface.

GREATER SANDEEL
Hyperoplus lanceolatus
Family Ammodytidae

32 cm. Long slender body with pointed lower jaw; a distinct black smudge on the sides of the snout.

Habitat: on clean sand from low tide mark to 150 m. Forms large schools. Often swims in oblique head-down posture. Dives into sand at great speed when alarmed. Eats fish eggs and young and crustaceans.

NILSSON'S PIPEFISH
Syngnathus rostellatus
Family Syngnathidae

17 cm. Body rings distinct, 13-17 rings between pectoral and anal fins; tail fins present.

Habitat: common on sandy bottoms in shallow water in northern Europe; also among floating seaweed and eel grass, especially in estuaries. Breeds in spring; the male carries eggs in brood pouch under the tail. Young about 14 mm at birth. Feeds on small crustaceans and larval fish.

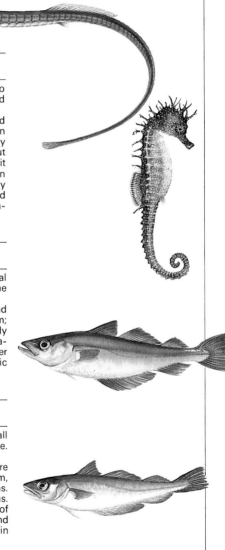

SEA HORSE
Hippocampus ramulosus

15 cm. Head set at angle to body; no tail fin. Snout long, more than a third of head length.
Habitat: lives among seaweed and eel grass in shallow water, but also in the open sea. Found mostly in the Bay of Biscay and the Mediterranean, but ocean currents occasionally carry it northwards to British and northern waters. Breeds in summer; males carry eggs and new-born young in brood pouch on tail. Feeds on small crustaceans.

POLLACK
Pollachius pollachius Family Gadidae

1·3 m. 3 dorsal and 2 anal fins. Lateral line dark and sharply curved over the pectoral fin.
Habitat: in loose schools around rocks and wrecks down to 100 m; young in shallow water over sandy bottoms. Feeds on fishes and crustaceans. Spawns in early spring in deeper water; the eggs and larvae are pelagic but drift shorewards.

WHITING
Merlangius merlangus

70 cm. 3 dorsal and 2 anal fins, all close together. Chin barbel minute. Dusky spot at base of pectoral fin.
Habitat: very common in inshore shallow water between 10 and 100 m, usually over sandy or muddy bottoms. Young mostly in shallower depths. Very young shelter among tentacles of jelly fishes. Eats small fishes and crustaceans, and spawns in spring in shallow water.

FIVE-BEARDED ROCKLING
Ciliata mustela

25 cm. Fine fringe of rays form first dorsal fin; second dorsal and anal fins long. 4 barbels on snout, 1 on chin.
Habitat: common among rocks and under weed, on shore and in shallow water down to 20 m on sand, mud and gravel bottoms. Feeds on small crustaceans and fishes. Breeds in winter in deep water; the young are silvery and surface-living and drift inshore with the tide.

CUCKOO WRASSE
Labrus mixtus Family Labridae

35 cm. Long dorsal fin with 16-18 spiny rays in front. Head pointed, with large mouth and strong teeth. Females and young males pinkish-orange with 3 brown blotches on back; adult males with blue heads and yellowish-orange sides.
Habitat: close to rocks in 10-100 m depth. Feeds on crabs, other crustaceans and molluscs. Spawns in spring in a seabed nest guarded by the male.

BASS
Dicentrarchus labrax
Family Percichthyidae

1 m. 2 dorsal fins, the first spiny; forward pointing spines on the lower edge of the gill cover.
Habitat: in schools over reefs, off rocky headlands, and in open bays, chiefly on ocean coasts. Young are common in estuaries and harbours and form large schools. An active predator, feeding mainly on fishes, squid and shrimps. Breeds in spring in inshore waters. Rare north of Britain.

LESSER WEEVER
Echiichthys vipera Family Trachinidae

14 cm. Short and deep-bodied; mouth strongly oblique; pectoral fin rounded. First dorsal fin jet black, with 4 venomous spines. Gill-cover spines also with venom glands.
Habitat: from low tide mark to 50 m, buried in clean sand. Forages up shore with return of tide, feeding on small crustaceans, fishes and worms. Venom spines give intensely painful sting which requires medical treatment.

RED MULLET
Mullus surmuletus Family Mullidae

40 cm. Reddish, with 2 long barbels on chin: young are blue-backed with silvery sides.
Habitat: bottom-living, most common on sand and mud in shallow water of 3-90 m. Probes the seabed with its barbels in search of food, mainly worms, molluscs and crustaceans; sometimes burrows into sand to seize food. Young are pelagic. Rare north of British waters.

SAND-SMELT
Atherina presbyter Family Atherinidae

21 cm. 2 dorsal fins, the first with slender spines. A bright silvery stripe along the sides: back clear green.
Habitat: a common inshore and estuarine fish, migrating northwards and closer inshore as the water warms in summer. Most abundant over sandy seabeds at 0-20 m depth. Eggs are attached to seaweed in mid-summer. Young are found in shore pools in late summer. Feeds on small crustaceans.

THICK-LIPPED GREY MULLET
Chelon labrosus Family Mugilidae

75 cm. Streamlined with a broad head; upper lip very thick and covered with coarse papillae.

Habitat: usually in schools near the surface of inshore waters, harbour mouths and estuaries. Feeds on rich organic mud, consuming soil and grit as well as the small animals and algae in it.

SHANNY
Lipophrys pholis Family Blenniidae

16 cm. Pelvic fins with two rays only; no tentacles on head.
Habitat: an abundant shore-fish living in rock pools, under stones and seaweed, and even in sandy shore pools where there is seaweed shelter. Also to depths of 30 m. Feeds on algae and a wide range of crustaceans; young fishes nip off the arms of barnacles. Eggs are laid on the underside of large stones or in rock crevices. The male guards the eggs.

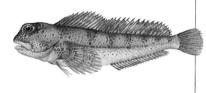

MACKEREL
Scomber scombrus Family Scombridae

66 cm. First dorsal fin with 11-13 slender spines; 2 small keels at the base of the tail fin.
Habitat: a schooling fish living near the surface and in mid-water in huge numbers; close to the coast in summer, when it moves northwards. Spawns in summer; both eggs and young are pelagic. Feeds on surface-living crustaceans and fishes, but in winter retires to deep water and feeds much less.

COMMON GOBY
Pomatoschistus microps Family Gobiidae

6·4 cm. Rather stout, with a broad head and thick lips. Scales moderate in size. A dusky triangular patch at the base of pectoral fin, and a dusky blotch at the base of tail fin. Pelvic fins are united to form a disc.
Habitat: abundant in tide pools; on muddy and sandy shores; also in river mouths and drainage ditches close to the sea. Migrates into deeper water in winter. Eggs are laid underneath shells, and guarded by the male. Feeds mainly on small crustaceans.

BUTTERFISH
Pholis gunnellus Family Pholidae

25 cm. Long, slender and compressed, with exceptionally slippery skin. Dorsal fin long, low and mostly spiny; pelvic fins minute spines.
Habitat: shallow seas close to the bottom and on the shore, mainly in rock pools, but also under damp rocks and seaweed. Depth range 0-100 m. Spawns January-February, the eggs laid in clumps in crevices or under shells and guarded by the adult. Eats worms, small crustaceans and molluscs. Rare south of Britain.

RED GURNARD
Aspitrigla cuculus Family Triglidae

40 cm. Heavy-headed with stout spines on the gill-covers. Lateral line with broad, flat scales. Bright red; pectoral fins greyish-red.
Habitat: shallow inshore waters from 20-200 m, usually on sand, gravel or mud. Eats bottom-living invertebrates and fishes, the former detected by the long, lower pectoral rays which act as feelers as the fish creeps over the sea-bed. Grunts loudly in water and when caught.

BRILL
Scophthalmus rhombus
Family Scophthalmidae

75 cm. Broad-bodied flatfish, lying on right side with its eyes on left side of head. Mouth large; front rays of dorsal fin branched and free of membrane. Body scaly.
Habitat: common inshore on sandy bottoms and gravel, less so on mud, mostly at depths of 9-73 m. Feeds on bottom-living and mid-water fishes, squid and crustaceans. Eggs and larvae are pelagic and, like all flatfishes, the young have an eye each side of head at first. As the fish grows, one eye moves over the top of the head, so that both are on the same side.

DAB
Limanda limanda Family Pleuronectidae

42 cm. Lies on left, with eyes on right side of head. Lateral line strongly arched above pectoral fin; scales very rough on coloured side.
Habitat: a common flatfish of sandy or shell grounds at 2-40 m depth. Feeds mainly on worms and small crustaceans, occasionally molluscs. Spawns in spring and early summer; the eggs and larvae are pelagic.

FLOUNDER
Platichthys flesus

51 cm. Eyes usually on right side of head, often on left. Prickles at bases of dorsal and anal fins, and above pectoral fin.
Habitat: common at 0-55 m depth, mostly on mud and sand. Regularly comes into fresh water and extremely common in river mouths. Feeds on molluscs, worms and crustaceans, and is most active at night. Breeds offshore in spring; eggs and larvae pelagic.

PLAICE
Pleuronectes platessa

91 cm. Lies on left, with eyes on right side of head. Scales smooth; a series of rounded bumps running from between eyes back to level of pectoral fins. Bright orange spots on coloured side.
Habitat: abundant on sand and gravel, less often on mud, from 0-200 m. Feeds on bottom-living invertebrates. Spawns in early spring; eggs and larvae pelagic.

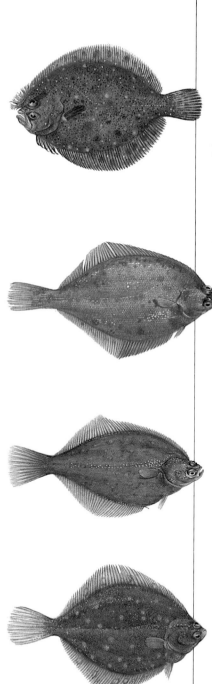

CHAPTER FIVE

INVERTEBRATES

The invertebrates are those animals which have no backbones. They belong to some 29 different phyla and far outnumber the vertebrates, or backboned animals, which belong to just one phylum – the Chordata. Invertebrates cannot compete in size with the largest vertebrates, but there are still some giants amongst them, including squids 15 m long (with their tentacles) and clams weighing 275 kg. These monstrous invertebrates are many thousands of times heavier than the smallest vertebrates. At the other end of the scale are the protozoans (see below) which cannot be seen without a microscope.

Many invertebrates have no skeleton at all and rely entirely on the pressure of their body fluids to maintain their shape. Many others, however, have external skeletons or shells, technically known as exoskeletons, which give them their shape and also afford a good deal of protection. Crabs and snails are obvious examples.

One-Celled Animals
The simplest invertebrates are the protozoans (Phylum Protozoa) whose bodies consist of just one microscopic cell. And yet within that one cell are carried on all the essential processes of life – breathing or respiration, the digestion of food and the elimination of waste, and reproduction. In addition, the cell is aware of its surroundings and can react to any changes. There are several distinct groups of protozoans, but they are well beyond the scope of a field guide.

The Major Groups of Invertebrates
Most of the invertebrates that you see belong to just five phyla, and the following pages are devoted to these five groups.

The largest of all the animal phyla is the Arthropoda. This name means 'jointed feet', and adult members of the group all have distinctly jointed limbs. Their bodies, too, are divided into a number of segments (although the divisions are sometimes obscured). All the members of the phyla are encased in tough and sometimes very hard exoskeletons. The main classes within the Arthropoda are the crustaceans, the insects, the arachnids (spiders and scorpions), the centipedes and the millipedes. They total more than a million known species.

The Phylum Mollusca, which includes the slugs and snails, the

REPRESENTATIVES OF THE FIVE MAIN PHYLA

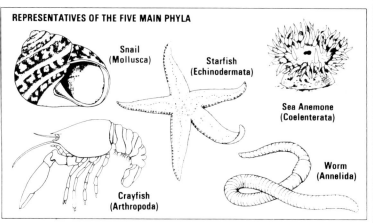

Snail (Mollusca)
Starfish (Echinodermata)
Sea Anemone (Coelenterata)
Worm (Annelida)
Crayfish (Arthropoda)

squids and all the sea shells, comes second to the Arthropoda but, with fewer than 100,000 species, it is a long way behind. The animals are all soft-bodied creatures which show no sign of segmentation. Most of them are protected by hard shells.

The Phylum Annelida includes a wide range of aquatic and terrestrial worms – mostly slender creatures whose bodies are clearly divided into segments. This segmentation separates the annelids from the roundworms or nematodes.

Members of the Phylum Echinodermata are confined to the sea. They include the starfishes and sea urchins and their relatives. All have rough and often very spiny skins and they are all built on a radially symmetrical (circular) plan. The fifth major phylum, the Coelenterata, is another radially symmetrical group. Entirely aquatic, it includes the sea anemones and jellyfishes.

Measurements and Dates

In the following pages the measurements given are the normal maximums for adults. A range of sizes is given for animals which are particularly variable. Unless otherwise stated, the sizes given indicate body length (without legs), but where insects are normally shown with their wings outstretched (butterflies and dragonflies, for example) the measurements indicate wingspans.

Most aquatic invertebrates can be found at any time of year. Many terrestrial species can also be found at all seasons, although some may go into hibernation in autumn. Many insects, however, are distinctly seasonal in their appearance and the times given are those at which the adults are most likely to be seen. In southern Europe they may appear earlier and continue later than indicated. Where no dates are given, it may be assumed that adults can be found at any time.

Echinoderms

The starfishes and sea urchins belong to the Phylum Echinodermata, whose members are built on a basically circular plan. Their skins are rough, often very spiny, and they all live in the sea. Many occur in coastal waters and can be found on the shore. Water-filled tubes run through the body, and slender branches, known as tube-feet, emerge from the surface. They are used for feeding and for locomotion and generally have disc-shaped suckers at their tips. Reproduction is extremely simple, most species merely releasing eggs and sperm into the water and leaving fertilization to chance. Most echinoderms have planktonic larvae which bear little resemblance to the adults.

There are five classes of echinoderms: starfishes (Asteroidea), brittle stars (Ophiuroidea), sea urchins (Echinoidea), sea cucumbers (Holothuroidea) and sea lilies (Crinoidea). This last group is not illustrated. The sea urchins have a chalky shell, called a test, just under the skin.

Sea Urchins

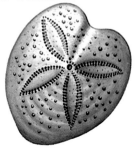

VIOLET HEART URCHIN
Spatangus purpureus
Family Spatangidae

Up to 12 cm long. Heart-shaped, having lost the radial symmetry. Spines are short and fur-like on top, but some on the underside are paddle-like and used for burrowing in sand and mud. Tube-feet lack suckers and mouth lacks teeth. It feeds on detritus. Test very thin.

EDIBLE SEA URCHIN
Echinus esculentus Family Echinidae

Up to 16 cm across, but usually less. Pink, red or purple and densely spined. Test deep pink with white spots: quite thick and often washed up on the shore intact. Long tube-feet, mostly with strong suckers, drag the animal along and also anchor it when necessary. Rocky and gravelly bottoms, usually just off-shore. It scrapes algae with strong teeth around the mouth. Edible parts are the bulky reproductive organs.

ROCK URCHIN
Paracentrotus lividus

Up to 6 cm across. Green, brown or violet with strong spines. Usually on soft limestone rocks in shallow water, often in rock pools. Often excavates a small cavity in the rock and may cover its upper surface with shell and seaweed fragments, held on by the tube-feet. Feeds mainly on debris. Mediterranean and Atlantic.

Sea Cucumbers

HOLOTHURIA FORSKALI
Family Holothuriidae

Up to 30 cm long. Dark brown to greenish-black with a leathery texture and only scattered chalky plates em-bedded in the skin. Suckered tube-feet on the lower surface move it about, while branched ones around the mouth scoop detritus from the seabed for food. Lives on mud and sand and in rocky crevices.

SEA GHERKIN
Cucumaria planci Family Cucumariidae

Up to 15 cm long. Leathery, with five rows of suckered tube-feet which it uses for climbing over rocks. Prefers stony bottoms with a certain amount of mud. The branching tentacles filter food particles from the water and also sweep up detritus from the surrounding rocks. Mediterranean.

Starfishes

SUNSTAR
Solaster papposus Family Solasteridae

Up to 25 cm across. Purple or red with 8-15 arms (sometimes more in old specimens). Tube-feet with suckers. On sand and stones, feeding on other echinoderms. English Channel north-wards.

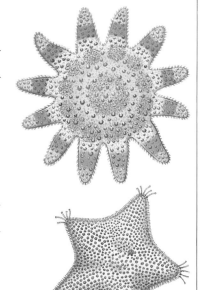

CUSHION STAR
Asterina gibbosa Family Asterinidae

Up to 7 cm across. Yellow or green (sometimes brick-red). On rocks and under stones. Suckered tube-feet allow it to climb. Eats molluscs and other echinoderms. Lays eggs under stones. English Channel southwards.

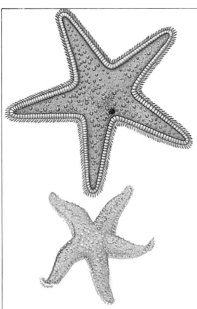

ASTROPECTEN IRREGULARIS
Family Astropectinidae

Up to 12 cm across. Red to purplish-brown. Often called a comb star because of the spines on the edges of the arms. Tube-feet without suckers. Eats worms, molluscs and other echinoderms.

COMMON STARFISH
Asterias rubens Family Asteriidae

Up to 30 cm across. Pale yellow, through red, to violet. Tube-feet with suckers. On stones and coarse sand, feeding mainly on bivalve molluscs: a pest on oyster farms.

Brittle Stars

OPHIOTHRIX FRAGILIS
Family Ophiotrichidae

Disc 2 cm across. Arms brittle and up to 7 cm long. Colour very variable. Tube-feet without suckers. Coils arms round stones to pull itself along and also uses them to filter food particles from the water. Common under stones and seaweeds near low-water mark.

SERPENT STAR
Ophiura texturata Family Ophiuridae

Disc 3 cm across. Arms up to 15 cm long: grey to reddish-brown. On mud and sand, burrowing when tide is out but roaming the seabed at other times and capturing prey with the arms.

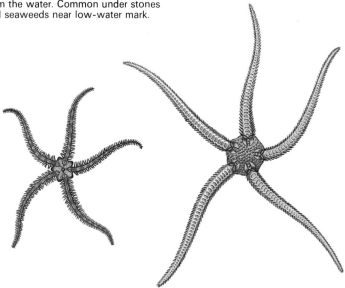

Molluscs

The molluscs (Phylum Mollusca) are soft-bodied invertebrates, mostly protected by a hard shell. There are nearly 100,000 known species, ranging from the highly mobile oceanic squids to the slow-moving slugs and snails of our gardens and the completely sedentary oysters. One of the few features present in all the major groups of molluscs is the mantle, a thick cloak of skin which envelops at least part of the body. The space between the mantle and the rest of the body is called the mantle cavity; this is connected to the outside world by one or more openings. In most aquatic molluscs the cavity contains gills: water is pumped in and out of the cavity and the gills absorb oxygen from it. In the bivalve molluscs the gills also play a major role in food collection (see pages 203–6). In land molluscs and many freshwater snails the mantle cavity acts as a lung: watch pond snails for a while and you will see them come to the surface and expel a bubble of stale air before taking in a fresh supply.

The mantle is also responsible for producing the shell. The latter has three layers: an outer horny layer which gives the shell much of its colour, a middle layer composed of columnar crystals of calcium carbonate, and a smooth inner layer which is often pearly.

Slugs and Snails

These animals belong to the Class Gastropoda, which is by far the largest group of molluscs. There are over 60,000 species living on land, in the sea and in fresh water. Gastropoda means 'belly-footed' and refers to the large muscular 'foot' on which the animals glide along. The head, with one or two pairs of tentacles, is not clearly separated from the foot. Most of the snail's internal organs are contained in the visceral hump, which is coiled over the foot and enclosed in the mantle and shell. The snail can pull its foot into the shell and many species, mainly those living in water, can close the shell with a horny disc called the operculum. Slugs are simply snails which have lost their shells during their evolution.

All gastropods have a rasp-like tongue called a radula. This is clothed with horny teeth and nibbles away at the animal's food rather like a cheese grater. Most gastropods have separate sexes, but many land snails and slugs are hermaphrodite, with both male and female organs in the same individual. They still pair up and mate, however, and often have very elaborate mating behaviour.

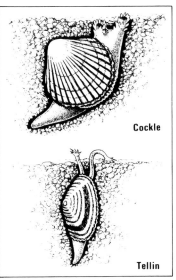

Cockle

Tellin

The cockle (top) feeds by sucking water in through its siphon. The tellin (above) uses its long siphon like a vacuum cleaner to suck debris from the seabed.

The Bivalves

These molluscs have two halves or valves to the shell and belong to the class Lamellibranchia. The two valves may or may not be alike, but each is asymmetrical in itself and usually has a prominent point called the umbo. The valves are hinged around the umbo, usually with interlocking teeth and a horny ligament. The shape and arrangement of the teeth can often help in the identification of empty shells. Strong muscles close the shell when the animal is alive; when the muscles relax the ligament causes the valves to gape. The attachment scars of the muscles are clearly visible in empty shells.

All the 20,000 or so species of bivalves live in water and all are filter feeders, using their large gills to strain food particles from the stream of water passing over them. The mantle edge is often drawn out to form two siphons: one to carry water in to the gills and one to carry it out again. Some bivalves have very long inlet siphons which they use to suck debris from the sea bed. Most have a muscular foot, with which they burrow into sand or mud, but none has a head. The sexes are normally separate; eggs or sperm are scattered into the water and left to meet by chance. Some females, however, retain their eggs in the mantle cavity, where they are fertilized by sperms drawn in with the water.

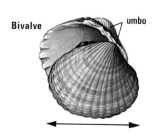
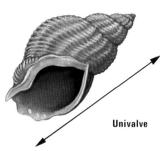

Above: Bivalve molluscs (left) have two valves hinged at the top. They are usually measured by width. Gastropods or univalves, which have a single, usually coiled valve (right), are measured by height. The opening of the gastropod shell is nearly always on the right of the shell (dextral condition) as you look at it.

Left: Tusk shells (Dentalium spp) belong to the Class Scaphopoda. The tubular shell is open at both ends and the animal protrudes from the wide end to feed in the sand or mud. Exclusively marine, the tusk shells live in fairly deep water, but their shells are often washed up on the beach.

Squid, Cuttlefish and Octopus
These animals form the class
Cephalopoda, in which the foot is
divided into several tentacles that
surround the mouth. There are
about 600 species, all marine and
all active predators with well-
developed eyes. There is no real
shell, although the squid's body
is supported by a horny plate
embedded in the mantle and the
cuttlefish is similarly supported
by the familiar chalky
'cuttlebone'. Behind the head,
the body is enclosed in a very
muscular mantle which opens by
way of a tubular funnel. Rapid
contraction of the mantle forces
water out through the funnel and
sends the animal speeding along
by jet propulsion. The sexes are
always separate and there are
often complex courtship rituals.

Other molluscs include the
tusk shells (see opposite) and
the chitons or coat-of-mail shells,
in which the flat, oval body is
protected by eight shell plates
(see page 203). These animals
glide over rocks on a broad foot,
and if detached can roll into a
ball.

Cephalopods

These are very mobile, predatory,
marine molluscs with a number
of sucker-covered arms and
extremely large and efficient eyes.
There is a horny, parrot-like beak
at the base of the arms and the
salivary glands secrete a poison
which quickly paralyzes prey.
The group contains the largest
of all invertebrates, but most
members are quite small and,
despite their sinister reputations,
most are quite harmless to
humans.

COMMON OCTOPUS
Octopus vulgaris Family Octopodidae

Up to 3 m across extended arms, but
usually much less: arms often under
50 cm long. Bag-like body grey to
brown, often mottled and changing
colour to match various backgrounds.
8 arms, each with 2 rows of suckers.
Lurks in rocky crevices on seabed and
darts out to catch fishes and crustaceans. A shy animal, it will inflict a
painful bite if handled. English Channel
southwards: rare in Britain.

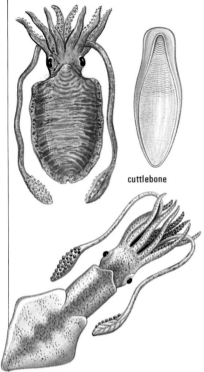

cuttlebone

COMMON CUTTLEFISH
Sepia officinalis Family Sepiidae

Up to 30 cm long. Flattened and oval with 8 short arms and 2 longer ones which can be shot out to catch shrimps and similar prey. Keeps close to sea bed, usually over sand or eel-grass, and can change colour to match different backgrounds. Swims by jet-propulsion or slowly by waving fin surrounding the mantle. Chalky white cuttlebone often washed up on the beach. One of several similar species.

COMMON SQUID
Loligo vulgaris Family Loliginidae

Up to 50 cm long. Slender, cylindrical body with diamond-shaped stabilizing tail fin. Cream or pink with purplish-brown spots. 8 short arms and 2 longer ones which can be shot out to catch prey. Free-swimming, often in large shoals. Often at surface; never on sea bed. Feeds mainly on fishes. Mainly Dutch coast southwards. One of several similar species.

Slugs and Snails

These are herbivorous or carnivorous gastropods, active mainly by night but also after daytime rain. They have two pairs of tentacles, usually with eyes at the tips of the longer ones. Slugs have a small saddle-like mantle, usually near the front. A coating of slime, especially thick and sticky in slugs, helps to prevent desiccation and also gives some protection from enemies. The animals may be active all year, but they hide away in very cold or dry weather. Snails often seal up their shells with slime which hardens into a parchment-like cap. Very few land snails have an operculum. All the species on these pages eat living or dead plant matter.

NETTED SLUG
Deroceras reticulatum Family Limacidae

Up to 5 cm. Cream to brown or grey, often speckled with black. Keel on hind end. Lung opening near back of mantle on right. Exudes milky slime when handled. A pest of vegetable crops.

GREAT GREY SLUG
Limax maximus

Up to 20 cm. Keel on hind end. Tentacles reddish-brown. Lung opening near back of mantle on right. Eats fungi and decaying matter.

BUDAPEST SLUG
Milax budapestensis Family Milacidae

Up to 6 cm. Pale to dark grey with yellow or orange keel along back. Lung opening near back of mantle on right. A serious crop pest, especially on roots. Mainly cultivated land.

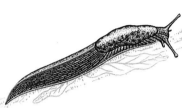

GREAT BLACK SLUG
Arion ater Family Arionidae

Up to 15 cm. May also be grey, brown, or orange, especially in south. A round-backed slug with no keel on back. Lung opening near front of mantle on right. Contracts to hemisphere and sways from side to side if disturbed. Eats rotting vegetation.

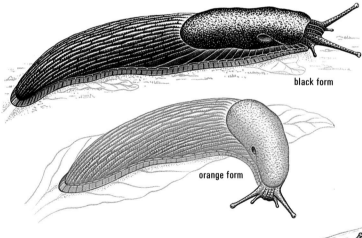

black form

orange form

BROWN-LIPPED SNAIL
Cepaea nemoralis Family Helicidae

Shell rounded, up to 20 mm high. Ground colour yellow, pink, or brown, with up to 5 spiral brown bands: often yellow with no bands in grassland. Shell lip is dark brown. Woods, hedgerows, grassland and gardens. *C. hortensis* is very similar, but shell has a white lip.

GARDEN SNAIL
Helix aspersa

Shell more or less globular, up to 3·5 cm high. Yellowish-brown with variable dark markings. A common garden pest, nibbling a wide range of plants. South and central Europe.

ROMAN SNAIL
Helix pomatia

Shell globular, up to 5 cm high. Creamy-white with pale brown bands. On lime-rich soils. South and central Europe: southern Britain only.

STRAWBERRY SNAIL
Trichia striolata

Shell flattened, up to 1·4 cm across. Sandy to purplish-brown, with a white rib just inside mouth when mature. Mainly damp places: a pest in gardens. Britain eastwards to Rhine Valley.

KENTISH SNAIL
Monacha cantiana

Shell slightly flattened, up to 2 cm across: creamy-white with reddish tinge near mouth. Often looks greyish with snail in it. Grassy places. South and central Europe.

GARLIC GLASS SNAIL
Oxychilus alliarius Family Zonitidae

Shell flattened, up to 7 mm across. Shining, translucent brown. Animal smells of garlic if touched. Damp places. Western Europe.

GREAT RAM'S HORN
Planorbis corneus Family Planorbidae

Deep-brown shell coiled in a flat spiral up to 3 cm across. Animal deep brown or red. Tentacles long and slender. No operculum. Weedy ponds, eating plant matter. An air-breather, but comes to the surface much less than some other species because body contains haemoglobin and can absorb oxygen from the water.

ROUND-MOUTHED SNAIL
Pomatias elegans Family Pomatiidae

Shell up to 1·3 cm high, with distinctly rounded whorls and a round opening. Thick: greyish to yellow. One of very few land snails with an operculum. Rough vegetation on lime-rich soils. Western Europe: not in north.

TWO-TOOTHED DOOR SNAIL
Clausilia bidentata Family Clausiliidae

Shell spindle-shaped, up to 1·2 cm high. Reddish-brown and sinistral – with opening on the left as you look at it. Damp walls and rocks, eating moss and algae.

GREAT POND SNAIL
Limnaea stagnalis Family Limnaeidae

Shell up to 6 cm long. Thin and pale brown. Tentacles flat, with eyes at base of hind pair. No operculum. Still and slow-moving water with plenty of lime and lots of weed. Eats plant and animal matter, living or dead. Air-breathing.

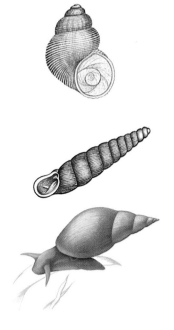

Sea Snails and Sea Slugs

These animals, like their terrestrial counterparts, belong to the Class Gastropoda. The head bears one or two pairs of sensory tentacles, usually with eyes at the base of one pair. The rasping radula (see page 193) is used to obtain either animal or vegetable food and can even be used to drill through the shells of other molluscs. Many sea snails have long inlet siphons through which water is drawn into the mantle cavity. The siphon is housed in a grooved extension of the lip of the shell, but can be extended way beyond the shell. Sea slugs have lost their shells and they have lost the mantle and mantle cavity as well. They breathe with the aid of false gills developed on the back. Sea snails and sea slugs live mainly on rocky sea beds and shores, sheltering under seaweeds when the tide goes out in the daytime but often moving about to feed in the damp air at night. Empty shells may be washed up on all kinds of beaches. Unless otherwise stated, the measurements given for snails are shell heights (see page 194).

COMMON ORMER
Haliotis tuberculata Family Haliotidae

Up to 8 cm long. Greenish-brown to brick-red, coiled only at apex and looking like half of a bivalve shell, but the row of small breathing holes identifies it. Very pearly inside. Among rocks and stones, eating algae. Channel Islands southwards.

COMMON LIMPET
Patella vulgaris Family Patellidae

Up to 6 cm in diameter. Shell conical and more or less circular at base. Those on highest parts of shore are taller than those further down. Greenish-grey or brown: pearly white inside. Foot more or less circular. Attaches itself very firmly to rocks of the upper and middle shore, where it wears a shallow groove into which it fits perfectly. Scrapes algae from rocks. Several similar species live on lower and middle shore. Western and northern shores.

BLUE-RAYED LIMPET
Patina pellucida

Up to 2 cm diameter. Shell conical with oval base. Translucent, yellowish with blue stripes. On oarweeds and related seaweeds. Western and northern shores.

PAINTED TOP SHELL
Calliostoma zizyphinum
Family Trochidae

Up to 4 cm. Orange, pink, or red with darker red spots. Outer layer often wears away to reveal thick pearly layer in places. On rocks on lower shore, browsing on seaweeds: usually below low-tide level in northern regions.

TOWER SHELL
Turritella communis Family Turritellidae

Up to 5 cm. Yellowish-brown to brick-red. Common in mud and sand just offshore, usually buried up to tip of spire. Feeds on algae and detritus.

NEEDLE SHELL
Bittium reticulatum Family Cerithiidae

Up to 1·5 cm. Tightly whorled, each whorl decorated with spiral rows of small bumps. Pale to dark brown, with short siphon canal at side of shell opening. Browses on seaweeds on mud and sand.

FLAT PERIWINKLE
Littorina littoralis Family Littorinidae

Up to 1·5 cm. Yellow to orange or pale brown, with or without banding. Flatter than other winkles, often almost circular in outline. Browses on seaweeds on rocks of middle shore.

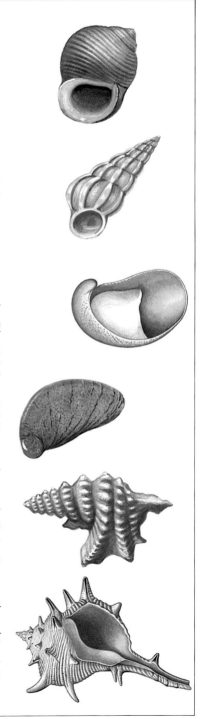

COMMON PERIWINKLE
Littorina littorea

Up to 3 cm. Dark greenish-grey or almost black, sometimes with paler bands. Shell thick. This is the familiar winkle of the fishmonger's slab. Browses on seaweeds on rocks and stones at around low-tide level.

COMMON WENTLETRAP
Clathrus clathrus Family Epitoniidae

Up to 4·5 cm. White to rusty or purplish-red, with prominent ridges crossing the tightly-packed whorls. In sand and mud below low-tide level. Carnivorous.

SLIPPER LIMPET
Crepidula fornicata Family Calyptraeidae

Up to 6 cm long. Cream to brown, often spotted with red. Resembles half a bivalve shell, but with a thick white plate extending half way across the underside. Often found in 'chains', with three or more shells fixed to each other. A filter-feeder. Often causes damage to mussel and oyster beds by settling all over the shells and denying them food. Introduced from America.

PELICAN'S FOOT
Aporrhais pespelecani
Family Aporrhaidae

Up to 5 cm. Yellow to dark brown. Named for the way in which lip of adult shell is drawn out into the shape of a bird's foot. Opening is straight and narrow. Burrows in mud and sand: eats detritus.

MUREX BRANDARIS
Family Muricidae

Up to 9 cm, with long spines and a very long siphon canal. Pale grey or yellowish. On mud and stones, eating other molluscs and carrion. Contains a rich purple dye. Mediterranean.

COMMON DOG WHELK
Nucella lapillus

Up to 4·5 cm. Very thick shell, brown or yellow and often banded with white. A short siphon groove. Abundant on rocks on middle shore. Feeds on other molluscs and barnacles, using the radula, which is at the end of a slender proboscis, to drill through their shells. Western and northern coasts.

STING WINKLE
Ocinebra erinacea

Up to 6 cm. Thick, with prominent ribbing. White to sandy grey. On stones and firm mud, especially among eelgrasses. Drills holes in other mollusc shells with radula, aided by chemical secretions.

COMMON WHELK
Buccinum undatum Family Buccinidae

Up to 12 cm, with short, curved siphon canal. White to sandy-grey. On sand, mud and stones. Eats carrion and also preys on bivalves, wedging the shells open with the lip of its own shell and inserting the radula on its long proboscis. Northern and western shores.

EUROPEAN COWRIE
Trivia monacha Family Cypraeidae

Up to 1·2 cm long. Oval shells, flattened on one side and with a long, narrow opening. Strongly ribbed, pale pink to greyish-brown with 4-6 darker spots. Mantle is folded back over shell in life. Rocky shores, feeding on small sea-squirts. Several similar species.

SEA HARE
Aplysia depilans Family Aplysiidae

Up to 25 cm long. Olive-green or brown with pale spots. 4 stout tentacles. Thin shell completely covered by mantle folds. Browses on algae on mud and sand, usually below low-tide level. Mediterranean. Several similar species.

SEA SLUG
Dendronotus frondosus
Family Dendronotidae

Up to 6 cm long. Cream, yellow or pale pink, with branched white tentacles and numerous branched gills on the back. No shell. Browses on small coelenterates on rocky shores. Northern and western coasts.

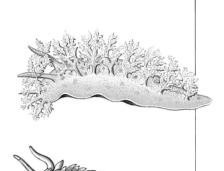

GREY SEA SLUG
Aeolidia papillosa Family Aeolidiidae

Up to 9 cm. Grey to brown, with many white-spotted, unbranched gills on the back. No shell. On sand and rocks, feeding on sea anemones. Bay of Biscay northwards. Several similar species.

Coat-of-Mail Shells

GREY CHITON
Lepidochitona cinerea
Family Lepidochitonidae

Up to 3 cm long. One of the coat-of-mail shells (see page 195) with 8 protective plates. Colour ranges from grey to green or brick-red. Clings tightly to other shells and to rocks in coastal zone: browses on algae. Several similiar species.

Bivalve Sea Shells

Huge populations of bivalves, belonging to hundreds of species, live on the seabed, usually burrowing in sand or mud. When they die, their empty shells are often cast up on the shore, sometimes forming huge banks. The hinges usually break as the shells are thrown about by the waves, and most of the shells on the shore are just single valves. The arrangement of the hinge teeth and muscle scars on the inside of the shell often help in identification, especially if the colours have faded. The habitats given are those preferred by the living animals. Measurements are taken across the width of the shell (see page 194).

PRICKLY COCKLE
Cardium echinatum Family Cardiidae

Up to 8 cm. Very thick shell with 20-30 ribs bearing short, blunt spines. White to mid-brown. In mud, usually below low-tide level.

COMMON COCKLE
Cardium edule

Up to 5 cm. White to mid-brown with 22-26 coarse ribs. Two main teeth close to the umbo. Abundant in mud and sand from lower shore downwards, including estuaries.

COMMON MUSSEL
Mytilus edulis Family Mytilidae

Up to 10 cm. Hinged on front (narrow) part of curved side; a few small teeth. Brown, blue or black. Attached to rocks and stones by tough, horny threads (the byssus): usually in exposed places where currents bring plenty of food.

QUEEN SCALLOP
Chlamys opercularis Family Pectinidae

Up to 9 cm. Almost circular with a straight, toothless hinge and slightly unequal 'ears'. One valve slightly more convex than the other. Yellow, through orange, to brown: 18-22 prominent ribs. Lies freely on coarse sand: swims by flapping valves.

BANDED WEDGE SHELL
Donax vittatus Family Donacidae

Up to 3 cm. Distinctly oblong with umbo very much off-centre. Shiny yellow to brown outside, with or without darker bands, and purplish or yellowish inside. Sand near low-tide level. Siphons long, as in tellins.

DOG COCKLE
Glycimeris glycimeris
Family Glycimeridae

Up to 10 cm. Almost circular. Straw-coloured to brick-red: many hinge teeth. Each valve with a broad, grooved inner rim. Sandy shores.

OYSTER
Ostrea edulis Family Ostreidae

Up to 15 cm. Almost circular. Grey with rough concentric growth lines. Left valve bowl-shaped and fixed to rocks and stones. Right valve flat and forms a lid. From low-tide level to depths of about 50 m.

PORTUGUESE OYSTER
Crassostrea angulata

Up to 10 cm. Similar to the oyster, but longer and narrower and left valve much deeper – usually with deeply-indented margins into which the lid fits very neatly. One purple muscle scar in each valve. Atlantic.

BLUNT TELLIN
Tellina crassa Family Tellinidae

Up to 5 cm. Cream or grey, sometimes with faint pink stripes and red umbo: orange inside. Like all tellins, it has long siphons and sucks debris from seabed. Sand: off-shore.

THIN TELLIN
Tellina tenuis

Up to 3 cm. Yellow, pink or red. Very thin, but hinge is tough and valves commonly remain joined after death. Sand near low-tide level.

RAYED ARTEMIS
Dosina exoleta Family Veneridae

Up to 5 cm. Thick shell with curved and pointed umbo. White or cream, usually with reddish-brown rays. 3 teeth under umbo. Sand.

BANDED CARPET SHELL
Venerupis rhomboides

Up to 5 cm. Sandy brown with 3 or 4 darker radiating stripes: often with zig-zag brown lines near the margin when mature. 3 converging teeth under umbo. Mud and sand.

LARGE RAZOR SHELL
Ensis siliqua Family Solenidae

Up to 20 cm. Open both ends. Hinged near one end, with 2 large teeth and dark external ligament. Lives vertically in sand and burrows very quickly. There are several similar, but smaller species, including *Ensis ensis* which is strongly curved.

RAYED TROUGH SHELL
Mactra corallina Family Mactridae

Up to 7 cm. Shell thin with a blunt umbo. Alternating yellowish and brown bands: numerous narrow white rays. Pink to violet inside. Sand.

COMMON OTTER SHELL
Lutraria lutraria Family Lutrariidae

Up to 14 cm. Distinctly elliptical. Dirty white to pinkish, with brown outer skin which flakes off in patches. Gapes slightly at each end. Burrows deeply in sand and mud: long siphons.

COMMON PIDDOCK
Pholas dactylus Family Pholadidae

Up to 12 cm. White and gaping at both ends. Valves thin, with no hinge ligament. A curved spine just under umbo in each valve. Front end of shell rasp-like and used to drill burrows in soft rocks.

SAND GAPER
Mya arenaria Family Myidae

Up to 15 cm. White to sandy, with darker concentric bands and peeling grey skin. Gapes at both ends. Left valve smaller and more domed than right and containing large, spoon-like tooth. Right valve has deep groove to hold tooth. Mud and sand.

Freshwater Bivalves

PAINTER'S MUSSEL
Unio pictorum Family Unionidae

Up to 14 cm. One of several rather similar bivalves living in still and slow-moving water with plenty of mud on the bottom. Yellowish-green to brown and tapering markedly towards the back. Named because artists once used the shells to hold their paints.

Crustaceans

The crabs and their relatives form the Class Crustacea, one of the major divisions of the arthropods. They nearly all live in water and they are covered with a hard exoskeleton heavily impregnated with calcium carbonate. The head bears two pairs of antennae, but otherwise the animals are extremely varied and it is impossible to give a simple description of the group. They range from minute floating creatures, such as water fleas, to lobsters and crabs weighing several kilogrammes.

Only a few of the more advanced species are shown here.

Woodlice

This is the only group of crustaceans that has really invaded the land, although several species still live in water and most are restricted to damp places. Most are flattened and all have seven pairs of similar legs. The woodlice belong to the order Isopoda.

ONISCUS ASELLUS
Family Oniscidae

12-16 mm. Glossy grey with a pale margin; sometimes all yellowish. Abundant under stones and in rotting wood. Feeds on decaying vegetable matter of all kinds.

SEA SLATER
Ligia oceanica Family Ligiidae

20-25 mm. Greyish-green, often blackish when young. Scavenges on the shore at night, hiding in rock crevices by day – usually close to high tide level.

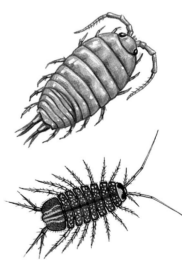

WATER LOUSE
Asellus aquaticus Family Asellidae

18-25 mm. Male much larger than female and often carries her about clasped to his belly. Abundant in weedy ponds and streams, where it feeds on assorted debris and sometimes on filamentous algae.

Amphipoda

An order of marine or freshwater crustaceans which have laterally compressed bodies, usually with three pairs of swimming legs and three pairs of jumping legs on the abdomen. There are four pairs of walking and grasping legs at the front.

FRESHWATER SHRIMP
Gammarus pulex Family Gammaridae

15-30 mm. Male larger than female and often carries her about in the breeding season. Grey to reddish-brown. Abundant in shallow streams, especially in lime-rich areas, usually hiding under stones and vegetation. Body curved at rest, but straightens when swimming – usually on one side. Feeds on detritus and also nibbles algae.

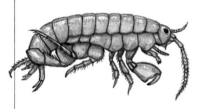

SAND HOPPER
Orchestia gammarella

10-20 mm. Greenish-brown to chestnut. Abundant on sea shore, under the piles of decaying seaweed and other rubbish on which it feeds. Leaps away vigorously when disturbed.

Decapoda

The creatures in this order are almost all marine, with five pairs of walking legs of which one or more pairs may bear pincers for catching food. Most are flesh-eaters, taking carrion as well as living food. The abdomen often bears five pairs of swimming legs (also used to carry eggs in female), but crabs have a very small abdomen tucked under thorax.

COMMON SHRIMP
Crangon crangon Family Crangonidae

4-7 cm. Grey or brown. Abundant in coastal waters, usually burrowing in sand or mud with just eyes showing.

LOBSTER
Homarus vulgaris Family Nephropidae

20-60 cm. The largest European crustacean and much in demand for food. Rocky coasts from low-tide level downwards, hiding in crevices by day and hunting at night. Becomes red when cooked.

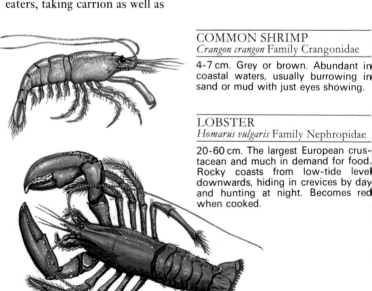

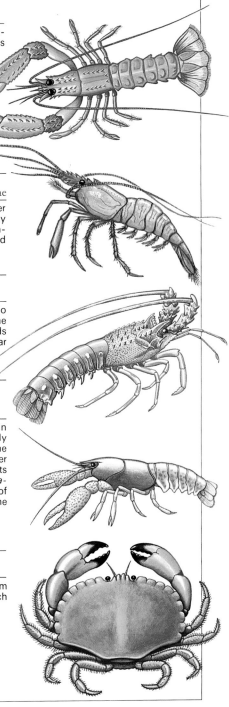

NORWAY LOBSTER
Nephrops norvegicus

10-20 cm. On sandy and muddy sea-beds from 30-200 m deep. Marketed as scampi or Dublin Bay prawns.

COMMON PRAWN
Palaemon serratus Family Palaemonidae

10 cm. Common in coastal waters over rocky bottoms, generally hiding by day and hunting by night. Easily distinguished from shrimp by the toothed rostrum on the head.

SPINY LOBSTER
Palinurus vulgaris Family Palinuridae

20-40 cm. Also called crawfish. No pincers, but the thick, spiny antennae can inflict damage. Rocky seabeds below 10 m. Mainly southern; as far north as Holland. A favourite food.

CRAYFISH
Potamobius pallipes
Family Potamobiidae

10 cm. A freshwater species found in clean streams with sandy or gravelly beds, usually in chalk and limestone areas. It usually hides by day under stones or in holes in the bank and hunts by night. The slightly larger *P. fluviatilis*, recognized by the red underside of its claws, is reared for food on the continent.

EDIBLE CRAB
Cancer pagurus Family Cancridae

7-20 cm. Lives on rocky coasts, from the shore to quite deep water. Much sought after for food.

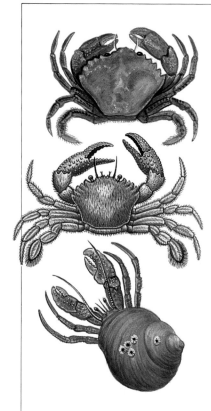

SHORE CRAB
Carcinus maenas Family Portunidae

4–6 cm. Common on sandy and rocky shores and, like most crabs, walks sideways. Often in estuaries.

VELVET CRAB
Portunus puber

6–7 cm. Named for its hairy coat, this is one of the swimming crabs. The hind legs are broad and flat and are used to row the crab through the water, although it can also crawl on the bottom. Rocky and sandy coasts.

HERMIT CRAB
Eupagurus bernhardus Family Paguridae

10 cm. Unlike true crabs, the abdomen is quite long, but it is very soft and the hermit crab protects it by taking up residence in empty shells. As it grows, it moves to larger shells. The large right claw is used to close the opening when the crab retires into the shell.

Cirripedia

ACORN BARNACLE
Semibatanus balanoides
Family Balanidae

5–15 mm diameter. Adults are cemented to inter-tidal rocks and surrounded by chalky plates. When submerged, feathery limbs emerge and comb food particles from the water. The plates close up when the tide recedes. Young stages are free-swimming.

Spiders and their Relatives

The spiders and their relatives, which include the scorpions and the mites and ticks, make up the class Arachnida – another major division of the arthropods. They are easily distinguished from insects by the four pairs of legs and the lack of antennae, although a pair of palps just behind the mouth may look like either legs or antennae. There are no real jaws, but there is always a pair of claw-like limbs called chelicerae just in front of the mouth. Most arachnids are carnivorous, although many of the mites are plant feeders.

Spiders (order Araneida) have two distinct body sections, the front one of which is covered by a fairly tough shield or carapace. The hind region is usually softer and rather bulbous. The front region carries all the legs, and there are usually six or eight eyes distributed over the front end. The palps are quite short and function like antennae, although they are swollen at the tips in males. The chelicerae are in the form of poison fangs. Some large spiders eat birds and lizards and even small mammals, but most spiders eat insects. Many spin elaborate webs to catch their prey, but other simply go hunting or lie in ambush for their prey. The venom from the fangs paralyzes the prey and the spider then sucks it dry.

Males are often much smaller than females and they usually put on some elaborate courtship displays to ensure that the females recognize them. Even so, many males are eaten by their mates. All spiders make silk, even if they do not make webs. It is used for many purposes, including wrapping up prey and protecting the eggs.

Spiders

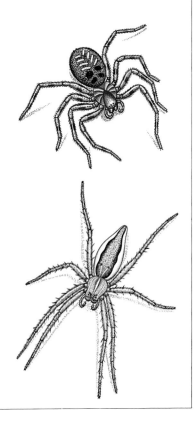

AMAUROBIUS SIMILIS
Family Amaurobiidae

6 mm (male); 12 mm (female). Lives in crevices in bark and old walls and also around window frames, making a rather irregular lacy web around its retreat. Crawling insects are entangled in the web and quickly drawn into the spider's lair, usually being pulled in by one leg. All year. *A. fenestralis* is very similar, but less common on buildings.

NURSERY-WEB SPIDER
Pisaura Mirabilis

12–15 mm. Abundant in dense vegetation, this is one of the wolf spiders which roam around in search of prey and chase after it. It often rests with the two front pairs of legs held close together and pointing forward at an angle of about 30° to the body. Female carries her egg cocoon about in her fangs, attaching it to a plant when the eggs are about to hatch and then covering it with a silken tent. She stands guard over it until the young have dispersed. Adult May–July.

HOUSE SPIDER
Tegenaria gigantea Family Agelenidae

11-15 mm. This is one of the spiders that commonly scuttle across the floor in the evening. It is especially common in outbuildings and also found out of doors. The web is a roughly triangular horizontal sheet (cobweb), spun in a corner with a tubular retreat in the angle. It is not sticky, but small insects get their feet entangled in the dense mat of threads and are easily caught by the spider. Adult in late summer and autumn. It is one of several similar species.

WATER SPIDER
Argyroneta aquatica

8-15 mm (sometimes much larger). Male often larger than female. It is the only spider living permanently under water. It builds a silken bell in ponds and other still waters and fills it with air brought from the surface among the body hairs. It sits in the bell by day, perhaps darting out after passing prey, and goes out to hunt at night. All year.

ENOPLOGNATHA OVATA
Family Theridiidae

3-6 mm. Upper side of abdomen may be all cream, all red, or just with the 2 red lines. Abundant among brambles, nettles and other dense vegetation including garden plants. Female rolls up a leaf to form a shelter and rests there with her blue-green egg cocoon. The web is a loose 3-dimensional scaffold with sticky threads on the outside. More silk is thrown over trapped victims. Adult June-August.

PARDOSA AMENTATA
Family Lycosidae

5-7 mm. A very common wolf spider which hunts on the ground and is regularly seen sunbathing on rockery stones and in other exposed places. The female carries her egg cocoon attached to the spinnerets at her hind end, and when the eggs hatch she carries the babies on her back for a few days. April-September. One of several very similar species.

DYSDERA CROCATA
Family Dysderidae

9-15 mm. A slow-moving hunter living under stones and logs, often in a silk-lined cell. It makes no web and hunts at night, specializing in woodlice, which it captures with its huge fangs: one pierces the underside of the wood-louse and the other goes in through the top. Early summer.

DOLOMEDES FIMBRIATUS
Family Pisauridae

9-13 mm (male); 13-25 mm (female). Another wolf spider, inhabiting marshes and the edges of ponds and streams. It often sits on a floating leaf with the front legs resting on the water, and if it senses an insect on the water nearby it skates after it. When alarmed, the spider may walk down plant stems into the water. May-July.

TARANTULA
Lycosa narbonensis Family Lycosidae

25 mm. This is the famous tarantula of southern Europe – a wolf spider whose bite was supposed to be fatal unless the victim embarked on a long and furious dance which became known as the tarantella. In fact, although the bite may be troublesome, it is not really dangerous. The spider lives in a burrow and hunts on the ground. Like all wolf spiders, it has large eyes. All year.

LINYPHIA TRIANGULARIS
Family Linyphiidae

5-6 mm. Abundant late summer and autumn, forming hammock webs on almost every bush and clump of grass. The spider hangs below the hammock, waiting for insects to collide with the scaffolding above and fall on to the sheet.

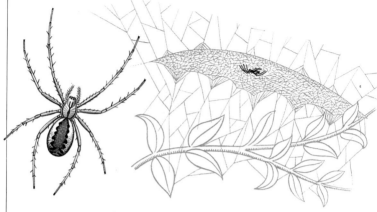

ZEBRA SPIDER
Salticus scenicus Family Salticidae

5-7 mm. Common on sunny rocks and walls, including house walls, this is one of the jumping spiders, with very large eyes. It hunts by sight like the wolf spiders, but when it spots prey it creeps slowly towards it and then, when within range, leaps on to it. The prey is held down by the sturdy front legs and then bitten by the fangs. The spider can leap many times its own length. April-September.

ORB-WEB SPIDERS Family Argiopidae

These spiders spin the circular webs which are so beautiful when covered with dew or frost in autumn. The spiders mature at this time and the webs are at their largest. The spider may rest at the centre of its web, but more often hides under a nearby leaf until an insect flies into the web. Eggs are laid in silken cocoons, often on walls and fences, and they hatch in spring.

ARGIOPE BRUENNICHI

4 mm (male): 11-14 mm (female). This striking spider makes a web with a zig-zag band of silk across the middle, usually from top to bottom, to strengthen it. August-October. Southern and central Europe: rare in southern Britain.

GARDEN SPIDER
Araneus diadematus

4-8 mm (male); 10-12 mm (female). One of the commonest of the orb-web spiders, abundant on fences and hedges August-October. Pale brown to almost black, the white cross on abdomen rather variable.

ARANEUS QUADRATUS

6-8 mm (male); 9-15 mm (female). The very rounded abdomen, usually with 4 distinct white spots, distinguishes this species which varies from greenish-yellow to dark brown. August-October, especially on heathland.

ARGIOPE LOBATA

7 mm (male); 20 mm (female). Makes a web similar to that of *A. bruennichi*. August-October. Mediterranean region.

ZYGIELLA X-NOTATA

3·5 mm (male); 6·5 mm (female). Colour varies, but usually a distinct leaf-like pattern on abdomen. Very common July-October, especially on and around buildings. Web has a missing segment (see illustration).

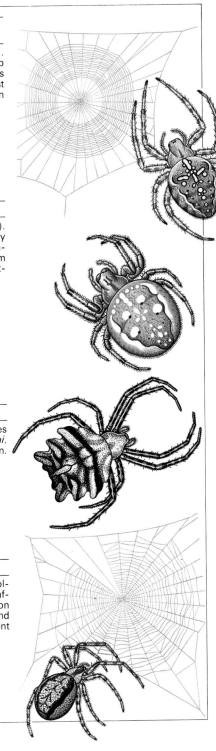

CRAB SPIDERS Family Thomisidae

Mostly crab-like in appearance with front two pairs of legs usually larger than the rest and often walking sideways. They spin no webs and usually lie in ambush for their prey, although they may hunt.

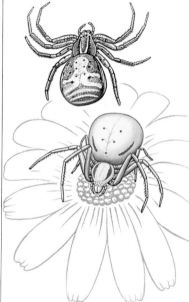

XYSTICUS CRISTATUS

4-7 mm. Very common in low herbage in spring and summer. Male sticks female down with silk before mating.

MISUMENA VATIA

3-4 mm (male); 10-11 mm (female). Greenish, yellow or white according to background. Usually lurks in flowers and catches insects that come to feed. May-July. Not in north.

Harvestmen

These arachnids (Order Opiliones) are often confused with spiders, but the body is not clearly divided into two sections. There are no poison fangs and the animals produce no silk. There are two eyes, perched on a turret near the middle of the back. Most species mature in late summer – hence their common name. They are mostly nocturnal and eat a wide range of living and dead animal matter.

PHALANGIUM OPILIO

4-9 mm. Female larger than male. Underside of body pure white. Chelicerae of male bear large, forward-pointing brown horns. Very common in rough herbage.

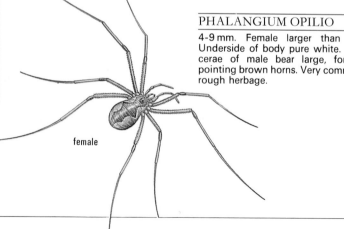

female

LEIOBUNUM ROTUNDUM

3·5-6 mm. Female longer than round-bodied male and heavily mottled. Abundant in rough herbage in all kinds of habitats, often resting on walls and tree trunks by day.

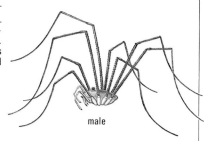

male

False Scorpions

These very small arachnids (Order Pseudoscorpiones) resemble scorpions in having relatively large claws but lack their tails. Many species, rarely more than 3 mm long, live in leaf litter and other debris, feeding on various small animals. *Lamprochernes nodosus* is a common example.

Scorpions

EUSCORPIUS FLAVICAUDIS
Family Chactidae

35 mm. One of the smallest scorpions, but endowed with the typical claws (modified palps) and long tail of the group. The sting is rarely, if ever, used and the animal is not dangerous. It hides in crevices, especially in old walls, with the claws protruding at night to capture small animals. Mainly southern Europe, but established elsewhere, including some port areas of Britain. All year. Scorpions belong to the order Scorpionidea.

Insects

The insects (Class Insecta) make up the largest class of the arthropods and are, in fact, the largest of all animal groups. There are roughly a million known species, arranged in about 30 orders, based mainly on the structure of the wings.

Adult insects can almost all be recognized by their three pairs of legs, one pair of antennae, and a body clearly divided into three sections – head, thorax and abdomen. Most adult insects also have two pairs of wings, although some have only one pair and many have none at all.

Very few insects live in the sea, but they can be found in almost every terrestrial and freshwater habitat, feeding on just about everything from nectar to wood and from blood to dried dung. To deal with such varied diets, they have an extraordinary range of mouthparts – from slender tubes for drinking nectar to the powerful jaws needed for chewing solid wood.

Insect Life Cycles

The insects exhibit two main types of life history. In the first, exemplified by the grasshopper, the youngster looks much like the adult except that it lacks functional wings. Known as a nymph, such a youngster usually eats the same kind of food as the adult. It moults its skin periodically and the wing buds on its back get larger at each moult. At the final moult the adult insect, complete with fully developed wings, emerges from the nymphal skin. This type of life history is called a partial metamorphosis. Bugs, dragonflies and earwigs all have this kind of life history.

The second type of life history, typified by the butterflies and moths, involves a youngster which is very different from the adult. It is called a larva or caterpillar and it often eats quite different food from the adult. The butterfly caterpillar, for example, eats leaves, while the adult sips nectar from flowers. The larva moults periodically, but does not gradually assume the adult form and shows no sign of wings. When fully grown, it turns into a pupa or chrysalis, and it is in this stage that the larval body is converted into that of the adult. This type of life history, shown by flies, bees and beetles as well as by butterflies and moths, is known as complete metamorphosis.

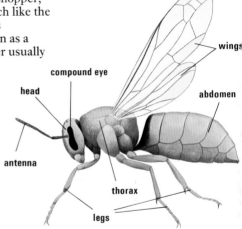

A typical insect, showing the clear division of the body into three parts. Legs and wings are all attached to the thorax.

Dragonflies

Dragonflies (Order Odonata) are long-bodied insects with 2 pairs of gauzy wings and very short bristle-like antennae. The eyes are very large. Dragonflies eat other insects which they scoop up in mid-air with their spiky legs. There are two main groups: the Anisoptera, or true dragonflies, and the Zygoptera, or damselflies. The true dragonflies are again divided into hawkers and darters. Hawkers spend most of their time on the wing, hawking to and fro in search of prey, while darters spend much time resting on the vegetation and simply dart out when prey approaches. Damselflies are much daintier than the hawkers and darters and generally fly rather slowly. They feed largely by plucking small insects from the vegetation. True dragonflies rest with wings outstretched, but damselflies normally fold their wings together over the body.

All dragonflies spend their early life in water. The nymphs are fiercely carnivorous, shooting out their spiky jaws to impale other small animals. The nymphs usually climb reeds when it is time for the adults to emerge. There is no chrysalis stage. Adult colours may take several days to develop fully. The larger dragonflies are strong fliers and often roam far from water, but the insects are most commonly seen close to ponds and streams. Sizes given are wingspans.

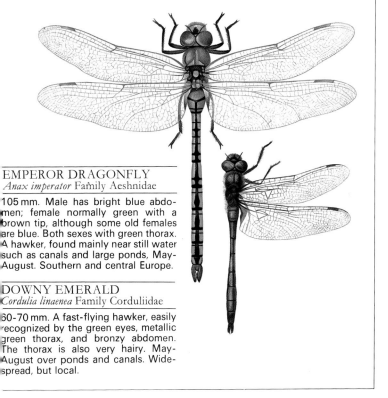

EMPEROR DRAGONFLY
Anax imperator Family Aeshnidae

105 mm. Male has bright blue abdomen; female normally green with a brown tip, although some old females are blue. Both sexes with green thorax. A hawker, found mainly near still water such as canals and large ponds, May-August. Southern and central Europe.

DOWNY EMERALD
Cordulia linaenea Family Corduliidae

60-70 mm. A fast-flying hawker, easily recognized by the green eyes, metallic green thorax, and bronzy abdomen. The thorax is also very hairy. May-August over ponds and canals. Widespread, but local.

BROWN AESHNA
Aeshna grandis Family Aeshnidae

100 mm. Only male has blue spots at front of abdomen. Hawks to and fro along a definite beat, usually over or along the edge of water, June-October. Prefers still or slow-moving water. Most of Europe, including the Arctic, but not Scotland.

GOLD-RINGED DRAGONFLY
Cordulegaster boltonii
Family Cordulegasteridae

100 mm. Hawks low over small streams May-September. Female uses her long ovipositor to dig her eggs into the silt at the bottom of the stream. The insect prefers upland areas and is common on heaths and moors in most parts of Europe. *C. bidentatus* of southern and central Europe is very similar but lacks the small yellow spots at hind edge of each segment.

BANDED AGRION
Agrion splendens Family Agriidae

60-65 mm. One of the largest of the damselflies. Female has a greener metallic body and uniform yellowish-green wings. Flies May-October, preferring quiet streams with muddy bottoms and plenty of weeds. Weak-flying female spends most of the time on the vegetation; males 'dance' quite rapidly over the waterside plants, often in large numbers. Most of Europe, but not Scotland.

LARGE RED DAMSELFLY
Pyrrhosoma nymphula
Family Coenagriidae

40-50 mm. Female has more black on the abdomen, including a black line down the centre. Legs black in both sexes (the Small Red Damselfly has red legs). It is one of the commonest damselflies and one of the first to appear in spring. It flies April-September, inhabiting still and slow-moving water, including peat bogs.

COMMON BLUE DAMSELFLY
Enallagma cyathigerum

35-40 mm. Male usually easily distinguished from similar blue and black
damselflies by the stalked black spot at
front of abdomen. Female is green and
black and may be recognized by a small
spine under 8th segment of abdomen.
Flies May-September at edges of still
and slow-moving water with plenty of
vegetation.

LIBELLULA DEPRESSA
Family Libellulidae

75 mm. A fast-flying darter. Female is
brown with yellow spots along sides of
abdomen: male is also like this when
young, but develops blue colour as he
matures. Dark patch at base of each
wing distinguishes this species from
several similar ones. Flies May-August
and perches more or less horizontally
on bushes and other vegetation, often
selecting a dead twig. Prefers still and
slow-moving water and will breed in
brackish pools by the sea.

FOUR-SPOTTED LIBELLULA
Libellula quadrimaculata

75 mm. Easily recognized by the 4
spots — one near the middle of the
front edge of each wing. Both sexes are
brown, but may be distinguished by
the larger claspers of the male. Flies
May-August, often rests on ground.
Prefers boggy pools and wet heaths.

RUDDY SYMPETRUM
Sympetrum sanguineum

55 mm. One of several similarly coloured darters, but male is distinguished
by the strongly constricted abdomen.
Female is orange-brown. Legs are
black without a yellow stripe in both
sexes. Flies June-September, breeding
in ponds and ditches where reedmace
and horsetails grow. Settles on bare
ground, rocks and twigs, often with
wings drooping.

Note: all illustrations of dragonflies
and damselflies show males.

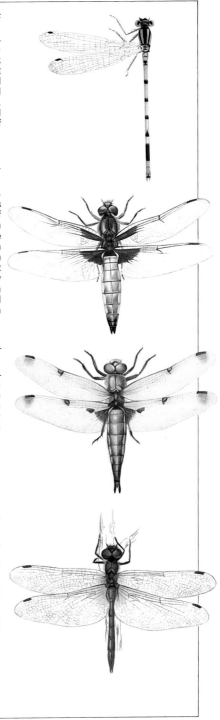

Grasshoppers and Crickets

These insects (Order Orthoptera) generally have tough front wings and membranous hind wings, although many species are wingless. The hind legs are long and used for jumping. The males of most species 'sing' by rubbing one part of the body against another. There is no chrysalis stage and young resemble adults.

MOLE CRICKET
Gryllotalpa gryllotalpa
Family Gryllotalpidae

35-45 mm. Front legs modified for digging; front wings short. Spends much time underground, feeding on roots and insect grubs, but can fly. Damp meadows in late summer and again in spring after hibernation. Very rare in Britain.

TRUE CRICKETS Family Gryllidae

The front wings, when present, form a box-like cover for the body, distinctly flattened on top. Males sing by rubbing the two front wings together. Females have a slender, spear-like ovipositor (egg-layer).

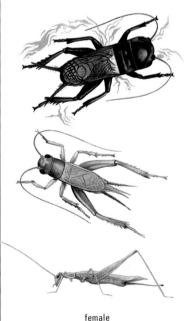

female

FIELD CRICKET
Gryllus campestris

20 mm. A warmth-loving insect of dry grassland. It is flightless and lives in burrows. Female is browner. Male has a shrill song. Spring and early summer, mainly diurnal. Southern and central Europe: now rare in Britain.

HOUSE CRICKET
Acheta domesticus

15 mm. Mainly nocturnal. Hind wings project like tails from end of body when folded. Both sexes fly well. Male has shrill song. Mostly in buildings. All year.

ITALIAN CRICKET
Oecanthus pellucens

9-15 mm. A delicate insect of shrubs and other tall vegetation. Female wings are much narrower on top than male's. Male has a beautiful soft warbling song at nightfall. July-October. Southern Europe.

BUSH CRICKETS Family Tettigoniidae

These insects differ from true crickets in having no large flat area on top. They are like grasshoppers in shape but have longer antennae. Males sing by rubbing the front wings together. Females have a broad, sabre-like ovipositor – long and straight or short and strongly curved. Most eat both plant and animal matter – usually insects – and are active mainly towards evening. They usually inhabit scrubby places and mature in late summer.

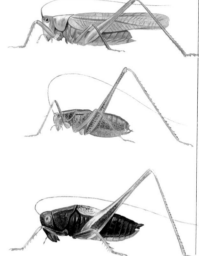

GREAT GREEN BUSH CRICKET
Tettigonia viridissima

40-50 mm. Bright green with brown on top of head and at base of male front wing. Song loud, in long bursts. Not in northern Britain.

SPECKLED BUSH CRICKET
Leptophyes punctatissima

9-17 mm. Bright green with dark spots. Wings minute; front ones forming a little saddle in male. Song almost inaudible. Ovipositor short and curved.

DARK BUSH CRICKET
Pholidoptera griseoaptera

13-20 mm. Yellowish-brown to black. Front wings are small flaps in male; female wingless. Ovipositor long. Song is a series of short chirps.

TYLOPSIS LILIIFOLIA

13-23 mm. Brown or green, with very long antennae. Both sexes fly well. Ovipositor short and curved. Song very faint. Southern Europe.

female

GRASSHOPPERS Family Acrididae

These are mostly sturdily-built, bullet-shaped insects with short antennae and narrow front wings, although many are wingless, especially montane species. Females are usually larger than males. Males sing by rubbing their back legs against veins on front wings, but many species are silent. They are usually active only in sunshine. All are vegetarian.

male

ARCYPTERA FUSCA

22-40 mm. Female longer and fatter than male but with shorter wings (flightless). Song very loud: starts with a few short notes, turns into a warble, and then dies away with a few more short notes. Grassy places in mountains July-September. Not Britain.

male

MEADOW GRASSHOPPER
Chorthippus parallelus

10-24 mm (female much larger than male). Colour may be any combination of green, brown, pink and red. Female front wings much shorter than male: hind wings absent in both sexes, therefore flightless. Song is a buzzing sound lasting for up to 3 seconds and getting louder. Most kinds of grassland July-November.

female

PODISMA PEDESTRIS

15-30 mm. Female larger than male. Flightless, with wings reduced to tiny flaps in both sexes. A montane species, rarely found below 1,000 metres. Stony ground in August and September. Not in Britain. (The closely related *P. alpina* has yellow hind tibiae.)

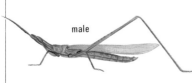

male

ACRIDA UNGARICA

30-75 mm. Female much larger than male. Green or brown, sometimes with light and dark patterns, and very hard to see when it is sitting upright among the grasses. July-October, mainly in the damper grasslands. Mediterranean.

OEDIPODA GERMANICA

15-30 mm. Female somewhat larger than male. At rest on the ground, the insect is well camouflaged, but if disturbed it flies away and flashes its red hind wings. It quickly drops to the ground again and this is believed to confuse the enemy, which continues to search for something red. The song is very quiet and produced only in the presence of a female. June-November in dry fields and hillsides, especially in stony areas. Southern and central Europe: not in Britain. (The closely related *O. coerulescens* has bright blue hind wings.)

MIGRATORY LOCUST
Locusta migratoria

30-50 mm. Male much smaller than female shown here. Colour varies, but males often brownish and females largely green. It forms huge swarms in some areas – especially in Africa – and is then greyish-brown or yellow. Most European specimens are of the solitary phase, always found alone and distinguished by the prominently domed thorax. They occur in all kinds of habitats July-November and may hibernate as adults to reappear in spring. Mainly in southern Europe, but it is strong-flying and occasionally migrates to Britain and other northern regions.

female

Bugs

This order (Hemiptera) is extremely varied, but all members possess a needle-like beak for piercing and sucking up fluids. Most have 4 wings, but many are wingless. There are two major divisions – the Heteroptera and the Homoptera. The front wings of the Heteroptera, when present, have a horny basal area and a membranous tip. The front wings of the Homoptera, when present, are of uniform texture throughout – either horny or membranous. There are also some differences in the beaks of the two groups. The Heteroptera include both plant and animal feeders and all the water bugs. The Homoptera are all terrestrial plant-feeders. Each group has many families. The young resemble the adults and there is no chrysalis stage.

HETEROPTERA

HAWTHORN SHIELD BUG
Acanthosoma haemorrhoidale
Family Acanthosomatidae

14 mm. One of many shield bugs, so called for their shape. It feeds on hawthorn leaves and berries in autumn and again after hibernation.

WATER SCORPION
Nepa cinerea Family Nepidae

20 mm. Creeps slowly around in ponds, mainly on the bottom, and catches other animals with its powerful front legs. It draws air from the surface through the tube at the back. All year.

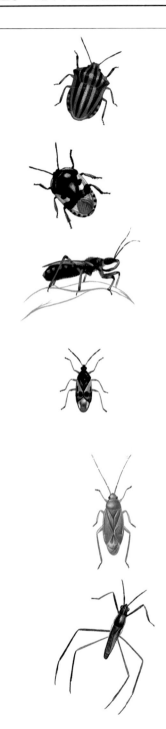

GRAPHOSOMA ITALICUM
Family Pentatomidae

10 mm. The bright colours of this shield bug warn of a most unpleasant taste. It feeds on a variety of umbelliferous plants August–October. Southern and central Europe: not in Britain.

PIED SHIELD BUG
Sehirus bicolor Family Cydnidae

5–7 mm. Feeds mainly on the sap of white deadnettle, on which it can be found at most times of the year. Adults hibernate under the ground.

RHINOCORIS IRACUNDUS
Family Reduviidae

12 mm. One of the assassin bugs - predatory species with strong, curved beaks. It feeds on a variety of insects, plunging its beak into them to drain out the fluids. Summer and autumn. Southern and central Europe: not in Britain.

COMMON FLOWER BUG
Anthocoris nemorum Family Anthocoridae

3–4 mm. A very common predatory bug found on leaves and flowers. It feeds on aphids and other small creatures, including the red spider mite which infests fruit trees. Spring to autumn: adults, especially females, hibernate under bark and in rubbish.

COMMON GREEN CAPSID
Lygocoris pabulinus Family Miridae

5–6 mm. Abundant on trees and shrubs in spring and on a wide range of herbaceous plants in summer. Often a pest of soft fruit, which it punctures with its beak.

COMMON POND SKATER
Gerris lacustris Family Gerridae

12 mm. Lives on the surface of still water, skating around on long 2nd pair of legs. Hind legs used as a rudder, and front legs for catching other small insects. April–November.

WATER BOATMAN
Corixa punctata Family Corixidae

12–13 mm. Antennae hidden, as in most aquatic bugs. Swims with hairy back legs and feeds on algae. All year.

HOMOPTERA

CICADETTA MONTANA
Family Cicadidae

15–25 mm. Female larger than male. The only cicada found in Britain (New Forest only), but widely distributed in Europe. Rests on tree trunks and branches and sucks sap with stout beak. Male makes a rather bubbling whistle. Nymphs feed underground on the roots of trees and shrubs. May–July. (Several larger cicadas with much louder calls live in southern Europe.)

COMMON FROGHOPPER
Philaenus spumarius Family Cercopidae

6 mm. Pattern varies. Abundant on trees and shrubs, leaping strongly when disturbed. Nymph lives in 'cuckoo spit', which protects it while it feeds on sap. June–September.

CERCOPIS VULNERATA

10 mm. This brightly coloured frog-hopper lives on various plants, mainly in wooded regions. The nymph lives on roots in a mass of solidified froth. April–August. Not in the north.

BUFFALO HOPPER
Stictocephala bisonia Family Membracidae

10 mm. The pronotal shield just behind the head is extended back to the tip of the body. A native of North America, it is now well established in southern Europe. July–October.

BLACKFLY
Aphis fabae Family Aphididae

2–3 mm. Also called the black bean aphid, this pest lives in large numbers on beans, spinach, sugar-beet and many other plants. In spring and summer all the aphids are females, giving birth to many young without mating. They may be winged or wing-less. April–October.

Butterflies

Butterflies, like moths, belong to the order Lepidopera. Their wings are clothed with minute scales. All have clubbed antennae. European butterflies fly by day and rest with the wings held vertically over the body. The front legs are reduced in some families. Sizes given are wingspans.

WHITES AND YELLOWS Family Pieridae

A worldwide group of about 2,000 medium-sized species, with about 40 species in Europe.
Males usually differ slightly from females in colour-pattern. All six legs are functional. The caterpillars lack spines and are usually green in colour. Most feed on legumes (Pea family) or crucifers (Cabbage family) and some are agricultural pests. The chrysalis is attached head-up to the foodplants, or elsewhere by tail hooks and a girdle of silk.

BRIMSTONE
Gonepteryx rhamni

50–62 mm. Overwinters as an adult and one of the first butterflies to appear in the spring. Flies on heaths and along hedges and the edges of woods during June and July, before hibernation and reappearing in February or March. Often in gardens.
The caterpillar feeds on Buckthorn (*Rhamnus catharticus*) and, less often on Alder Buckthorn (*Frangula alnus*). It is green, spotted with black and striped with darker green and white.
Identification: the males are easily distinguished by their bright yellow wings. Females are greenish-white. The Cleopatra butterfly of southern Europe is similar but the male has a deep orange patch on the front wing.

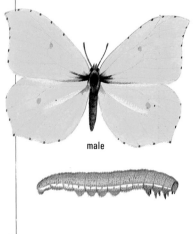

male

BLACK-VEINED WHITE
Aporia crataegi

57–67 mm. This butterfly is common along hedgerows, in fields of Lucerne (*Medicago sativa*) and open country in some parts of Europe, North Africa and temperate Asia, and can be a pest in orchards. In Britain it is now extinct. The single generation flies in May, June and July. The female fore wing is almost transparent.
The caterpillar feeds in groups on the foliage of hawthorn (*Crataegus*), Blackthorn (*Prunus spinosa*) and apple (*Malus*), and rests in a large silken nest. It is black, lined with orange, above, and grey, spotted with white, below. The partly grown caterpillars overwinter inside the nest.

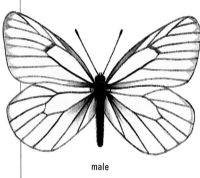

male

LARGE WHITE
Pieris brassicae

56–67 mm. A common butterfly in gardens, agricultural land and hill slopes up to 2,000 metres. There are two or three generations each year, on the wing from April to August. Found in North Africa, in most of Europe and across Asia to the Himalayas. Often migrates in large numbers.

The caterpillar feeds in groups on cabbage (*Brassica*) and other crucifers, but also on garden Nasturtium (*Tropaeolum*). It is green striped with yellow, and mottled with black.

SMALL WHITE
Pieris rapae

46–54 mm. A common species in most of Europe, North Africa, northern Asia and North America. In gardens, meadows and agricultural land during most of the summer, with usually two generations in northern and up to four in southern Europe. Sometimes migrates in large numbers. Cabbage (*Brassica*) is a common foodplant, but wild crucifers like Hedge Mustard (*Sisymbrium officinale*) are also eaten.

The caterpillar is green lined with yellow, and often chooses sheltered places on fences in which to pupate.

Identification: two southern European whites resemble the Small White: the Mountain Small White (*P. ergane*), which lacks black spots on the underside of the wings, and the Southern Small White (*P. mannii*), which has a larger black marking at the outer edge of the forewing.

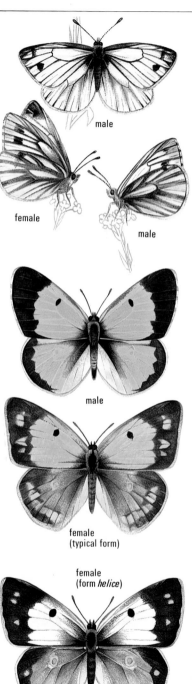

male

female

male

GREEN-VEINED WHITE
Pieris napi

39–51 mm. A migratory butterfly (less so than the Small White), but usually not a pest. Prefers meadows and hedgerows and often visits flowers. Except at high altitudes, there are usually two generations flying in May and June and in July and August. Found in North Africa, most of Europe, temperate Asia and North America.
The caterpillar is pale green lined with dark green and yellow. It feeds mainly on Charlock (*Sinapis arvensis*) and other wild crucifers.

male

female
(typical form)

female
(form *helice*)

CLOUDED YELLOW
Colias croceus

47–61mm. Migrates northwards during the summer, but a year-long resident in southern Europe, south-western Asia and North Africa. Flies from early spring until October in a succession of generations. Found in meadows up to about 1,500 metres, and often common in fields of lucerne and clover.
The caterpillar is green, with a line of yellow and red, and a row of black spots on the side. It feeds on clovers and lucerne and other legumes and changes into a chrysalis on the food-plant. The last generation of the year overwinters in the caterpillar stage.
Identification: the normal female is slightly paler than the male and has yellow spots in the black borders. There is, however, a very pale variety of the female with dusky hind wings. Known as *helice*, it makes up about 10 per cent of the female population. It is easily confused with the female Pale Clouded Yellow, but the black margins are much less extensive in this latter species and the underside of the hind wing is a much brighter yellow, without any grey clouding.

ORANGE-TIP
Anthocharis cardamines

33–48 mm. The butterflies of the single yearly generation usually emerge between March and July. They fly along hedgerows and in meadows, often near woods, and are frequently attracted to flowers. Found in most of Europe as far north as the Arctic Circle and across Asia to Japan.

The caterpillar is green with black spots and white lines. It feeds on Cuckoo Flower (*Cardamine pratensis*) and other crucifers and eventually changes into a chrysalis on or near the foodplant.

male

female

SWALLOWTAILS Family Papilionidae

A group with over 500 mostly large and colourful butterflies, mainly tropical. Most have tailed hind wings and all have 3 pairs of functional legs. The caterpillar has a retractable fleshy process behind the head. The pupa is usually attached to the foodplant in an upright position by tail hooks and a girdle of silk.

SWALLOWTAIL
Papilio machaon

60–98 mm. Flies between April and August in meadows and on flowery hillslopes in the lowlands and mountains up to about 2,000 metres. Occurs in North Africa, through most of Europe and across Asia as far as Japan. It is common in parts of continental Europe, but rare in Britain and found only in the marshy fens of East Anglia. There is usually one generation in the north but up to three in warmer parts of Europe.

The caterpillar feeds exclusively on the leaves of umbellifers, chiefly those of the Milk Parsley (*Peucedanum palustre*) in England, but on other species elsewhere. The caterpillar is at first black and white and looks like a bird-dropping, but later becomes green, ringed with black and orange, and has an orange retractable process behind the head.

ADMIRALS, EMPERORS, VANESSIDS AND FRITILLARIES Family Nymphalidae

A worldwide group of several thousand medium-sized species, with about 70 representatives in Europe. All the species have reduced forelegs and most are colourful, strongly flying butterflies. The upper-side colour-pattern usually differs from that of the underside, but males and females resemble each other fairly closely. The caterpillars are generally covered with spines. The chrysalids are often ornamented with shiny gold or silver markings, and are suspended from hooks at the tail end.

male

LESSER PURPLE EMPEROR
Apatura ilia

64-70 mm. A rather scarce butterfly of open woodlands, up to about 1,500 metres. On the wing between April and June and again in August and September, but with only one generation in the north and the Alps. Found in southern and central Europe (not Britain or Scandinavia) and in temperate Asia as far east as Japan.
The caterpillar is green, spotted and striped with yellow, and has two processes on the head. It feeds mainly on Black Poplar (*Populus nigra*) and other poplars, but probably also on willow (*Salix*) and other trees. The caterpillar overwinters.
Identification Separated from the Purple Emperor (*A.iris*) by the orange margin around the dark spot near the edge of the upper side of the forewing.

PEACOCK
Inachis io

56-68 mm. Regularly visits *Buddleia* in gardens and attracted to knapweeds (*Centaurea*) and other flowers. The main flight is from June onwards, the survivors overwintering until the following spring to produce the next year's generation. Generally common in Europe up to about 1,500 metres, except in Arctic Scandinavia, and across Asia to Japan. The unusual colour-pattern of the upper side possibly scares away small birds when the butterfly suddenly opens its wings.
The caterpillar feeds in a group on the young leaves of nettles (*Urtica*). It is black, spotted with white, and has numerous branched, black spines.

PURPLE EMPEROR
Apatura iris

64-80 mm. Males usually fly around the upper branches of oak trees (*Quercus*), but may be attracted to rotting animal material and damp patches on the ground. Fairly common in July and August up to about 1,500 metres in much of Europe, including Britain, but not in Sweden or Norway.

The caterpillar, which overwinters, is green, marked with yellow and white, and has two long horns on the head. It feeds mostly on sallows (*Salix*), resting along the middle of a leaf on a layer of silk.

WHITE ADMIRAL
Limenitis camilla

52-60 mm. A woodland species often attracted to Bramble (*Rubus*) flowers and decaying animal matter. Fairly common in a single flight during June and July up to 1,500 metres in most of Europe, except for the extreme south and north, and also found in temperate Asia as far east as Japan.

The caterpillar is green, striped with purple and white. It feeds on Honeysuckle and overwinters on the food-plant.

SMALL TORTOISESHELL
Aglais urticae

44-52 mm. One of the most abundant European butterflies wherever there are flowers, and a common visitor to Ice-plant (*Sedum*) and *Buddleia* flowers. This species does migrate, but not in great numbers. It overwinters as an adult butterfly and can be seen as early as March, flying until September or October in two or more generations. Found throughout Europe and temperate Asia to Japan from sea-level to 3,500 metres.

The caterpillar lives with others in a large web on nettles (*Urtica*). It is usually black above and greenish below, with several rows of spines.

Identification Best separated from the Large Tortoiseshell by the uniformly black base to the hind wing.

RED ADMIRAL
Vanessa atalanta

56-68 mm. A generally common species of meadows, hedgerows, orchards and gardens, and attracted to flowers and rotten fruit. Possibly overwinters as an adult in Britain, but usually first appears in May as a migrant from the south and produces a main flight in late summer together with further migrants. Found in much of Europe and across Asia to India, in North Africa, and in North and Central America.

The caterpillar is mainly black, with brown and yellow spines. It feeds alone, in a web, usually on nettles.

PAINTED LADY
Cynthia cardui

54-65 mm. Sometimes common in northern Europe and even in Iceland as a migrant, but overwinters probably only in warmer regions. Flies in gardens, often visiting *Buddleia* flowers, and up to 3,000 metres in open country and woodland clearings. Occurs throughout the year in the tropics but has only two generations in the north. Almost worldwide in distribution but not known in South America.

The caterpillar feeds alone in a web under leaves of thistles (*Carduus* and *Cirsium*), nettles (*Urtica*) and other plants. It is mainly black, and is covered with yellow or yellow and black spines.

COMMA
Polygonia c-album

44-54 mm. First-brood insects fly June to August, and a 2nd brood, much darker than 1st, flies August to October. The 2nd-brood insects then hibernate and reappear in March and April. Found in orchards and gardens and along hedgerows and woodland margins in most of Europe. Often attracted to *Buddleia* and ice plant (*Sedum*) flowers.

The caterpillar lives alone in a small web under a leaf, usually on nettles (*Urtica*). It is black, marked with yellow and white, and is covered with white or yellow spines.

Identification Differs from the Southern Comma (*P.egea*) in the distinctly comma-like white marking under the hind wing (Y-shaped in *egea*).

MAP BUTTERFLY
Araschnia levana

32-40 mm. First brood insects (April to early July) are orange and black, those of the second generation (July and August) black and white. Generally a lowland species, but sometimes occurs up to about 1,000 metres. Found fairly commonly in France and Germany, but not in Britain nor in most of southern Europe or Scandinavia. Also occurs in Japan and much of temperate Asia.
The caterpillar feeds on nettles (*Urtica*), at first in a group but later alone. It is black or brown, with many long yellow and black spines.

male
(first
generation)

male
(first
generation)

male
(second
generation)

KNAPWEED FRITILLARY
Melitaea phoebe

40-48 mm. Found mainly in grassy hilly country, up to 2,000 metres, and can be locally common. At high altitudes flies only in July, but at lower elevations has two or three generations flying between April and August. A resident of North Africa, central and southern Europe, and Asia as far as China.
The caterpillar is spiny and grey, striped with black and white, and feeds on knapweeds (*Centaurea*), plantains (*Plantago*) and other plants.

QUEEN OF SPAIN FRITILLARY
Issoria lathonia

36-48 mm. A rare migrant in Britain and northern Scandinavia, but often common in continental Europe, North Africa and temperate Asia in rough grassy country, regularly visiting scabious, thistles and other flowers. The single northern generation flies in May and June, but there are up to three generations in the south between February and October. Migrants to the north may breed and produce another generation, but the offspring never overwinter successfully.
The caterpillar is black, marked with white, and has many black and brown spines. It feeds on Violets (*Viola*). Autumn caterpillars overwinter.
Identification The large silver spots on the underside readily identify this species.

female

male

SILVER-WASHED FRITILLARY
Argynnis paphia

56-74 mm. Flies in or near woods between June and September in a single yearly generation, and can be quite common up to about 1,000 metres. Often visits Bramble (*Rubus*) flowers. Found in most of Europe, including Britain, but not in Arctic Scandinavia. **The caterpillar** feeds chiefly on Dog Violet (*Viola riviniana*), but in the first few months of its life it overwinters in the crevices of the bark of oaks (*Quercus*) and pines (*Pinus*).

HEATH FRITILLARY
Mellicta athalia

36-42 mm. One of the most common Fritillaries in Europe on heaths, in grassland and in woodland clearings up to 1,800 metres. There is a single midsummer flight in the north, but two generations are on the wing in the south between May and September. Rare in southern England.
The caterpillar is black, spotted with white, and covered with short, hairy spines. It feeds with others in a web on plantains (*Plantago*), Cow-wheat (*Melampyrum pratense*) and on other plants. Autumn-generation caterpillars overwinter.

MARSH FRITILLARY
Eurodryas aurinia

34-46 mm. Flies between April and July in a single flight, and can be common locally in marshy land and wet moors up to about 2,000 metres. Found in much of Europe (including Britain, but excluding northern Scandinavia), in North Africa and in temperate Asia eastwards to Korea.
The caterpillar, which overwinters, spins a web and lives in a large group on plantains (*Plantago*), gentians (*Gentiana*) and other plants. It is mostly black, marked with white, and has several short, black spines along the body.
Identification Separable from other similarly patterned Fritillaries by the combination of a strongly marked upper side and a usually pale underside to the forewing.

BROWNS Family Satyridae

This large family, with over 3,000 species, is most abundant in temperate regions. Over 100 species live in Europe, many of them in the mountains. Most have eye-spots on the wings, and the males of many species have a dark patch near the centre of the front wing. This patch, known as a scent brand, consists of scent-emitting scales used during courtship. The caterpillars are usually green or brown, finely hairy, and tapered at both ends. There is a short forked 'tail'. They feed almost entirely on grasses. The chrysalids either hang from tail hooks or lie in a loose cocoon on the ground.

MARBLED WHITE
Melanargia galathea

45-56 mm. A common butterfly of open, flowery grassland up to 1,800 metres. Flies in June and July in a single generation and has a characteristic, slow flight. Found in southern and central Europe, including southern England. Several similar species live in southern Europe.
The caterpillar is green or brown; it hibernates soon after hatching, and starts to feed early the next year on fescues (*Festuca*) and other grasses.

WOODLAND GRAYLING
Hipparchia fagi

65-76 mm. A locally common butterfly of open woodlands and scrubland, usually below 1,000 metres. Often rests on tree-trunks, where it is well camouflaged. Usually emerges in July and August in a single flight. Found in central and southern Europe. Not found in Britain.
The caterpillar is brown, striped with dark brown and yellow, and feeds at night on Creeping Soft Grass (*Holcus mollis*) and other grasses.

female

GREAT BANDED GRAYLING
Brintesia circe

65–73 mm. Common at times in open oak woods at low elevations during June, July and August in a single flight. Often rests on tree-trunks or branches, and if disturbed flies long distances before resettling. Resident in southern and central Europe (as far north as central France and Germany) and in south-western Asia.

The caterpillar is brown, striped with black and darker brown, and feeds on Rye-grass (*Lolium*) and other grasses. It overwinters partly grown.

GATEKEEPER
Pyronia tithonus

36–42 mm. Common in places, especially near woods and along hedge-rows, and often attracted to the flowers of Wood Sage (*Teucrium scorodonia*). Appears in July and August in a single flight, usually at low elevations but up to 1,000 metres in southern Europe. Found in most of Europe but not in Scandinavia or northern Britain.

The caterpillar is either green or brown, striped along the body with black, brown and white. It feeds on Cocksfoot (*Dactylis glomerata*) and other grasses, and overwinters partly grown.

Identification: separable from the Southern Gatekeeper (*P. cecilia*) by the presence of eye-spots on the underside of the hind wing.

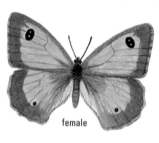

female

SMALL HEATH
Coenonympha pamphilus

27–34 mm. On the wing, usually in two or more generations, from April onwards, often settling on flowers or on the ground. A common species of grassy places from sea-level to 2,000 metres in western Asia and most of Europe, including Britain but not the extreme north of Scandinavia.

The caterpillar is green, spotted with white, and striped with darker green, and feeds on various species of grass. In northern Europe some caterpillars from each generation overwinter.

SPECKLED WOOD
Pararge aegeria

35–45 mm. A butterfly of woodlands and old hedgerows, where its colour-pattern makes it difficult to see in broken sunlight. Flies in a series of generations from March onwards, but with only one flight in parts of Scandinavia. Found in North Africa, Madeira, the Canaries, most of Europe (except for northern Scotland and northern Scandinavia), and across Asia to the Ural mountains.
The caterpillar is green, striped with dark green and yellow, and feeds on Couch Grass (*Agropyron*) and other grasses. Some of the Autumn generation overwinter as caterpillars, others in the chrysalis stage.
Identification: occurs in two distinct forms: in south-west Europe (Italy, southern France, and Iberia) the pale spots are orange, while elsewhere they are creamy white.

Britain

S.W. Europe

SCOTCH ARGUS
Erebia aethiops

40–53 mm. The single flight of this species takes place between July and early September, the butterflies seldom taking to the wing unless the weather is sunny. Found in Scotland and northern England, central and south-eastern Europe and in western Asia. Restricted to grassy areas, usually near forests in hills and mountains up to 2,000 metres, but also occurs near the coast in Belgium.
The caterpillar is usually yellow-brown, striped with darker and lighter brown. It feeds on Couch Grass (*Agropyron*) and other grasses, and overwinters when partly grown.

WOODLAND BROWN
Lopinga achine

48–54 mm. Occurs in widely separated colonies up to 1,000 metres in woodland meadows and along edges of woods in central and northern Europe (excluding Britain and north-western Germany), and across temperate Asia to Japan. Appears in a single flight between June and August, the males emerging before the females.
The caterpillar is green, striped with dark green and white, and feeds on Rye-grass (*Lolium*), various other grasses and sedges (*Carex*). It overwinters.

female

female

female

male

GRAYLING
Hipparchia semele

48-60 mm. Widespread and common in open, grassy places and on heaths up to 1,500 metres in a single flight between May and September. Often visits thyme (*Thymus*) flowers, but usually rests on the ground with the closed wings inclined towards the sun so that little shadow is cast, making the butterfly difficult to detect. Found in most of Europe.

The caterpillar is yellow, striped along the body with brown and dull yellow. It feeds on various kinds of Grass and overwinters when half grown.

TREE GRAYLING
Neohipparchia statilinus

46-53 mm. Locally common, but becoming more rare in some areas. On the wing between July and October in a single flight, the males always emerging several days before the females. Found on heaths and in rocky places on mountain slopes in southern and central Europe (not Britain or Scandinavia) and in western Asia.

The caterpillar is yellow, striped with brown and feeds on fescues (*Festuca*), meadow grass (*Poa*) and other grasses. It overwinters, partly grown, at the base of the grass.

DRYAD
Minois dryas

54-63 mm. A butterfly of damp moors and meadows, often near woods, usually below 1,000 metres. Usually emerges in July and August in a single generation, flying quite slowly and close to the ground. Occurs in colonies in central Europe (not Britain or Scandinavia), and in temperate Asia including Japan.

The caterpillar is yellow-grey, striped with dark grey and brown. It feeds on Purple Moor Grass (*Molinia caerulea*) and other grasses, and overwinters partly grown.

Identification The blue-centred eye-spots readily distinguish this species from the very similar Great Sooty Satyr (*Satyrus ferula*), which has white-centred eye-spots. It also has white bands on the underside of hind wing.

RINGLET
Aphantopus hyperantus

40-50 mm. Generally common near and in woods and along old hedgerows up to about 1,500 metres in a single flight during June and July. Often visits flowers. Found in most of Britain and continental Europe (except for southern Spain and Italy and Arctic Scandinavia), and also in northern Asia as far east as Siberia.

The caterpillar, which overwinters, is yellow-brown with darker stripes, and feeds on meadow grasses (*Poa*) and other grasses, and rarely on sedges (*Carex*).

MEADOW BROWN
Maniola jurtina

44-50 mm. Often very common on grass and heathland up to about 1,500 metres in much of Europe, including Britain but excluding northern Scandinavia. Found also in Asia as far east as the Ural mountains of central Russia and in North Africa and the Canaries. There is probably only one generation each year, which is on the wing from June to September. Upper side of male darker than female, with very little orange.

The caterpillar is green, spotted with black, and striped with white and dark green. It feeds on grasses, often meadow grasses (*Poa*), and overwinters partly grown.

LARGE WALL BROWN
Lasiommata maera

44-54 mm. Common in rocky, grassy places in or near woodlands, up to about 2,000 metres in the Alps. The single northern and high-elevation flight is in June and July, but there are two generations on the wing elsewhere between May and September. Resident in North Africa, much of Europe (but not Britain), and in western Asia as far east as the Himalayas.

The caterpillar is green, striped with white and dark green, and feeds on various species of grasses. Autumn generation caterpillars overwinter.

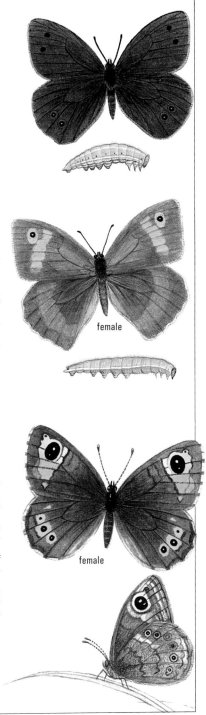

female

female

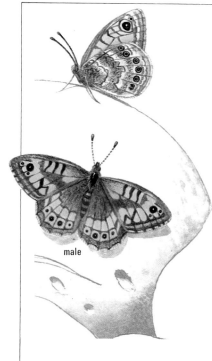

male

WALL BROWN
Lasiommata megera

35-40 mm. Prefers sunny, dry places and often basks in the sunshine on a wall, rock or pathway. Attracted to *Buddleia* and other garden flowers. Often common up to about 1,200 metres from March onwards, usually in two or more generations. Found in Europe (including Britain, but excluding northern Scandinavia), North Africa, Madeira, the Canaries and western Asia.

The caterpillar is blue-green, striped along the body with dark green and white, and feeds on Cocksfoot (*Dactylis glomerata*) and other grasses. Autumn caterpillars overwinter, some feeding throughout the winter.

Identification Separable from male Large Wall Brown (*L.maera*) chiefly by the presence of two dark-brown bars across the cell on the upper side of the forewing.

LARGE HEATH
Coenonympha tullia

35-40 mm. A butterfly of wet meadows, moors and bogs, on the wing in a single flight during June and July, at low elevations in the north but up to 2,000 metres in the mountains of southern Europe. Much less common in Britain now than in the past, probably as a result of improved land drainage. Found in isolated colonies in most of Europe, including Britain but excluding Arctic Scandinavia and south-western and south-eastern Europe. Occurs also in northern Asia and North America.

The caterpillar is green, spotted with white, and striped with dark green and white. It feeds on Beak-sedge (*Rhynchospora*) and various grasses, and overwinters at the base of the foodplant.

Identification Resembles the Small Heath (*C. pamphilus*), but on the upper side has a wider grey band along the outer edge of the wings. A rather variable species.

HAIRSTREAKS, COPPERS AND BLUES
Family Lycaenidae

A worldwide group of several thousand, mainly small species, best represented in the tropics of the Old World but with about 100 species in Europe. The wings are mostly blue, brown, orange or red above, but usually very differently coloured on the underside. Most Hairstreaks have one or more short tails to the hind wing. All three pairs of legs are fully developed. Females usually differ from the males in colour-pattern.

The chrysalis is short and stout. It may hang from its tail end, be fixed in an upright position by a girdle of silk, or lie on the ground.

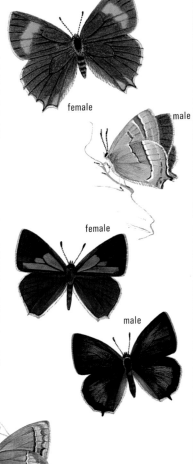

female

male

female

male

male

BROWN HAIRSTREAK
Thecla betulae

34-36 mm. This butterfly normally flies high up amongst the branches of Oak trees, but is sometimes attracted to flowers at ground level. Appears in August and September in a single flight, and is fairly common locally up to 1,500 metres in central and northern Europe (including Ireland and southern England). Overwinters in the egg stage.
The caterpillar is green, striped with yellow, and feeds chiefly on Blackthorn (*Prunus spinosa*).

PURPLE HAIRSTREAK
Quercusia quercus

24-29 mm. Emerges in a single flight between June and August, and often common in oak forests, flying high up in the trees but occasionally attracted to flowers near the ground. Found in North Africa, western Asia and much of Europe, including Britain but excluding Arctic Scandinavia. Overwinters in the egg stage.
The caterpillar is brown, marked with black and white, and looks rather like the oak buds on which it feeds.

GREEN HAIRSTREAK
Callophrys rubi

25-30 mm. A well-camouflaged butterfly when the wings are closed and the green of the underside blends with a background of green leaves. The upper side is dull brown in both sexes, but the male can be recognized by a small dark scent brand near the front edge of the front wing.

Appears between April and July in a single flight, and is generally common along overgrown hedgerows, thickets and the edges of woods from sea-level up to about 2,000 metres. Widely distributed in Europe (including Britain and the Arctic), North Africa, temperate Asia and North America.

The caterpillar is green and yellow and feeds on the buds and shoots of gorse (*Ulex*), *Vaccinium* and other shrubs and low-growing plants.

SMALL COPPER
Lycaena phlaeas

25-30 mm. A common butterfly of dry fields and heaths, often visiting flowers or chasing away other butterflies in quick darting flights. The first European emergence is in April or May, the second in July and August and there is sometimes a third flight except in the north. Found in most of Europe, up to 2,000 metres, and in North and central Africa, the Canaries, Madeira, temperate Asia (including Japan), and North America.

The caterpillar is green, spotted with white and usually also with red. It feeds on sorrel (*Rumex*) and knotgrass (*Polygonum*), and overwinters either partly or full-grown.

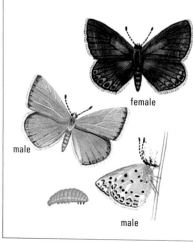

female

male

male

COMMON BLUE
Polyommatus icarus

25-33 mm. The commonest European Blue in grassy, flowery places from the Arctic to the Mediterranean; found also in North Africa, the Canary Islands, and much of temperate Asia. Appears between May and July in the north, but in two or three flights in the south between April and October.

The caterpillar is green, striped with dark green and white, and feeds on trefoils (*Lotus*) and other legumes. Autumn-generation caterpillars overwinter at the base of the foodplant in a frail, silken shelter.

HOLLY BLUE
Celastrina argiolus

20-32 mm. Widely distributed and common in gardens, heaths and along hedgerows; usually in two flights in temperate climates, the first as early as April. Often rests on Ivy and holly leaves. Found up to 1,500 metres in most of Europe (including Britain), North Africa, North and Central America and much of temperate Asia.

The caterpillar is green, marked with darker and lighter green, and feeds on the shoots, flowers and berries of holly, ivy, gorse, dogwoods and other shrubs.

CHALK-HILL BLUE
Lysandra coridon

29-36 mm. A common species of chalk and limestone grassland up to 3,000 metres, emerging during July or August. Attracted to flowers and animal droppings. Found in most of Europe but absent from much of the south-west, Ireland, Scotland and Scandinavia.

The caterpillar overwinters on the foodplant as a caterpillar inside the unbroken egg-shell. When full grown it is green, striped with yellow, and feeds at night on the leaves and flowers of Wild Liquorice (*Astragalus glycyphyllos*), and other legumes, attended by ants.

SCARCE COPPER
Heodes virgaureae

32-35 mm. Locally distributed at low elevations in the north and up to 2,000 metres in the Alps in woodland meadows and more open, grassy places, especially near water. On the wing during June, July and August in a single flight. Probably bred in Britain over 200 years ago but now extinct. Absent also in western France and Holland, but found in much of central and northern Europe, including the Arctic. Overwinters in the egg stage.

The caterpillar is green, striped with yellow, and feeds on Sheep's Sorrel (*Rumex acetosella*) and other species of *Rumex*. It is often attended by ants.

male

male

female

male

female

male

female

DUKE OF BURGUNDY FRITILLARY
Hamearis lucina Family Riodinidae

27-34 mm. Flies in woodland clearings and along the edges of woods during May and June in a single northern generation, or from May to August in the south where there are two flights. Usually rests on a leaf but is sometimes attracted to Bugle (*Ajuga reptans*) flowers. Found in Spain, Sweden, much of central Europe (not the Low Countries), and in western Asia. Prefers limestone regions in Britain and is absent from Ireland and northern Scotland.

The caterpillar is brown and feeds on Primrose (*Primula vulgaris*) and other species of *Primula*.

SKIPPERS Family Hesperiidae

The skippers are mostly small species, with a broad head and body, and most make only short, swift, darting flights. The club of the antenna is usually rather pointed and curved; all six legs are well developed. Many are sombrely coloured above, and the underside provides the best guide to identity. Females differ little from the males in colour-pattern, but the males of several species have a dark scent brand on the front wing. They rest either with the wings folded together above the back or held in a tent-like fashion.

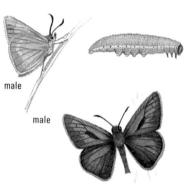

male

male

LARGE SKIPPER
Ochlodes venatus

27-35 mm. Inhabits meadows up to 1,800 metres, flying from May to August in one or more generations. Found in much of Europe, including Britain, and across Asia to Japan.

The caterpillar is mostly green, and lives in a silk tube on brome (*Bromus*) and other grasses. It overwinters at the grass base in a silk shelter.

Identification Similar to the Silver-spotted Skipper (*Hesperia comma*), but has yellow spots on the underside instead of silvery ones.

GRIZZLED SKIPPER
Pyrgus malvae

20-29 mm. Found in grassy places up to 1,700 metres, and usually fairly common. There is usually a single flight in the north during May and June, but two flights in the south from April to August. The range includes North America, western Europe (excluding northern Scotland, Ireland and northern Scandinavia).

The caterpillar is green, striped with pink and brown, and feeds on strawberry (*Fragaria*), mallow (*Malva*) and other plants.

Identification The row of white spots close to the outer margin on the upper side of the forewing separates this species from other European Skippers.

Moths

Like the butterflies, the moths belong to the order Lepidoptera and their wings are clothed with minute scales. There are over 100,000 known species, in many different families. There is no single difference between all the moths on the one hand and all the butterflies on the other, but the antennae are a good guide. Moth antennae vary a great deal but, with the exception of the burnets and a few other groups, they are not clubbed, whereas all European butterflies have clubbed antennae. Moth antennae are often feathery, especially in the males. Most species are nocturnal and generally well camouflaged during the daytime when they are at rest. The caterpillars are with or without hairs and they normally pupate either in silken cocoons or in subterranean chambers.

The measurements given in the following pages indicate wingspan.

HAWKMOTHS Family Sphingidae

These are fast-flying, stout-bodied moths with relatively narrow, pointed front wings. Some do not feed as adults, but others have enormously long tongues which they plunge deep into flowers while hovering in front of them. The family is found mainly in the tropics, but 23 species occur in Europe. Nine are resident in the British Isles and eight more occur as regular or irregular immigrants. The caterpillars are hairless, often with diagonal stripes, and most have a curved horn at the end.

PRIVET HAWKMOTH
Sphinx ligustri

100-120 mm. The largest resident British moth, this species flies June-July and regularly visits flowers at dusk. At rest, the wings are pulled tightly back along the sides of the body and the insect resembles a broken twig. Brownish front wings, pink bands on hind wings, and blackish thorax distinguish it from the Convolvulus

Hawkmoth. Most of Europe, but mainly southern in Britain.
Caterpillar: reaches 75 mm and is bright green with purple and white stripes and a black horn. It feeds on privet, ash and lilac July-September and is very well camouflaged by its stripes. It often sits with the front end raised in a sphinx-like attitude. Several other hawkmoth larvae do this, and in America the insects are known as sphinx moths.

ELEPHANT HAWKMOTH
Deilephila elpenor

70 mm. Flying in June, this moth is very fond of Honeysuckle flowers. At rest, with its wings swept back like an arrowhead – a feature of many hawk-moths – it is very hard to see on the vegetation. Most of Europe.
Caterpillar: up to 85 mm, is brown (rarely green) with 2 pairs of pink eye-spots just behind the thorax. When disturbed, the head and thorax are pulled into the abdomen, causing the eye-spots to swell. The caterpillar then sways to and fro and frightens birds away. It feeds on willowherbs and bedstraws July-August.

HUMMINGBIRD HAWKMOTH
Macroglossum stellatarum

50 mm. This day-flying moth is most often seen as a brown blur as it hovers to feed at flowers. It flies all year in southern Europe, where it has three or four generations, although the adults hibernate in the coldest months. Large numbers fly north in spring and breed all over Europe in summer.
Caterpillar: up to 60 mm long, is green or brown with white spots and a bluish horn. It feeds on bedstraws.

SWIFT MOTHS Family Hepialidae

The swifts are rather primitive, fast-flying moths with all four wings of similar shape. The antennae are very short and the adults do not feed. The wings are folded along the sides of the body at rest. The caterpillars, usually white with brown heads, all feed on roots from summer to late spring.

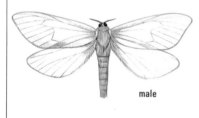

male

GHOST MOTH
Hepialus humuli

46 mm. The male, silvery-white above and dull brown below, drifts ghost-like over grassy places at dusk June-July. The female is brownish-yellow. North-ern and central Europe.

male

COMMON SWIFT
Hepialus lupulinus

25-40 mm. Female is larger than male and often has virtually no wing mark-ings. It flies May-July in most of Europe.

CLEARWING MOTHS Family Sesiidae

The clearwings are day-flying moths which, because the wings are largely devoid of scales, bear striking resemblances to various bees and wasps, especially when in flight. They like to sunbathe on leaves. The caterpillars are pale and maggot-like and most live inside the stems or roots of trees and shrubs, usually for two years. A few tunnel in the roots of herbaceous plants.

HORNET CLEARWING
Sesia apiformis

30-40 mm. One of the largest of the clearwings, this species resembles a wasp, except that it lacks the narrow waist. It flies May-July in most parts of Europe.
Caterpillar: about 25 mm long, tunnels in the roots and lower parts of the trunks of poplars.

BURNETS and FORESTERS Family Zygaenidae

These are mostly brightly coloured, day-flying moths with rather sluggish flight. Many species live in Europe, especially in the south. The burnets have clubbed antennae, but the tip thickens more gradually than in the butterflies. The foresters have toothed antennae.

SIX-SPOT BURNET
Zygaena filipendulae

30 mm. The deep metallic green (often appearing black) and red colours are typical of the burnets and advertise their poisonous nature, although the red is replaced by yellow in some individuals. The two outer spots of each front wing may join up. It flies May-August in flowery grasslands.
Caterpillar: up to 25 mm long, is cream with black spots. It feeds on trefoils and related plants in autumn and spring. Like most burnets, it pupates in a papery cocoon.

COMMON FORESTER
Adscita statices

20 mm. Bluish or bronzy green front wings. It flies in damp, flowery meadows May-July. Most of Europe.
Caterpillar: about 25 mm long, is yellowish with darker spots. It feeds on sorrel in autumn and spring.

TIGER MOTHS Family Arctiidae

Most of these moths are brightly coloured and very hairy, warning birds that they are distasteful. The adults often do not feed. The caterpillars are also very hairy in most species and pupate in cocoons made largely from the hairs.

GARDEN TIGER
Arctia caja

50-80 mm. Extremely variable in size and also in the wing pattern, with the dark markings sometimes linking up and sometimes almost absent. The hind wing may be yellow instead of orange. It flies July-August and is common all over Europe.
Caterpillar: reaches 60 mm in length and is commonly known as a 'woolly bear' because of its dense fur coat made up of long black hairs with white tips, and shorter brown hairs. It feeds on a wide variety of low-growing plants, beginning in late summer but hibernating when small and feeding up in the spring.

CINNABAR
Tyria jacobaeae

35-45 mm. The red markings vary a little in size and sometimes join up. Very rarely they are replaced by yellow. The moth flies May-July in grassy places. Although nocturnal, it is easily disturbed by day and it flies weakly away to find another resting place. It occurs in most parts of Europe, but is mainly coastal in the north — often on sand dunes.
Caterpillar: up to 25 mm long, is easily identified by its black and yellow banding. It feeds on ragwort July-August, freely exposed but well protected by its efficient warning coloration. It has been used in some places in attempts to control ragwort in grazing land.

NOCTUID MOTHS Family Noctuidae

Sometimes known as owlet moths, or simply noctuids, the members of this large family are all nocturnal. They have fairly stout bodies and relatively sombre front wings which provide good camouflage when at rest by day. Most also have dull hind wings. The caterpillars are mostly without conspicuous hairs and nearly all pupate in the soil. The pupae are normally shiny and bullet-shaped.

LARGE YELLOW UNDERWING
Noctua pronuba

50-60 mm. One of several species with yellow hind wings, this very common moth flies June-September. Front wings range from pale greyish-brown (female only) to deep chestnut or almost black (male only). At rest, they lie flat over the body. When disturbed, the moth flies rapidly away and the flashing yellow of hind wings confuses a pursuing bird: the moth drops quickly to the ground and covers hind wings, leaving the bird searching unsuccessfully for something yellow. All Europe.
Caterpillar: 50 mm long and tapering towards the front, is usually brown with black dashes at the sides. It feeds July-April on a wide variety of herbaceous plants at about ground level and often under the ground.

RED UNDERWING
Catocala nupta

70-90 mm. One of several very similar species, it flies July-October in most parts of Europe. When disturbed, it behaves like the yellow underwings.
Caterpillar: reaches 70 mm and feeds on poplar and willow April-July. Its greyish-brown body blends perfectly with the twigs on which it lies at rest.

HERALD MOTH
Scoliopteryx libatrix

40-50 mm. The attractive front wings conceal plain grey-brown hind wings. It flies August-October and then hibernates in hollow trees and outhouses before reappearing to fly again March-June. Most of Europe.
Caterpillar: 45 mm long, is slender and bright green. It feeds on willows and poplars June-August.

SILVER Y
Autographa gamma

30-45 mm. Named for the silvery mark in middle of front wing, this common moth flies by day and night. Resident in southern Europe, it spreads north to nearly all parts in summer and breeds there.
Caterpillar: up to 40 mm, is green with black dots and faint white lines. It has only 2 pairs of prolegs in front of the claspers. It feeds in summer on various low-growing plants.

FAMILY SATURNIIDAE

This family contains some of the world's largest moths, including the giant silkmoths. Adults do not feed. Most are tropical; 4 species live in Europe, including the Giant Peacock Moth – Europe's largest moth, spanning about 15 cm. Only the Emperor moth lives in Britain.

female

EMPEROR MOTH
Pavonia pavonia

50–80 mm. Male much brighter than female shown here, with orange hind wings. On the wing April–May in most parts of Europe, inhabiting heathland, scrub and hedgerow. Male flies by day, picking up female's scent with his large antennae. She flies by night.
Caterpillar: orange and black when young, becoming green with black rings. It reaches 70 mm and feeds May–July on bramble, blackthorn, heather and many other plants. It pupates in a tough silken cocoon.

EGGAR MOTHS Family Lasiocampidae

The moths in this family are mostly rather stout and furry. Females are larger than males. Antennae are feathery in both sexes, but especially so in the males. Adults do not feed. The caterpillars are generally hairy and often brightly coloured.

OAK EGGAR
Lasiocampa quercus

60–90 mm. The female, illustrated below, flies by night to scatter her eggs. The male is much darker, with a yellowish band across the outer part of the wings, and he flies by day in search of resting females for mating. The moths fly May–August on heathlands and lightly-wooded places. Northern specimens may be darker.
Caterpillar: up to 90 mm, is brown and very furry and feeds on heather, bramble and many other plants, including hawthorn. It begins to feed in summer, but then hibernates and completes its growth in spring. It pupates in a silken cocoon, usually among dead leaves on the ground.

female

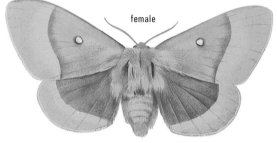

TUSSOCK MOTHS Family Lymantriidae

A family of fairly stout and hairy moths, many of them known as tussocks. Female is usually larger than male and often has a dense tuft of hair at tip of abdomen. Antennae are strongly feathered in male. Adults do not feed.

Caterpillars are very hairy, often with dense tufts or tussocks on various parts of the body. Hairs often cause irritation if handled. Pupation occurs in a silken cocoon incorporating many of the larval hairs.

VAPOURER
Orgyia antiqua

35–40 mm (male only). Female wingless. Adult June–October, with 2–3 broods in southern regions, the male flies by day and seeks out females, which never venture further than the surface of their cocoons. Eggs are laid on the cocoon.
Caterpillar: reaches 40 mm. It feeds on a wide range of deciduous trees and shrubs April–September.

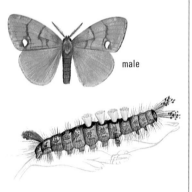

male

GEOMETER MOTHS Family Geometridae

Collectively known as geometers, the moths in this very large family are mostly rather flimsy and slender-bodied. The majority rest with wings held flat, sometimes covering the abdomen and sometimes held well out to the sides. A few species rest with wings held vertically over the body like butterflies. The larvae, often known as loopers or inchworms, have only 2 pairs of

prolegs at the hind end, including the claspers. They move by alternately stretching the front end forward and then bringing the hind end up to it, throwing the body into a high loop in the process. This habit is also responsible for the name geometer, which means 'ground measurer'. Many species pupate in cocoons in the vegetation, but others pupate under the ground.

MAGPIE MOTH
Abraxas grossulariata

35–40 mm. Pattern variable, but easily recognized; bold colours warn of its unpleasant taste. Very common in gardens and hedgerows June–August. Most parts of Europe.
Caterpillar: reaches 40 mm and has same colours as adult. Feeds on various shrubs, especially blackthorn and gooseberry, August–June. Pupates in a flimsy cocoon.

True Flies

The true flies belong to the order Diptera and have only one pair of functional wings. The hind wings are reduced to tiny pin-like bodies called halteres, which help to maintain balance in flight. A few parasitic species, such as the sheep ked, are completely wing-less. All flies are liquid-feeders, either mopping up free fluids, such as nectar, or piercing other animals to suck blood. The larvae are all legless, but otherwise are extremely varied. Many of them live in water.

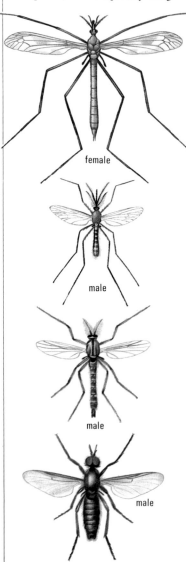

female

male

male

male

CRANE-FLY
Tipula maxima Family Tipulidae

50-60 mm. Largest of many quite similar species which are also known as daddy-long-legs. Male abdomen not pointed. Summer, especially in woods. The larva lives in waterlogged soil. The larvae of some other species are the notorious leatherjackets which damage plant roots.

MOSQUITO
Culex pipiens Family Culicidae

12 mm. One of the commonest mosquitoes, especially in buildings. As in all mosquitoes, only male has feathery antennae and only female sucks blood (this species rarely attacks humans): male prefers nectar. One of many species holding abdomen parallel to surface on which they are resting. Larva lives in stagnant water. All year.

MIDGE
Chironomus annularis
Family Chironomidae

15 mm. Mosquito-like, but with no piercing beak: probably does not feed as adult. Males often dance in large swarms. Rests with wings roof-like over body, but wings much shorter than abdomen. Only male has feathery antennae. Larva is a 'blood-worm' living in stagnant water. All year.

ST MARK'S FLY
Bibio marci Family Bibionidae

20 mm. Common in gardens and fields March-May. Flies lethargically, males often in swarms, and visits flowers. Female eyes much smaller than those of male. Larvae feed on roots and decaying matter in soil.

ROBBER-FLY
Asilus crabroniformis Family Asilidae

35-45 mm. A fast-flying insect, catching other insects in mid-air and sucking them dry. Late summer. Larvae live in cow dung.

HORSE-FLY
Tabanus sudeticus Family Tabanidae

30-50 mm. Female larger than male and usually seen around horses and other livestock from which she sucks blood. Male frequents flowers. Mainly on pastureland, especially near water, June-August. The larvae feed on other animals in damp soil.

HORSE-FLY
Chrysops relictus

15-20 mm. One of several similar flies with beautiful iridescent eyes. Females often attack people. June-August, usually near water and often in wooded country.

BEE-FLY
Bombylius major Family Bombyliidae

25 mm. A very bee-like fly commonly seen hovering over low-growing flowers in spring. The larva lives as a parasite in nests of solitary bees.

HOVER-FLY
Syrphus ribesii Family Syrphidae

20-25 mm. As in all hover-flies, some veins turn and run parallel to hind edge of wing, forming a false margin. Abundant on hogweed and other umbels in summer, protected by wasp-like coloration. Maggot-like larva eats aphids.

larva

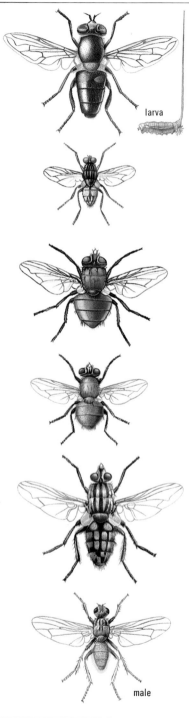

larva

DRONE-FLY
Eristalis tenax Family Syrphidae

20-30 mm. Named for its bee-like appearance, this hover-fly is common on spring flowers. A superb hoverer. The larva is the rat-tailed maggot, living in muddy ditches and breathing with a telescopic 'snorkel'.

HOUSE-FLY
Musca domestica Family Muscidae

15 mm. Common in houses for much of the year, but not the commonest fly indoors. Abundant in stables. Mops up all kinds of liquid food. Larva is a white maggot living in decaying matter.

BLUEBOTTLE
Calliphora vomitoria
Family Calliphoridae

20-25 mm. Metallic blue. Buzzes noisily indoors. Maggot feeds on dead flesh. Most of the year.

GREENBOTTLE
Lucilia caesar

20 mm. One of several similar flies. Less common indoors than bluebottle. Maggot feeds on living and dead flesh.

FLESH-FLY
Sarcophaga carnaria

25 mm. Common near buildings, but rarely indoors. Adults visit flowers and carrion. Female gives birth to young maggots on carrion. Most of the year.

DUNG-FLY
Scathophaga stercoraria
Family Scathophagidae

20 mm. Abundant on cow-pats and other dung from early spring onwards. Female is greyer and less furry. Larvae feed in dung: adults prey on smaller flies.

male

Bees, Wasps, Ants and their Relatives

These insects all belong to the order Hymenoptera, an extremely variable group with well over 100,000 species. They have little in common except that most have two pairs of membranous wings, often with few veins and several large cells. The hind wings are often quite small and are linked to the front wings by a row of tiny hooks. All have biting jaws, although the bees have suctorial mouthparts as well for nectar-feeding.

There are two distinct sub-orders – the Symphyta and the Apocrita. The Symphyta contains the sawflies, in which the thorax and abdomen are broadly joined without any 'waist'. These insects get their name because most of the females have tiny saw-like ovipositors (egg-layers) with which they cut slits in plants before laying their eggs there. Most larvae feed on leaves and look like moth caterpillars except that they have more stumpy legs on the abdomen. Some live inside plants and have no abdominal legs. Adult sawflies feed mainly on pollen.

The Apocrita contains all the other hymenopterans, all with the typical 'wasp waist'. The ichneumons and many others are parasites, the females using needle-like ovipositors to lay eggs inside the young stages of other insects. The parasitic grubs gradually destroy their hosts, but not until the parasites themselves are fully grown and ready to pupate. Gall wasps lay their eggs in plants and the presence of the developing larvae causes the plant tissues to swell and form galls,

with the grubs feeding on the nutritious tissues inside them.

Social behaviour is well developed in some bees and wasps and in all the ants. The insects live in large colonies which are always founded by females, or queens. All the other members of a colony are the queen's children. Most of them are sterile females called workers, and these do all the building and food-gathering chores as well as tending their younger sisters. The females of the bees and wasps and many of the ants have powerful stings, which are modified ovipositors. Many wasps use their stings to paralyze prey, but otherwise the stings are used for defence. Having laid the foundations of their nests, the queens do nothing but lay eggs. The queen honey bee does not even do any building: she always has a band of workers to help her right from birth. Males occur only at certain times of year among the social insects and do nothing but mate with the new queens.

Most bees and wasps are actually solitary insects, each female excavating or constructing a small nest – often in the ground – and laying a few eggs in it. The nests are always stocked with food – pollen and nectar for the bees, and paralyzed insects or spiders for the wasps (although adult wasps feed mainly on fruit and nectar). Because the larvae are always surrounded by food and do not need to move, they are all legless. This is true of the social and parasitic hymenopterans as well.

BEES Family Apidae
SOLITARY BEES

female

male

TAWNY MINING BEE
Andrena fulva

20–25 mm. One of several species with flattened abdomens which dig nest burrows in lawns and similar places. Female is bright orange-brown: male is much duller. Very common in spring, especially on blackthorn blossom and also on garden currants and gooseberries, which it pollinates very efficiently. It has a short tongue and cannot reach the nectar in deep-throated flowers. After stocking the nest and laying her eggs, the female seals it up and abandons it, like most other solitary bees and wasps.

LEAF-CUTTER BEE
Megachile centuncularis

15–20 mm. Resembles a small honey bee, but venation is different and the abdomen is fringed with golden hairs, especially on the lower surface. The female cuts neat semi-circular pieces from leaves, especially rose leaves, and uses them to construct neat sausage-shaped cells in a hollow stem or some other suitable crevice. The cells are then stocked with food and an egg is laid in each. May–August in northern and central Europe.

LONG-HORNED BEE
Eucera longicornis

20–25 mm. Named for the great length of the male's antennae. Female antennae are of normal length and she has pale, wedge-shaped marks on the sides of her abdomen. Female makes a nest in the ground. April–July.

CARPENTER BEE
Xylocopa violacea

40–50 mm. This striking, fast-flying bee appears in late summer, feeding on a wide variety of flowers to stock up with nectar before going into hibernation. It reappears in spring and the female excavates a nest burrow in a dead tree or other timber. Mainly southern Europe, but occasionally further north.

SOCIAL BEES

These insects include the honey bee and the bumblebees, all of which make their nests with wax from their own bodies. Honey bee colonies are perennial, but bumblebee colonies last for just one season: the young mated queens hibernate and begin new colonies in the spring. The social bees all have long tongues and can obtain nectar from deep-throated flowers. They carry pollen on their hind legs, held by stiff hairs which form the pollen baskets.

HONEY BEE
Apis mellifera

20–25 mm (worker). Male (drone) and queen are larger, but queen is not normally seen outside the hive. There are many races, some with orange patches on the front of the abdomen. Originally a tropical insect, it is now almost world-wide. Most honey bees live in artificial hives, but wild colonies live in hollow trees and similar places. The nest consists of vertical sheets of 6-sided cells. The bees survive the winter on honey stored up during the previous summer.

worker

WHITE-TAILED BUMBLEBEE
Bombus lucorum

20–40 mm. One of several similar bees, but the bright yellow bands distinguish it. Queens spend a lot of time at flowers in spring, being especially fond of sallow blossom. They usually nest just under the ground, often in old mouse holes. Small workers are soon reared and they take over the building and foraging work. Later workers are larger, and those reared in late summer are almost as large as the queen. New queens and males are reared in late summer.

queen

RED-TAILED BUMBLEBEE
Bombus lapidarius

20–40 mm. Male, seen only in late summer, has a yellow collar just behind the head. Life cycle is just like that of the previous species. It often nests under stones.

queen

queen

CARDER BEE
Bombus pascuorum

20-32 mm. A very common bumble bee, particularly fond of white dead-nettle flowers. Its life cycle is like that of the previous species, but the nest is usually built in rough grass.

SOCIAL WASPS Family Vespidae

These insects all form annual colonies like those of the bumble bees (page 259), but they build their nests with paper, which they make by chewing wood. The larvae are fed insects and other animal matter. Queen usually much larger than workers.

COMMON WASP
Vespula vulgaris

25-45 mm. One of several very similar black and yellow species. Usually with an anchor-shaped mark on face. Nests under the ground or in roof cavities, building a football-sized nest of yellowish paper: cells are enclosed by delicate, overlapping 'shells'. Spring to autumn. Up to 6,000 wasps in a colony.

HORNET
Vespa crabro

30-50 mm. The largest European wasp. Nests in hollow trees, often reducing entrance holes with its brittle yellow paper. No more than a few hundred colony members. April-October.

PAPER WASP
Polistes dominulus

20-25 mm. Lives in small colonies of just a few dozen insects. Nest is a small umbrella with a few dozen cells. Queens no larger than workers. Spring to autumn in southern and central Europe: not in Britain.

SOLITARY WASPS

ECTEMNIUS CEPHALOTES
Family Sphecidae

15-30 mm. One of several rather similar digger wasps. Makes nest in rotten tree stumps and stocks it with paralyzed flies. June-September.

BEMBEX ROSTRATA

25-35 mm. Another digger wasp, nesting in sandy soil and stocking up with flies. June-August, from southern Scandinavia southwards: not in Britain.

AMMOPHILA SABULOSA

25 mm. Often called a sand wasp, it nests in sandy soil and stocks the nest with caterpillars. June-September.

BEE-KILLER WASP
Philanthus triangulum

16-35 mm. Female much larger than male. Catches bees on flowers, paralyzes them and puts them in nest – usually in sandy ground. July-September. Southern and central Europe: rare in Britain.

ANOPLIUS VIATICUS
Family Pompilidae

20-30 mm. Female larger than male. Long legs are a feature of this wasp and its relatives, all of whom capture spiders to stock their subterranean burrows. All summer.

SPINY MASON WASP
Odynerus spinipes Family Eumenidae

15-20 mm. Nests in vertical sandy banks and also in the mortar of old walls. Stocks nest with small caterpillars. May-August.

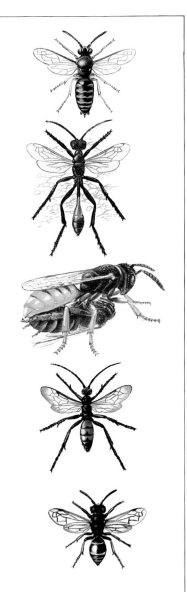

ANTS Family Formicidae

Social insects in which the workers are usually much smaller than queens and always wingless. Queens and males are winged for mating flight, but queens lose wings before starting nest. The nests have no elaborate cells of wax or paper. Insects active in all but coldest months.

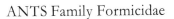

WOOD ANT
Formica rufa

5-11 mm long. Nests in large mounds in woods, covering mounds with twigs and leaves. Omnivorous.

BLACK ANT
Lasius niger

3-5 mm long. Nests under stones and paths, and even under houses. Very common. Eats other insects and is very fond of honeydew from aphids.

RED ANT
Myrmica ruginodis

5-10 mm. 'Waist' of 2 distinct segments. Has a sting. Very common; nests in soil and in tree stumps. Mainly carnivorous, but enjoys honeydew.

SAWFLIES

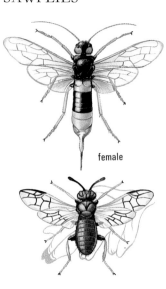

female

HORNTAIL
Urocerus gigas Family Siricidae

40-60 mm. Female has a drill-like ovipositor with which she lays eggs in pine trunks. Summer.

HAWTHORN SAWFLY
Trichiosoma tibiale Family Cimbicidae

30-35 mm. Fast-flying: May-June. Larva is pale green with a brown head and eats hawthorn leaves in summer.

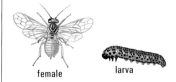

female   larva

GOOSEBERRY SAWFLY
Nematus ribesii Family Tenthredinidae

10-15 mm. Male is smaller than female and has much black on abdomen. All summer on gooseberries and currants. Larvae live in groups and strip leaves.

PARASITIC HYMENOPTERA

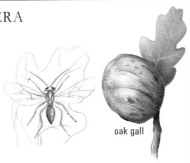

oak gall

GALL WASP
Biorhiza pallida Family Cynipidae

10 mm. Develops inside oak apples on oak twigs. June-July.

APANTELES GLOMERATUS
Family Braconidae

4 mm. Grows up in large white butterfly larvae and pupates in silken cocoons around empty skin. Spring and summer.

ICHNEUMON FLY
Ophion luteus Family Ichneumonidae

30 mm. One of several species developing in moth caterpillars. Summer.

RUBY-TAILED WASP
Chrysis ignita Family Chrysididae

14 mm. Found on walls and tree trunks spring and summer. A parasite of various solitary bee and wasp larvae.

SCOLIA HIRTA
Family Scoliidae

35 mm. Common on flowers in sandy places June-September. Larva parasitizes various beetles. Southern and central Europe: not in Britain.

Beetles

The beetles form the order Coleoptera which, with about 250,000 known species, is the largest of all the insect groups. They exhibit a tremendous range of size, shape and habits. The front wings, known as elytra, are tough and horny and they conceal the membranous hind wings.

They also conceal the whole abdomen as a rule, although some beetles, such as the rove beetles, have short elytra. Most beetles can fly, but some have no hind wings and in some ground-living beetles the elytra are fused together for extra protection. Water beetles carry their air supply under the elytra, renewing it from time to time at the surface. All beetles have biting mouthparts, and between them they feed on just about every-thing. The larvae are also extremely varied, but they all have powerful jaws and often feed on the same kinds of foods as the adults.

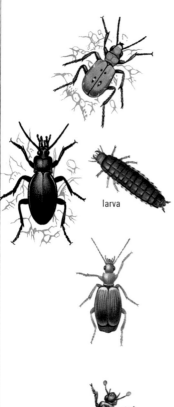

larva

GREEN TIGER BEETLE
Cicindela campestris Family Cicindelidae

10–15 mm. A fast-flying and fast-running predator of ants and other insects. Active only in sunshine, it lives mainly on heathland. Spring and summer. The larva lives in a burrow and darts out to catch prey in its large jaws.

VIOLET GROUND BEETLE
Carabus violaceus Family Carabidae

20–30 mm. A flightless, nocturnal predator of slugs and other small invertebrates. Often found under logs and stones by day. The violet sheen is especially marked on edges of thorax and elytra. All year. The larva is also an active hunter.

BOMBARDIER BEETLE
Brachinus crepitans

7–10 mm. A carnivorous beetle named because, when alarmed, it fires a puff of volatile, corrosive liquid from its anus, accompanied by a slight bang. Ground-living on well-drained soils: mainly on chalk in Britain. Most common in early summer.

BURYING BEETLE
Nicrophorus vespillo Family Silphidae

15–20 mm. One of several similarly-coloured species, but distinguished by two uninterrupted orange bands and the strongly curved hind legs. Also known as sexton beetles, these insects bury the corpses of small birds and mammals by digging soil from under them. The beetles usually work in pairs and eggs are laid on the buried corpse. The grubs feed on the decaying meat and also on fly maggots and other scavengers. Adults are active mainly in the summer and often fly to lights at night.

BURYING BEETLE
Nicrophorus humator

18–30 mm. Antennal club is reddish-yellow. The beetle's habits are just like those of *N. vespillo*.

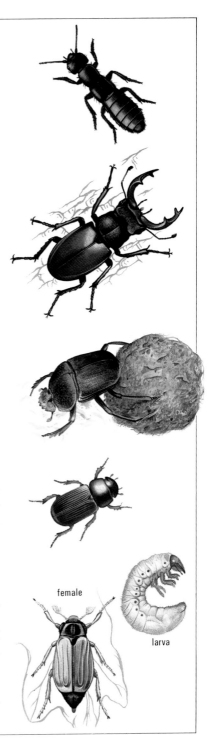

DEVIL'S COACH-HORSE
Staphylinus olens Family Staphylinidae

20–30 mm. This ground-living predator is one of the rove beetles, with very short elytra. When disturbed, it opens its huge jaws and bends the abdomen forward over the rest of the body in a threatening attitude – leading to its alternative name of cocktail. Commonly found under stones and in compost heaps, it comes out to hunt at night.

STAG BEETLE
Lucanus cervus Family Lucanidae

Male 50–70 mm. Female lacks the 'antlers', which are really enlarged jaws, and is 20–40 mm long. Males use antlers to fight over females, just like male deer. Flies well on summer evenings. Found mainly in and around old woodland and parks with old trees. Larva is like the cockchafer, but feeds for several years in old tree trunks and decaying stumps. Southern and central Europe.

SCARAB BEETLE
Scarabaeus sacer Family Scarabaeidae

25 mm. One of a number of dung beetles famed for their habit of rolling balls of dung about until they find a suitable spot in which to bury them. Eggs are then laid in the dung and the larvae feed on it. Adults also eat dung and sometimes fight over possession of it. All year in Mediterranean region.

APHODIUS RUFIPES

10–12 mm. A very common dung beetle which tunnels in cow-pats and other dung in both adult and larval stages. All legs are quite broad for tunnelling and, as in all other dung beetles and chafers, the antennal club is composed of a number of very thin leaf-like flaps.

COCKCHAFER
Melolontha melolontha

20–25 mm. Female has much smaller flaps to antennal club. Also known as the May-bug. It usually flies around trees and feeds on the leaves, often causing great damage when present in numbers. Larvae feed on roots and do much damage to cereals and other crops.

female

larva

male

CLICK BEETLE
Corymbites cupreus Family Elateridae

11-16 mm. Female antennae are less feathery than those of male seen here. Lives in grassland, especially in upland regions, in summer. Northern and central Europe. It is one of numerous slender beetles known as click beetles because, when turned on their backs, they leap into the air and right themselves with a loud click.

larva

CLICK BEETLE
Athous haemorrhoidalis

10-13 mm. One of the commonest click beetles, found almost everywhere in spring and early summer. Especially common on hedgerow flowers. The larva is one of the notorious wireworms which live in the soil and feed on plant roots. This species prefers pasture to arable land, but does a lot of damage to potatoes and cereal roots. It is also fond of dock roots.

SOLDIER BEETLE
Rhagonycha fulva Family Cantharidae

10-15 mm. Elytra rather soft. Abundant everywhere on flower-heads of hogweed and other umbellifers where it catches other small insects throughout the summer. The beetles are called bloodsuckers in many country areas because of their red colour, but they are harmless. There are several similar species, some known as sailor beetles.

male

GREAT DIVING BEETLE
Dytiscus marginalis Family Dytiscidae

30 mm. Female has ridged elytra and no swelling on front leg. A fierce predator in ponds and streams. Flies well at night. Larva has huge curved jaws for piercing prey. All year.

GLOW-WORM
Lampyris noctiluca Family Lampyridae

Only the male (10-13 mm long) looks like a beetle, with soft brown elytra that gape slightly at the hind end. A broad shield covers the head and thorax. Female (10-18 mm) is wingless and looks more like a flat brown woodlouse except that she has only three pairs of legs. Pale yellow patches on the underside of her abdomen give out a strong greenish light as she sits in the grass at night (above). The light attracts the flying males, and if you pick up a glowing female in the dark you will often find a male with her. The larva is very like the adult female and feeds on small snails, often going right inside their shells to devour them. Adults rarely feed. Mainly in chalk and limestone areas, especially in more more northerly parts, and absent from northern Britain. Appears to be getting rarer. May-August.

The related Firefly, *Luciola lusitanica*, lives in parts of southern Europe. The males flash their lights as they fly and are answered by flashes from the females on the ground.

CARDINAL BEETLE
Pyrochroa coccinea Family Pyrochroidae

13-18 mm. A flattened, predatory beetle commonly seen on flowers May-July. The larvae, very flat and shiny brown, feed on small animals under loose bark. Northern and central Europe.

7-SPOT LADYBIRD
Coccinella 7-punctata
Family Coccinellidae

5–8 mm. Famed for its aphid-eating habits in both larval and adult stages this is one of the commonest ladybirds. found on a wide variety of plants for much of the year. It goes into hibernation in autumn, often in huge colonies, in attics and outhouses. The larva is steely blue with a few yellow spots. There are several similar species, varying in spot pattern.

ROSALIA ALPINA
Family Cerambycidae

15-38 mm. A beautiful longhorn from the mountain beechwoods of central Europe. Flies in summer. Rare.

male

female

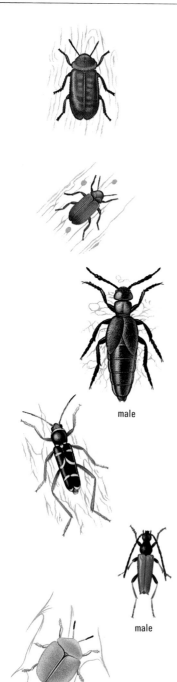

DEATH-WATCH BEETLE
Xestobium rufovillosum
Family Anobiidae

5-7 mm. Head almost covered by thoracic shield (pronotum). Larvae tunnel in dead trees in the wild and are very serious pests of timbers in old buildings, especially oak. Young adults knock their heads against the timber to attract mates and the loud ticking sound was once thought to herald a death in the house. April-June.

FURNITURE BEETLE
Anobium punctatum

3-5 mm. Head almost covered by pronotum. Larvae (woodworm) bore in dead trees and also in furniture and other household timbers. Small holes show where adults have emerged. May-July.

OIL BEETLE
Meloe proscarabaeus Family Meloidae

13-32 mm. Female larger than male but with even shorter elytra and less of a bulge in antennae. Flightless. Discharges an oily fluid when alarmed. Larvae parasitize various bees in their nests. March-June; mainly southern.

male

WASP BEETLE
Clytus arietis Family Cerambycidae

9-18 mm. One of the longhorn beetles. Flies well in sunshine May-July, often visiting flowers for pollen and nectar. Harmless, but protected by wasp-like colours and movements. Larva lives in dead wood.

LEPTURA RUBRA

10-20 mm. Another longhorn beetle. Female larger than male, with redder elytra and reddish-brown thorax. Larvae live in fallen conifers. Summer.

male

TORTOISE BEETLE
Cassida viridis Family Chrysomelidae

7-10 mm. One of several similar leaf beetles. Very hard to see at rest on leaves. Summer.

COLORADO BEETLE
Leptinotarsa decemlineata

6-12 mm. 5 black stripes on each elytron. Native to North America, this leaf beetle is now a serious potato pest in many parts of Europe. Adult and fleshy pink larva both eat potato leaves (and also related plants). All year, but hibernates in winter. Not in Britain: report it at once if you do find one.

BLOODY-NOSED BEETLE
Timarcha tenebricosa

11-18 mm. This large flightless leaf beetle roams in grassy places in spring, eating bedstraws and other low-growing plants. When alarmed, it exudes bright red blood from its mouth. The blood has a burning taste and birds soon learn to leave the beetle alone. Southern and central Europe.

CHRYSOMELA POPULI

10-12 mm. May-August on sallow and related trees. Adults and larvae all nibble the leaves.

NUT WEEVIL
Curculio nucum Family Curculionidae

6-9 mm. Snout is longer than in most weevils, especially in female, who uses it to drill into young hazel nuts where she lays her eggs. Larvae feed in the developing kernels. Adult visits various flowers in spring.

PHYLLOBIUS POMACEUS

7-9 mm. A very common weevil, showing the typical snout or rostrum of the group. Clothed with metallic green or golden scales, but these easily rub off and black elytra commonly show through. Abundant on nettles and many other plants in spring and summer. There are many similar species.

ELM BARK BEETLE
Scolytus scolytus Family Scolytidae

3-6 mm. The infamous carrier of the Dutch elm disease fungus which has killed millions of elm trees. The larvae live under the bark, making the familiar galleries as they chew through the nutritious tissues. Adults emerge through small holes May-July.

Mayflies

The mayflies (order Ephemeroptera) fly weakly on flimsy wings: hind wings small and sometimes absent. 2 or 3 tails. Antennae very short. Adults short-lived and do not feed: always near water in which young grow up. There is no pupal stage.

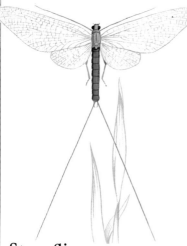

ISONYCHIA IGNOTA
Family Isonychidae

30 mm. Female often with large egg mass protruding from her body, ready to be dropped into the water. Lakes and rivers in southern and central Europe: not in Britain. Summer.

grow up in water – usually in fairly fast streams, but some species in still water. Adults feed little: many nibble algae and pollen. They rest with wings flat over body or wrapped tightly round it. There are 2 tails, sometimes very short.

Stoneflies

The stoneflies (order Plecoptera) are weak-flying insects which

PERLODES MICROCEPHALA
Family Perlodidae

30–40 mm (female). Male has short wings. Stony streams. March–July.

Earwigs

Easily recognized by the pincers at the hind end, which are quite strongly curved in males and straighter and thinner in females. Front wings short and horny: hind wings extremely thin and elaborately folded under front wings, protruding as little triangular flaps. Hind wings often lacking, however, and many species lack front wings as well. Mainly nocturnal, earwigs eat both plant and animal matter. They hide by day under stones and loose bark. Female looks after eggs and young. The earwigs belong to the order Dermaptera.

COMMON EARWIG
Forficula auricularia Family Forficulidae

9–17 mm. Male sometimes has much longer pincers. All year in many habitats. The only earwig commonly seen in Britain.

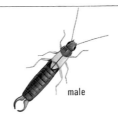

male

Cockroaches and Mantids

These insects (order Dictyoptera) have long, spiky legs and the front wings (when present) are leathery. Cockroaches are nocturnal scavengers, while mantids are fierce predators, catching other insects in their strongly-spined front legs. Mantids lay their eggs in frothy masses which become tough and horny as they dry. Cockroach eggs are laid in horny 'purses'. There is no pupal stage.

GERMAN COCKROACH
Blattella germanica Family Blattellidae

9–14 mm. A native of North Africa, now a widely distributed pest in warehouses, bakeries and other buildings; also on rubbish dumps. All year.

PRAYING MANTIS
Mantis religiosa Family Mantidae

40–80 mm (female usually longer than male and stouter). Stalks prey or lies in wait in low vegetation. Flies well in warm weather. Southern and central Europe: not in Britain.

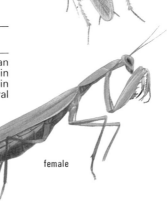

female

Thrips

These minute black, brown or yellow insects (order Thysanoptera) have four feathery wings. They suck juices from a wide variety of plants, including fungal threads. Many are found in flowers, and in thundery weather they often take to the air in millions. Many hibernate as adults in our houses. There is no pupal stage.

ONION THRIPS
Thrips tabaci Family Thripidae

1-2 mm. Yellow or brown. Attacks leaves and flowers of many plants, including various crops, and often causes stunting. All year.

Booklice and Barklice

The booklice and barklice (order Psocoptera) are very small, winged or wingless, with relatively large eyes and long antennae. Many live on tree trunks, chewing algae and pollen grains: others live in debris and some are household pests. There is no pupal stage.

COMMON BOOKLOUSE
Liposcelis terricolis Family Liposcelidae

1-2 mm. One of several very similar wingless species found in buildings, where they chew all kinds of starchy materials, including the glue of book-bindings and wallpaper. Can be a pest in stamp collections. All year.

Scorpion Flies

Named because the males of most species have a scorpion-like tail although the insects are quite harmless. Jaws at the tip of a stout beak. Omnivorous scavengers. Larvae are caterpillar-like and live in damp soil. The scorpion flies belong to the order Mecoptera.

PANORPA COMMUNIS
Family Panorpidae

30 mm. May-August in hedgerows and gardens and other shady places: especially fond of nettle beds. One of several very similar species.

Lacewings and their relatives

A variable order of carnivorous insects (Neuroptera), mostly with densely netted wings held roof-wise over the body at rest. They undergo a complete metamorphosis, the young stages being bristly, shuttle-shaped larvae.

ALDER FLY
Sialis lutaria Family Sialidae

30 mm. Weak-flying and rarely far from the still or slow-moving water in which larva lives. Rests on stones and plants: rarely feeds. May-July.

SNAKE FLY
Raphidia notata Family Raphidiidae

25 mm. Mainly on trees and shrubs, feeding on aphids. Rests with long, snake-like neck raised. Larva eats insects under bark and in dead wood. One of several similar species. May-August in woodland.

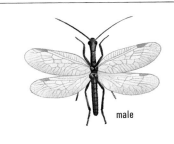

male

GREEN LACEWING
Chrysopa septempunctata
Family Chrysopidae

30-40 mm. One of several similar species. Adult and larva eat aphids. Nocturnal. Woods, hedges and gardens. May-August. Not in north.

LIBELLOIDES COCCAJUS
Family Ascalaphidae

50 mm. Fast-flying, catching other small insects in mid-air. May-August in grassy places, mainly in hills. Southern and central Europe: not in Britain.

PALPARES LIBELLULOIDES
Family Myrmeleonidae

100 mm. Slow-flying, catching other insects in flight or on vegetation. It is one of the antlions, some of whose larvae dig pits to trap ants. May-August. Southern Europe.

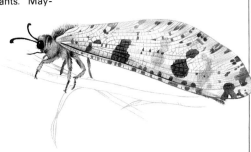

Caddis Flies

Mostly brownish, rather moth-like insects, but wings are clothed with hairs instead of scales and there is no tongue or proboscis. They rarely feed and the mouthparts are often vestigial. Most fly by night. The number of stout spines on the leg helps to distinguish the numerous species. The larvae nearly all live in water and many make portable shelters or cases with sand grains or plant fragments. Each species has its own case pattern. The caddis flies belong to the order Trichoptera.

PHRYGANEA GRANDIS
Family Phryganeidae

35-40 mm. Breeds in still water with plenty of vegetation, the case being made of leaf fragments. Summer.

larva in case

Centipedes

The centipedes form the class of arthropods known as the Chilopoda. They are elongate animals with one pair of legs on each body segment. They are mostly fast–moving and all are carnivores, catching and killing other animals with a pair of poison claws surrounding the head. Most are active at night.

SCUTIGERA COLEOPTRATA
Family Scuterigidae

30 mm. 15 pairs of long legs, the hind pair extremely long and thin. The antennae are also extremely long. A very fast runner. Native in Mediterranean region, in caves and rocky places: found in buildings further north, rarely in Britain.

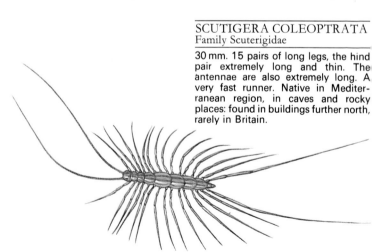

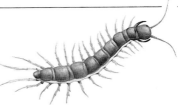

LITHOBIUS FORFICATUS
Family Lithobiidae

18-30 mm. 15 pairs of legs when mature, including the hind legs which trail behind body and act rather like antennae. Hides under stones and loose bark by day.

HAPLOPHILUS SUBTERRANEUS
Family Himantariidae

50-70 mm. 77-83 pairs of legs (always an odd number), the last pair resembling the antennae. Lives in soil and leaf litter.

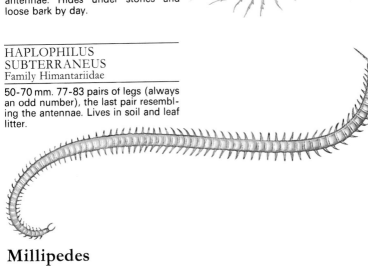

Millipedes

Millipedes (Class Diplopoda) are elongate arthropods with two pairs of legs on most body segments. They are relatively slow-moving herbivores.

TACHYPODIULUS NIGER
Family Iulidae

50 mm. One of several very similar cylindrical species which curl up like watch springs when disturbed. Very common in many habitats, especially on lime-rich soils. Often climbs trees.

PILL MILLIPEDE
Glomeris marginata Family Glomeridae

20 mm. Much stouter than other millipedes and often confused with woodlice, but has 17-19 pairs of legs compared with the 7 pairs of the woodlouse. It is also much shinier than the woodlouse, which distinguishes it when rolled up. Turf and leaf litter.

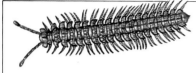

POLYDESMUS ANGUSTUS
Family Polydesmidae

25 mm. One of the flat-backed millipedes, most common in leaf litter and other decaying matter.

Worms

The name worm is given to several quite distinct groups of animals with long, thin bodies, including the tapeworms (Phylum Platyhelminthes) and roundworms (Phylum Nematoda) that live parasitically in the bodies of other animals. The most familiar worms, however, are the segmented worms or annelids (Phylum Annelida), whose bodies are divided into many rings or segments. There are three classes. In the Oligochaeta, which includes the earthworms and various aquatic worms, each body segment has just a few bristles. The leeches belong to the Hirudinea and have suckers fore and aft, but no bristles. Most are aquatic and generally prey on other animals, but some are blood-suckers. The Polychaeta contains the bristleworms, in which there are many bristles on each segment. The sides of the segments are often expanded to form simple paddle-like limbs and it is possible that the arthropods evolved from worms of this kind. Bristleworms are all marine and include both free-swimming and sedentary forms. The latter filter food particles from the water or mud, but the free-swimming species are often predatory. Quite a number of species can be found on the sea shore.

COMMON EARTHWORM
Lumbricus terrestris Family Lumbricidae

9-30 cm. 110-160 segments. Reddish-brown above, yellowish below. Front end pointed, hind end flattened. The swollen region known as the clitellum or saddle covers segments 32-37 in adult worms. Like all earthworms, the species is hermaphrodite, with both male and female organs in each individual. Feeds by swallowing soil as it tunnels and digesting the organic matter in it. May come to the surface at night. All year, but goes very deep to avoid winter cold.

HORSE LEECH
Haemopis sanguisuga Family Hirudidae

30 cm when extended, but can contract to an oval blob. Green, brown or black. Swims with beautiful sinuous movements, but actually spends much time hunting worms and other soft-bodied animals in damp soil near the water's edge. The prey is crushed with the leech's blunt teeth and usually swallowed whole. The leech cannot pierce even human skin to suck blood and has nothing to do with horses. It can be found all year in muddy ponds and ditches.

Bristleworms

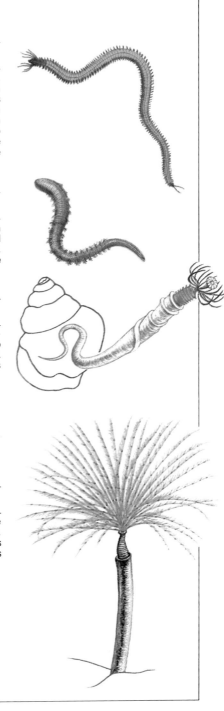

RAGWORM
Nereis diversicolor Family Nereidae

10 cm. 90-120 segments. Green to red, but usually yellowish and always with a red line on the back. Lives in burrows in muddy and sandy shores, often in estuaries. Strong jaws may snatch passing animals, but the worm also feeds by straining particles from the mud and water. It can crawl on the mud and also swim weakly.

LUGWORM
Arenicola marina Family Arenicolidae

Up to 35 cm. Green to black, with feathery red gills. Lives in U-shaped burrow in muddy and sandy shores. Sucks in sediment, digests the edible content and voids the rest at surface.

SERPULA VERMICULARIS
Family Serpulidae

5 cm. Secretes a trumpet-shaped lime-stone tube around itself, attached to stones or shells in shallow water. Filters food particles from water. Closes tube with a stopper.

PEACOCK WORM
Sabella pavonina Family Sabellidae

Up to 25 cm. Lives in a slender tube built of sand grains and filters food. Usually below low-tide level. Tentacles withdrawn if uncovered, leaving tubes sticking up like pencils.

Coelenterates

These animals belong to the Phylum Coelenterata. They have no skeleton, no head, and no real sense organs, although a simple network of nerves runs through the body. There is just one opening, through which food is taken in and waste is passed out. It is usually surrounded by food-catching tentacles. The animals are carnivorous and usually well-endowed with stinging cells which are fired into the prey like tiny harpoons. There are two main types of body – the polyp, which is fixed and roughly cup-shaped, and the free swimming medusa or jellyfish type. The sea anemones and the corals form the Class Anthozoa, which is entirely marine. Jellyfishes (Class Scyphozoa) are also entirely marine, but the Class Hydrozoa contains several freshwater animals, such as *Hydra,* as well as marine ones.

Hydrozoa

PORTUGUESE MAN O'WAR
Physalia physalis Family Physalidae

A colonial animal, consisting of numerous small polyps clustered under a gas-filled blue or pink float. The colony drifts with the wind and current, trailing long tentacles in the water. The tentacles, armed with stinging cells powerful enough to cause severe injury to people, capture small fishes and pull them up to the feeding polyps just under the float for digestion. The food is then shared by the whole colony. Usually seen off-shore in the Atlantic and Mediterranean.

BROWN HYDRA
Hydra oligactis Family Hydridae

Up to 10 mm long when extended, this slim animal lives in ponds and streams, attached to water plants; often hangs down from water lily leaves. The relatively few slender tentacles capture water fleas and other small animals and push them into the mouth, causing prominent bulges in the body until they are digested. Small buds often grow on the body and develop into new individuals which eventually drop off and become independent. Hydra can also reproduce sexually by producing sperm and egg cells in autumn. It then passes the winter in the embryonic stage, surrounded by a tough coat. There are several similar green or brown species.

Anthozoa

DAHLIA ANEMONE
Tealia felina Family Actiniidae

Up to 15 cm long when stretched, but usually about 5 cm. Normally 80 short tentacles clothed with stinging cells. Attached to rocks and common in rock pools quite high on the shore, especially where shaded by seaweeds. When uncovered by the tide, the animal pulls its tentacles right inside the body and contracts to a blob of jelly. One of many colourful species, it often gathers small stones and shells and sticks them to its body.

Scyphozoa

COMMON JELLYFISH
Aurelia aurita Family Aureliidae

Up to 40 cm across. Easily recognized by the four circular violet reproductive organs. Often floats in large shoals. It feeds on small planktonic animals, which it catches by means of the stinging cells on the long lips surrounding the mouth. It is often washed up on the shore.

Comb Jellies

Marine animals once grouped with the coelenterates, but they have no stinging cells and now form the Phylum Ctenophora.

SEA GOOSEBERRY
Pleurobrachia pileus
Family Pleurobrachiidae

2-3 cm diameter. Drifts through the water by beating the iridescent cilia which form 8 rows along the body. Small animals are caught with sticky lasso-like threads on the retractile tentacles and then brought up to the mouth. Often washed up on beaches, like soft crystal-clear marbles.

English Names

Accentor, Alpine 139
 Hedge 139
Adder 161
Admiral, Red 234
 White 233
Aeshna, Brown 220
Agama 154
Agrion, Banded 220
Alder Fly 272
Amphibians 153–168
Anchovy 182
Anemone, Dahlia 279
Ant, Black 262
 Red 262
 Wood 262
Ants 261–262
Argus, Scotch 239
Artemis, Rayed 205
Asp (fish) 174
Asp Viper (snake) 161
Auk, Little 104
Avocet 98

Badger 49
Barbel 179
Barnacle, Acorn 210
Bass 184
Bat, Common Long-eared 26
 Daubenton's 27
 Free-tailed 25
 Greater Horseshoe 24
 Greater Mouse-eared 26
 Natterer's 27
 Noctule 27
 Whiskered 26
Bear, Brown 41
Beaver, European 32
Bee, Carder 260
 Carpenter 258
 Honey 259
 Leaf-cutter 258
 Long-horned 258
 Tawny Mining 258
Bee-Eater, European 111
Bee-fly 255
Beetle, Bloody-nosed 269
 Bombardier 264
 Burying 264
 Cardinal 267
 Click 266
 Colorado 269
 Death-Watch 268
 Devil's Coach-Horse 265
 Elm Bark 269
 Furniture 268
 Great Diving 266
 Green Tiger 264
 Oil 268
 Scarab 265
 Soldier 266
 Stag 265
 Tortoise 268
 Violet Ground 264
 Wasp 268
Birch Mouse, Northern 40
Birds of Prey 79–84
Bitterling 176
Bittern, Great 70
 Little 70
Bivalves 194
Blackbird 127
Blackcap 135

Blackfly 227
Bleak 176
Blue, Chalk Hill 245
 Common 244
 Holly 245
Bluebottle 256
Bluethroat 130
Boa, Sand 158
Boar see Wild Boar
Boatman, Water 227
Booklouse, Common 272
Brambling 149
Bream, Common 177
 Silver 177
Brill 187
Brimstone 229
Bristleworms 277
Brittle Stars 192
Brown, Large Wall 241
 Meadow 241
 Wall 242
 Woodland 239
Buffalo Hopper 227
Bug, Common Flower 226
 Hawthorn Shield 225
 Pied Shield 226
Bullfinch 147
Bullhead 180
Bumblebee, Red-tailed 259
 White-tailed 259
Bunting, Cirl 149
 Corn 149
 Ortolan 150
 Reed 150
 Snow 151
Burbot 179
Burnet, Six-spot 249
Bush Cricket, Dark 223
 Great Green 223
 Speckled 223
Bustard, Little 91
Butterfish 186
Butterflies 228–246
Butterfly, Map 235
Buzzard, Common 83
 Rough-Legged 83

Caddis Flies 274
Capercaillie 87
Capsid, Common Green 226
Carp 176
 Crucian 175
Cat see Wild Cat
Centipedes 274
Cephalopods 195
Chaffinch 147
Chamois 54
Charr, Arctic 171
Chiffchaff 135
Chiton, Grey 203
Chough, Alpine 120
 Red-billed 120
Chub 174
Cinnabar 250
Clearwing, Hornet 249
Clouded Yellow 230
Coat-of-Mail Shells 203
Cockchafer 265
Cockle, Common 204
 Dog 204
 Prickly 203
Cockroach, German 271
Coelenterates 278
Colubrid Snakes 158

Comb Jellies 279
Comma 234
Conger 182
Coot, Common 91
Copper, Scarce 245
 Small 244
Cormorant, Great 65
 Pygmy 65
Corncrake 90
Cowrie, European 202
Coypu 33
Crab, Edible 209
 Hermit 210
 Shore 210
 Velvet 210
Crab Spiders 216
Crake, Baillon's 90
 Little 91
 Spotted 90
Crane, Common 89
Crayfish 209
Crane-fly 54
Cricket, Field 222
 House 222
 Italian 222
 Mole 222
Crossbill, Common 148
 Parrot 148
Crow, Carrion 119
 Hooded 119
Crustaceans 207–210
Cuckoo, Common 106
 Great Spotted 107
Curlew, Eurasian 95
Cushion Star 191
Cuttlefish, Common 196

Dab 187
Dabchick see Grebe, Little
Dace 173
Damselfly, Common Blue 221
 Large Red 220
Deer, Fallow 57
 Red 55
 Roe 55
 Sika 57
Desman, Pyrenean 21
Dipper 124
Diver, Black-throated 62
 Great Northern 62
 Red-throated 62
Dogfish, Lesser Spotted 180
Dog Whelk, Common 202
Dormouse, Common 31
 Fat 32
 Garden 31
Dotterel 93
Dove, Collared 105
 Rock 106
 Stock 105
 Turtle 105
Dragonfly 219
 Gold-ringed 220
Drone-fly 256
Dryad 240
Duck, Ferruginous 74
 Tufted 75
Dung-fly 256
Dunlin 96
Eagle, Bonelli's 80
 Booted 81
 Golden 81
 Imperial 81
 Short-toed 80
 White-tailed 82

Earthworm, Common 276
Earwig, Common 271
Echinoderms 190–192
Eel 178
Eggar, Oak 252
Egret, Great White 69
  Little 69
Eider, Common 73
Elk 57
Emerald, Downy 219
Emperor, Lesser Purple 232
  Purple 233

False Scorpions 217
Fieldfare 126
Firecrest 138
Flamingo, Greater 70
Flesh-fly 256
Flounder 187
Flycatcher, Collared 138
  Pied 137
  Red-breasted 137
  Spotted 137
Flies 254–256
Forester, Common 249
Fox, Arctic 42
  Red 43
Fritillary, Duke of Burgundy 246
  Heath 236
  Knapweed 235
  Marsh 236
  Queen of Spain 235
  Silver Washed 236
Frog, Common 166
  Common Tree 165
  Edible 165
  Marsh 166
  Painted 163
  Parsley 165
Froghopper, Common 227
Fulmar 66

Gadwall 72
Game Birds 86–89
Gannet, Northern 65
Gaper, Sand 206
Garfish 182
Garganey 72
Gatekeeper 238
Gecko, Moorish 154
Genet 49
Glow-worm 267
Goat, Domestic 53
Goby, Common 186
Godwit, Bar-tailed 95
  Black-tailed 95
Goldcrest 138
Goldeneye, Common 74
Goldfinch 144
Goosander 75
Goose, Barnacle 76
  Bean 77
  Brent 76
  Canada 76
  Greylag 77
  Pink-footed 76
  White-fronted 77
Gooseberry, Sea 279
Goshawk, Northern 82
Grasshopper, Meadow 224
Grayling (butterfly) 240
  Great Banded 238
  Tree 240
  Woodland 237

Grayling (fish) 172
Grebe, Black-necked 64
  Great Crested 63
  Little 64
  Red-necked 63
  Slavonian or Horned 64
Greenbottle 256
Greenfinch 144
Greenshank, Common 96
Grosbeak, Pine 148
Grouse, Black 87
  Hazel 86
  Red 86
  Willow 86
Gudgeon 175
Guillemot, Black 104
  Common 103
Gull, Black-headed 101
  Common 101
  Glaucous 100
  Great Black-backed 100
  Herring 101
  Lesser Black-backed 101
  Little 100
Gurnard, Red 186

Hairstreak, Brown 243
  Green 244
  Purple 243
Hamster, Common 34
Hare, Brown 29
  Mountain 28
Harrier, Hen 83
  Marsh 82
  Montagu's 83
Harvestmen 216
Hawfinch 145
Hawkmoth, Elephant 248
  Hummingbird 248
  Privet 247
Hazel Grouse
Heath, Large 242
  Small 238
Hedgehog, Western 20
Heron, Grey 69
  Night 68
  Purple 68
  Squacco 68
Herring 182
Hobby 84
Honey-buzzard 81
Hoopoe 112
Hopper, Buffalo 227
  Sand 208
Hornet 260
Horntail 262
Horse 262
Horse-fly 255
House-fly 256
Hover-fly 255
Hydra, Brown 278
Hydrozoa 278

Ichneumon 263
Ide 173
Insectivores 20–23
Insects 218–273

Jackal 43
Jackdaw, Eurasian 118
Jay 120
Jellyfish, Common 279

Kestrel, Common 85
Kingfisher 111
Kite, Black 82
  Red 84
Kittiwake 102

Lacewing, Green 273
Ladybird, Seven-spot 267
Lammergeier 80
Lampern 170
Lamprey 170
Lapwing, Northern 93
Lark, Crested 115
  Horned 116
  Sky 116
  Wood 116
Leech, Horse 276
Lemming, Wood 35
Libellula, Four-spotted 221
Limpet, Blue-rayed 200
  Common 200
  Slipper 201
Linnet 145
Lizard, Common Wall 155
  Green 156
  Ocellated 156
  Sand 157
  Viviparous 157
Loach, Pond 177
  Spined 177
  Stone 177
Lobster 208
  Norway 209
  Spiny 209
Locust, Migratory 225
Louse, Water 207
Lugworm 277
Lynx 51

Mackerel 186
Magpie 121
Mallard 71
Mantis, Praying 271
Marmot, Alpine 30
Marten, Beech 47
  Pine 46
Martin, Crag 117
  House 116
  Sand 117
Mayfly 270
Merganser, Red-breasted 75
Merlin 85
Midge 254
Millipede, Pill 275
Mink, European 47
Minnow 175
Moderlieschen 173
Mole, Northern 21
Mole-Rat, Greater 35
Molluscs 193–206
Mongoose, Egyptian 50
Moorhen 91
Mosquito 254
Moths 247–253
Moth, Emperor 252
  Ghost 248
  Herald 251
  Magpie 253
Mouflon 54
Mouse, Harvest 39
  House 39
  Striped Field 40
  Wood 39
  Yellow-necked Field 38

Mullet, Red 185
    Thick-lipped Grey 185
Muntjac 56
Muskrat 35
Mussel, Common 204
    Painter's 206

Nase 174
Natterjack 165
Newt, Alpine 167
    Marbled 167
    Palmate 168
    Smooth 167
    Warty 167
Nightingale, Rufous 129
Nightjar, European 109
Noctuid Moths 250–251
Nutcracker 120
Nuthatch, Wood 123

Octopus, Common 195
Orange-tip 231
Oriole, Golden 118
Ormer, Common 199
Osprey 85
Otter 48
Ouzel, Ring 127
Owl, Barn 107
    Eagle 109
    Eurasian Scops 108
    Little 108
    Long-eared 107
    Pygmy 108
    Short-eared 109
    Tawny 108
Oyster, Flat 204
    Portuguese 205
Oystercatcher 92

Painted Lady 234
Partridge 88
    Grey 88
    Red-legged 89
    Rock 88
Peacock 232
Pelican, Dalmatian 66
    White 66
Pelican's Foot 201
Perch 179
Perching Birds 115–151
Peregrine Falcon 84
Periwinkle, Common 201
    Flat 200
Phalarope, Red-necked 98
Pheasant, Common 88
Piddock, Common 206
Pike 172
Pintail, Northern 72
Pipefish, Nilsson's 183
Pipistrelle, Common 25
Pipit, Meadow 140
    Rock 140
    Tawny 140
    Tree 139
    Water 140
Plaice 187
Plover, European Golden 93
    Great Ringed 92
    Grey 93
    Kentish 93
    Little Ringed 92
Pochard, Common 74
Polecat, Marbled 44
    Steppe 45
    Western 45

Pollack 183
Pond Skater, Common 226
Porcupine, North African Crested 33
Portuguese Man o'War 279
Powan 172
Prawn, Common 209
Praying Mantis 271
Ptarmigan 87
Puffin 104

Quail, Common 89

Rabbit 28
Raccoon 50
Raccoon-Dog 43
Ragworm 277
Rail, Land see Corncrake
    Water 90
Ram's Horn, Great 198
Rat, Black or Ship 37
    Common or Norway 38
Raven 119
Ray, Sting 181
    Thornback 181
Razorbill 104
Redpoll 146
    Arctic 146
Redshank, Common 96
Redstart, Common 128
    Black 129
Red wing 127
Reedling see Tit, Bearded
Reindeer 56
Reptiles 153–168
Ringlet 241
Roach 173
Robber-fly 255
Robin 130
Rockling, Five-bearded 184
Rodents 29
Roller, European 111
Rook 118
Rudd 174
Ruff 97
Ruffe 179

St Mark's Fly 254
Salamander, Alpine 168
    Fire 168
    Spectacled 168
Salmon 171
Sandeel, Greater 182
Sanderling 97
Sandpiper, Common 94
    Green 95
    Wood 94
Sand-Smelt 185
Sawfly, Gooseberry 262
    Hawthorn 262
Scallop, Queen 204
Scaup, Greater 74
Scorpion 217
Scorpion Fly 272
Scorpion, Water 225
Sea Gherkin 191
Sea Hare 202
Sea Horse 183
Seal, Common 58
    Grey 59
    Monk 59
Sea Slug 203
    Grey 203
Sea Urchin, Edible 190

Serin, European 147
Serpent Star 192
Shag 65
Shanny 185
Shearwater, Cory's 66
    Great 67
    Manx 67
    Sooty 67
Shelduck, Common 73
Shell, Banded Carpet 205
    Banded Wedge 204
    Common Otter 206
    Large Razor 205
    Needle 200
    Painted Top 200
    Rayed Trough 206
    Tower 200
Shoveler, Northern 73
Shrew, Bicoloured White-toothed 23
    Common 22
    Greater White-toothed 22
    Pygmy 22
    Pygmy White-toothed (Etruscan) 23
    Water 23
Shrike, Great Grey 143
    Lesser Grey 143
    Red-backed 143
    Woodchat 144
Shrimp, Common 208
    Freshwater 208
Silver Y 251
Siskin 145
Skink, Three-toed 155
Skipper, Grizzled 246
    Large 246
Skua, Arctic 99
    Great 99
Slater, Sea 207
Slow Worm 155
Slug, Budapest 196
    Great Black 196
    Great Grey 196
    Netted 196
Smelt 172
Snail, Brown-lipped 197
    Garden 198
    Garlic Glass 198
    Great Pond 199
    Kentish 198
    Roman 198
    Round-mouthed 199
    Strawberry 198
    Two-toothed Door 199
Snake, Cat 161
    Grass 160
    Horseshoe Whip 159
    Ladder 159
    Leopard 160
    Montpellier 158
    Smooth 160
    Viperine 160
    Western Whip 159
Snake Fly 273
Snipe, Common 94
    Jack 94
Snowfinch 152
Spadefoot, Common 164
Sparrowhawk, Eurasian 82
Sparrow, House 151
    Rock 152
    Tree 151

Spider, Garden 215
  House 212
  Nursery Web 211
  Orb-web 214
  Water 212
  Zebra 214
Spiders 210–217
Spurdog 181
Squid, Common 196
Squirrel, Flying 29
  Grey 30
  Red 30
Starfish, Common 192
Starling, Common 152
Stickleback, Nine-spined 180
  Three-spined 180
Stilt, Black-winged 98
Stoat 46
Stonechat 29
Stone-curlew 99
Stonefly 270
Stork, White 70
Storm petrel, European 67
  Leach's 67
Sturgeon 170
Sunstar 191
Swallow, Barn 117
  Red-rumped 117
Swallowtail 231
Swan, Bewick's 78
  Mute 78
  Whooper 78
Swift (bird) 110
  Alpine 110
  Common 110
Swift (moth), Common 249
Sympetrum, Ruddy 221

Tarantula 213
Teal, Common 71
Tellin, Blunt 205
  Thin 205
Tench 175
Tern, Arctic 102
  Black 102
  Common 102
  Little 102
  Whiskered 102
Terrapin, European Pond 162
  Stripe-necked 162
Thrips, Onion 272
Thrush, Blue Rock 127
  Mistle 126
  Rock 126
  Song 126
Tiger (moth), Garden 250
Tit, Bearded 124
  Blue 122
  Coal 122
  Crested 121
  Great 121
  Long-tailed 122
  Marsh 122
  Willow 122
Toad, Common 164
  Green 165
  Midwife 164
  Yellow-bellied 164
Toothcarp, Spanish 178
Tortoise, Hermann's 162
Tortoiseshell, Small 233
Treecreeper, Eurasian 125
  Short-toed 125

Trout, Brown 171
  Rainbow 171
Turnstone 93
Twite 146

Underwing, Large Yellow 251
  Red 251
Urchin, Rock 190
  Violet Heart 190

Vapourer 253
Vendace 172
  Viper, Asp 79
  Lataste's 79
Vole, Bank 36
  Field 36
  Northern Water 36
Vulture, Egyptian 79
  Griffon 79
  Monk 80

Waders 92–99
Wagtail, Grey 141
  Pied 141
  White 141
  Yellow 142
Wallcreeper 124
Warbler, Barred 134
  Bonelli's 136
  Cetti's 131
  Dartford 136
  Garden 133
  Grasshopper 131
  Great Reed 131
  Icterine 134
  Marsh 132
  Melodious 134
  Moustached 130
  Olivaceous 134
  Orphean 133
  Reed 132
  Savi's 132
  Sedge 133
  Willow 136
  Wood 136
Wasp, Bee-killer 261
  Common 260
  Gall 263
  Paper 260
  Ruby-tailed 263
  Spiny Mason 261
Waterfowl 71–78
Waxwing, Bohemian 142
Weasel 44
Weever, Lesser 184
Weevil, Nut 269
Wels 178
Wentletrap, Common 201
Wheatear, Black 128
  Black-eared 128
  Northern 128
Whelk, Common 202
Whimbrel 96
Whinchat 129
White, Black-veined 228
  Green-veined 230
  Large 229
  Marbled 237
  Small 229
Whitethroat, Common 135
  Lesser 135
Whiting 183
Wigeon, Eurasian 72

Wild Boar 52
Wild Cat 52
Winkle, Sting 202
Wolf 42
Wolverine 48
Wood, Speckled 239
Woodcock 97
Woodlice 207
Woodpecker, Black 112
  Great Spotted 115
  Green 113
  Grey-headed 113
  Lesser Spotted 114
  Middle Spotted 114
  Three-toed 113
  White-backed 114
Woodpigeon 105
Worm, Peacock 277
Wrasse, Cuckoo 184
Wren 125
Wryneck 114

Yellowhammer 150

Zander 179

Scientific Names

Abramis brama 177
Abraxas grossulariata 253
Acanthosoma haemorrhoidale 225
Accipiter gentilis 82
    nisus 82
Acheta domesticus 222
Acipenser sturio 170
Acrida ungarica 224
Acrocephalus arundinaceus 131
    melanopogon 130
    palustris 132
    schoenobaenus 133
    scirpaceus 132
Adscita statices 249
Aegithalos caudatus 123
Aegypius monachus 80
Aeolidia papillosa 203
Aeshna grandis 220
Agama stellio 154
Aglais urticae 233
Agrion splendens 220
Alauda arvensis 116
Alburnus alburnus 176
Alca torda 104
Alcedo atthis 111
Alces alces 57
Alectoris graeca 88
    rufa 89
Alle alle 104
Alopex lagopus 42
Alytes obstetricus 164
Amaurobius similis 211
Ammophila sabulosa 261
Anas acuta 72
    clypeata 73
    crecca 71
    penelope 72
    platyrhynchos 71
    querquedula 72
    strepera 72
Anax imperator 219
Andrena fulva 258
Anguilla anguilla 178
Anguis fragilis 155
Anobium punctatum 268
Anoplius viaticus 261
Anser albifrons 77
    anser 77
    brachyrhyncus 76
    fabalis 77
Anthocharis cardamines 231
Anthocoris nemorum 226
Anthus campestris 140
    pratensis 140
    petrosus 140
    spinoletta 140
    trivialis 139
Apanteles glomeratus 263
Apatura ilia 232
    iris 233
Aphanius iberus 178
Aphantopus hyperantus 241
Aphis fabae 227
Aphodius rufipes 265
Apis mellifera 259
Aplysia depilans 202
Apodemus agrarius 40
    flavicollis 38
    sylvaticus 39
Aporia crataegi 228
Aporrhais pespelecani 201
Apus apus 110

    melba 110
Aquila chrysaetos 81
    heliaca 81
Araneus diadematus 215
    quadratus 215
Araschnia levana 235
Arctia caja 250
Arcyptera fusca 224
Ardea cinerea 69
    purpurea 68
Ardeola ralloides 68
Arenaria interpres 93
Arenicola marina 277
Argiope bruennichi 214
    lobata 215
Argynnis paphia 236
Argyroneta aquatica 212
Arion ater 197
Arvicola terrestris 36
Asellus aquaticus 207
Asilus crabroniformis 255
Asio flammeus 109
    otus 107
Aspitrigla cuculus 186
Aspius aspius 174
Asterias rubens 192
Asterina gibbosa 191
Astropecten irregularis 192
Athene noctua 108
Atherina presbyter 185
Athous haemorrhoidalis 266
Aurelia aurita 279
Autographa gamma 251
Aythya ferina 74
    fuligula 75
    marila 74
    nyroca 74
Barbus barbus 176
Belone belone 182
Bembex rostrata 261
Bibio marci 254
Biorrhiza pallida 263
Bitium reticulatum 200
Blattella germanica 271
Blicca bjoerkna 177
Bombina variegata 164
Bombus lapidarius 259
    lucorum 259
    pascuorum 260
Bombycilla garrulus 142
Bombylius major 255
Bonasa bonasia 86
Botaurus stellaris 70
Brachinus crepitans 264
Branta bernicla 76
    canadensis 76
    leucopsis 76
Brintesia circe 238
Bubo bubo 109
Buccinum undatum 202
Bucephala clangula 74
Bufo bufo 164
    calamita 165
    viridis 165
Burhinus oedicnemus 99
Buteo buteo 83
    lagopus 83

Calidris alba 97
    alpina 96
Calliostoma zizyphinum 200
Calliphora vomitoria 256
Callophrys rubi 244
Calonectris diomedea 66

Cancer pagurus 209
Canis aureus 43
    lupus 42
Capra hircus 53
Capreolus capreolus 55
Caprimulgus europaeus 109
Carabus violaceus 264
Carassius carassius 175
Carcinus maenas 210
Cardium echinatum 203
    edule 204
Carduelis cannabina 145
    carduelis 144
    chloris 144
    flammea 146
    flavirostris 146
    hornemannia 146
    spinus 145
Cassida viridis 268
Castor fiber 32
Catocala nupta 251
Celastrina argiolus 245
Cepaea nemoralis 197
Cepphus grylle 104
Cercopis vulnerata 227
Certhia brachydactyla 125
    familiaris 125
Cervus dama 57
    elaphus 55
    nippon 57
Cettia cetti 131
Chalcides chalcides 155
Charadrius alexandrinus 93
    dubius 92
    hiaticula 92
    morinellus 93
Chelon labrosus 185
Chironomus annularis 254
Chlamys opercularis 204
Chlidonias hybrida 103
    niger 103
Chondrostoma nasus 174
Chorthippus parallelus 224
Chrysis ignita 263
Chrysomela populi 269
Chrysopa septempunctata 273
Chrysops relictus 255
Cicadetta montana 227
Cicindela campestris 264
Ciconia ciconia 70
Ciliata mustela 184
Cinclus cinclus 124
Circaetus gallicus 80
Circus aeruginosus 82
    cyaneus 82
    pygargus 82
Clamator glandarius 107
Clathrus clathrus 201
Clausilia bidentata 199
Clethrionomys glareolus 36
Clupea harengus 182
Clytus arietis 268
Cobitis taenia 178
Coccinella 7-punctata 267
Coccothraustes coccothraustes 145
Coenonympha pamphilus 238
    tullia 242
Colias croceus 230
Coluber hippocrepis 159
    viridiflavus 159
Columba livia 106
    oenas 105
    palumbus 105
Conger conger 182

Coracias garrulus 111
Cordulegaster boltonii 220
Cordulia linaenea 219
Coregonus albula 172
   lavaretus 172
Corixa punctata 227
Coronella austriaca 160
Corvus corax 119
   corone cornix 119
   corone corone 119
   frugilegus 118
   monedula 118
Cottus gobio 180
Coturnix coturnix 89
Crangon crangon 208
Crassostrea angulata 205
Crepidula fornicata 201
Crex crex 90
Cricetus cricetus 34
Crocidura leucodon 22
   russula 22
Ctenicera cuprea 266
Cuculus canorus 106
Cucumaria planci 191
Culex pipiens 254
Curculio nucum 268
Cygnus columbianus 78
   cygnus 78
   olor 78
Cynthia cardui 234
Cyprinus carpio 176

Dasyatis pastinaca 181
Deilephila elpenor 248
Delichon urbica 116
Dendrocopos leucotos 114
   major 115
   medius 114
   minor 114
Dendronotus frondosus 203
Deroceras reticulatum 196
Dicentrarchus labrax 184
Discoglossus pictus 163
Dolomedes fimbriatus 213
Donax vittatus 204
Dosina exoleta 205
Dryocopus martius 112
Dysdera crocata 213
Dytiscus marginalis 266

Echichthys vipera 184
Echinus esculentus 190
Ectemnius cephalotes 260
Egretta alba 69
   garzetta 69
Elaphe scalaris 159
   situla 60
Eliomys quercinus 31
Emberiza cirlus 149
   citrinella 150
   hortulana 150
   schoeniclus 150
Emys orbicularis 162
Enallagma cyathigerum 221
Engraulis encrasicolus 182
Enoplognatha ovata 212
Ensis siliqua 205
Equus caballus 53
Erebia aethiops 239
Eremophila alpestris 116
Erinaceus europaeus 20
Eristalis tenax 256
Erithacus rubecula 130
Eryx jaculus 158

Esox lucius 172
Eucera longicornis 258
Eupagurus bernhardus 210
Eurodryas aurinia 236
Euscorpius flavicaudis 217

Falco columbarius 84
   peregrinus 84
   subbuteo 84
   tinnunculus 84
Felis lynx 51
   sylvestris 52
Ficedula albicollis 138
   hypoleuca 137
   parva 137
Forficula auricularia 271
Formica rufa 262
Fratercula arctica 104
Fringilla coelebs 147
   montifringilla 149
Fulica atra 91
Fulmarus glacialis 66

Galemys pyrenaicus 21
Galerida cristata 115
Gallinago gallinago 94
Gallinula chloropus 91
Gammarus pulex 208
Garrulus glandarius 120
Gasterosteus aculeatus 180
Gavia arctica 62
   immer 62
   stellata 62
Genetta genetta 49
Gerris lacustris 226
Glaucidium passerinum 108
Glis glis 32
Glomeris marginata 275
Glycimeris glycimeris 204
Gobio gobio 175
Gonepteryx rhamni 228
Graphosoma italicum 226
Grus grus 89
Gryllotalpa gryllotalpa 222
Gryllus campestris 222
Gulo gulo 48
Gymnocephalus cernuus 179
Gypaetus barbatus 80
Gyps fulvus 79

Haematopus ostralegus 92
Haemopis sanguisuga 276
Haliaeetus albicilla 82
Halichoerus grypus 59
Haliotis tuberculata 199
Hamearis lucina 246
Haplophilus subterraneus 275
Helix aspersa 198
   pomatia 198
Heodes virgaureae 245
Hepialus humuli 248
   lupulinus 248
Herpestes ichneumon 50
Hieraaetus fasciatus 80
   pennatus 81
Himantopus himantopus 98
Hipparchia fagi 237
   semele 236
Hippocampus ramulosus 183
Hippolais icterina 134
   pallida 134
   polyglotta 134
Hirundo daurica 117

rustica 117
Holothuria forskali 191
Homarus vulgaris 208
Hydra oligactis 278
Hydrobates pelagicus 67
Hyla arborea 165
Hyperoplus lanceolatus 182
Hystrix cristata 33

Inachis io 232
Isonychia ignota 270
Issoria lathonia 235
Ixobrychus minutus 70

Jynx torquilla 114

Labrus mixtus 184
Lacerta agilis 157
   lepida 156
   viridis 156
   vivipara 157
Lagopus lagopus lagopus 86
   mutus 87
   scoticus 86
Lampetra fluviatilis 170
Lamprochernes nodosus 217
Lampyris noctiluca 267
Lanius collurio 143
   excubitor 143
   minor 143
   senator 144
Larus argentatus 101
   canus 101
   fuscus 101
   hyperboreus 100
   marinus 100
   minutus 100
   ribundus 101
Lasiocampa quercus 252
Lasiommata maera 241
   megera 242
Lasius niger 262
Leiobunum rotundum 217
Lepidochitona cinerea 203
Leptinotarsa decemlineata 269
Leptophyes punctatissima 223
Leptura rubra 268
Lepus capensis 29
   timidus 28
Leucaspius delineatus 173
Leuciscus cephalus 174
   idus 173
   leuciscus 173
Libelloides coccajus 273
Libellula depressa 221
   quadrimaculata 221
Ligia oceanica 207
Limanda limanda 187
Limax maximus 197
Limenitis camilla 233
Limnaea stagnalis 199
Limosa lapponica 95
   limosa 95
Linyphia triangularis 214
Lipophrys pholis 185
Liposcelis terricolis 272
Lithobius forficatus 275
Littorina littoralis 200
   littorea 201
Locusta migratoria 225
Locustella luscinioides 132
   naevia 131
Loligo vulgaris 196
Lopinga achine 239

Lota lota 179
Loxia curvirostra 148
  pytyopsittacus 148
Lucanus cervus 265
Lucilia caesar 256
Lululala arborea 116
Lumbricus terrestris 276
Luscinia megarhyncos 129
  svecica 130
Lutra lutra 48
Lutraria lutraria 206
Lycaena phlaeas 244
Lycosa narbonensis 213
Lygocoris pabulinus 226
Lymnocryptes minimus 94
Lysandra coridon 245

Macroglossum stellatarum 248
Mactra corallina 206
Malpolon monspessulanus 158
Maniola jurtina 241
Mantis religiosa 271
Marmota marmota 30
Martes foina 47
  martes 46
Mauremys caspica 163
Megachile centuncularis 258
Melanargia galathea 237
Meles meles 49
Melitaea phoebe 235
Mellicta athalia 236
Meloe proscarabaeus 268
Melolontha melolontha 265
Mergus merganser 75
  serrator 75
Merlangus merlangus 183
Merops apiaster 111
Micromys minutus 39
Microtus agrestis 36
Milax budapestensis 197
Miliaria calendra 149
Milvus migrans 82
  milvus 84
Minois dryas 240
Misgurnus fossilis 177
Misumena vatia 216
Monacha cantiana 198
Monachus monachus 59
Monticola saxatilis 126
  solitarius 127
Montifringilla nivalis 152
Morus bassanus 65
Motacilla alba alba 141
  alba yarrelli 141
  cinerea 141
  flava 142
Mullus surmuletus 185
Muntiacus reevesi 56
Murex brandaris 201
Musca domestica 256
Muscardinus avellanarius 31
Muscicapa striata 137
Mus musculus 39
Mustela erminea 46
  eversmanni 45
  lutreola 46
  nivalis 44
  putorius 45
Mya arenaria 206
Myocastor coypus 33
Myopus schistocolor 35
Myotis daubentoni 27
  myotis 26
  mystacinus 26

nattereri 27
Myrmica ruginodis 262
Mytilus edulis 204

Natrix maura 160
  natrix 160
Nematus ribesii 262
Neohipparchia statilinus 240
Neomys fodiens 23
Neophron percnopterus 79
Nepa cinerea 225
Nephrops norvegicus 209
Nereis diversicolor 277
Nicrophorus humator 264
  vespillo 264
Noctua pronuba 251
Noemacheilus barbatulus 177
Nucella lapillus 202
Nucifraga caryocatactes 120
Numenius arquata 95
  phaeopus 95
Nyctalus noctula 27
Nyctereutes procyonoides 43
Nycticorax nycticorax 68

Oceanodroma leucorhoa 67
Ochlodes venatus 246
Ocinebra erinacea 202
Octopus vulgaris 195
Odynerus spinipes 261
Oecanthus pellucens 222
Oedipoda germanica 224
Oenanthe hispanica 128
  leucura 128
  oenanthe 128
Ondatra zibethicus 35
Oniscus asellus 207
Ophion luteus 263
Ophiothrix fragilis 192
Ophiura texturata 192
Orchestia gammarella 208
Orgyia antiqua 253
Oriolus oriolus 118
Oryctolagus cuniculus 28
Osmerus eperlanus 172
Ostrea edulis 204
Otus scops 108
Ovis musimon 54
Oxychilus alliarius 198

Palaemon serratus 209
Palinurus vulgaris 209
Palpares libelluloides 273
Panarus biarmicus 124
Pandion haliaetus 85
Panorpa communis 272
Papilio machaon 231
Paracentrotus lividus 190
Pararge aegeria 239
Pardosa amentata 213
Parus ater 122
  caeruleus 122
  cristatus 121
  major 121
  montanus 122
  palustris 122
Passer domesticus 151
  montanus 151
Patella vulgaris 200
Patina pellucida 200
Pavonia pavonia 252
Pelecanus crispus 66
  onocrotalus 66
Pelobates fuscus 164

Pelodytes punctatus 165
Perca fluviatilis 179
Perdix perdix 88
Perlodes microcephala 270
Pernis apivorus 81
Petromyzon marinus 170
Petronia petronia 152
Phalacrocorax aristotelis 65
  carbo 65
  pygmeus 65
Phalangium opilio 216
Phalaropus lobatus 98
Phasianus colchicus 88
Philaenus spumarius 227
Philanthus triangulum 227
Philomachus pugnax 97
Phoca vitulinum 58
Phoenicopterus ruber 70
Phoenicurus ochruros 129
  phoenicurus 128
Pholas dactylus 206
Pholidoptera griseoaptera 223
Pholis gunnellus 186
Phoxinus phoxinus 175
Phryganea grandis 274
Phyllobius pomaceus 269
Phylloscopus bonelli 136
  collybita 135
  sibilatrix 136
  trochilus 136
Physalia physalis 278
Pica pica 121
Picoides tridactylus 113
Picus canus 113
  viridis 113
Pieris brassicae 229
  napi 230
  rapae 229
Pinicola enucleator 148
Pipistrellus pipistrellus 25
Pisaura mirabilis 211
Planorbis corneus 198
Platichthys flesus 187
Plecotus auritus 26
Plectrophenax nivalis 151
Pleurobrachia pileus 279
Pleuronectes platessa 187
Pluvialis apricaria 93
  squatarola 93
Podarcis muralis 155
Podiceps auritus 64
  cristatus 63
  grisegena 63
  nigricollis 64
  ruficollis 64
Podisma pedestris 224
Polistes dominulus 260
Pollachius pollachius 183
Polydesmus angustus 276
Polygonia c-album 234
Polyommatus icarus 244
Pomatias elegans 199
Pomatoschistus microps 186
Portunus puber 210
Porzana parva 91
  porzana 90
  pusilla 90
Potamobius pallipes 209
Procyon lotor 50
Prunella collaris 139
  modularis 139
Pteromys volans 29
Ptyonoprogne rupestris 117
Puffinus gravis 67

-riseus 67
-uffinus 67
-ngitius pungitius 180
-gus malvae 246
-ochroa coccinea 267
-onia titthonus 238
-rhocorax graculus 120
-pyrrhocorax 120
-rhosoma nymphula 220
-rhula pyrrhula 147

-ercusia quercus 243

-a clavata 181
-llus aquaticus 90
-na esculenta 165
-ridibunda 166
-temporaria 166
-ngifer tarandus 56
-ohidia notata 273
-ttus norvegicus 38
-rattus 37
-curvirostra avosetta 98
-gulus ignicapillus 138
-regulus 138
-inocoris iracundus 226
-inolophus ferrumequinum 24
-odeus sericeus 176
-aria riparia 117
-sa tridactyla 102
-salia alpina 227
-picapra rupicapra 54
-tilus rutilus 173

-bella pavonina 277
-lamandra atra 168
-salamandra 168
-terdigitata 168
-lmo gairdneri 121
-salar 121
-trutta 121
-ticus scenicus 214
-lvelinus alpinus 171
-rcophaga carnaria 256
-xicola rubetra 129
-torquata 129
-arabaeus sacer 265
-ardinius erythrophthalmus 174
-iurus carolinensis 30
-vulgaris 30
-olia hirta 263
-oliopteryx libatrix 251
-olopax rusticola 97
-olytus scolytus 269
-omber scombrus 186
-ophthalmus rhombus 187
-utigera coleoptrata 274
-yliorhinus canicula 180
-hirus bicolor 226
-mibalanus balanoides 210
-pia officinalis 196
-rinus serinus 147
-rpula vermicularis 277
-sia apiformis 249
-alis lutaria 272
-cista betulina 40
-lurus glanis 178
-tta europaea 123
-laster papposus 191
-materia mollissima 73
-rex araneus 22
-minutus 22
-oalax microphthalmus 35
-atangus purpureus 190

Sphinx ligustri 247
Squalus acanthias 181
Stercorarius parasiticus 99
  skua 99
Sterna albifrons 102
  hirundo 102
  paradisaea 102
Stictocephala bisonia 227
Stizostedion lucioperca 179
Straphylinus olens 265
Streptopelia decaocto 105
  turtur 105
Strix aluco 108
Sturnus vulgaris 152
Suncus etruscus 23
Sus scrofa 52
Sylvia atricapilla 135
  borin 133
  communis 135
  curruca 135
  hortensis 133
  nisoria 134
  undata 136
Sympetrum sanguineum 221
Syngnathus rostellatus 183
Syrphus ribesii 255

Tabanus sudeticus 255
Tachypodiulus niger 275
Tadarida teniotis 25
Tadorna tadorna 73
Talpa europaea 21
Tarentola mauritanica 154
Tealia felina 279
Tegenaria gigantea 212
Telescopus fallax 161
Tellina crassa 205
  tenuis 205
Testudo hermanni 162
Tetrax tetrax 91
Tetrao tetrix 87
  urogallus 87
Tettigonia viridissima 223
Thecla betulae 243
Thrips tabaci 272
Thymallus thymallus 172
Tichodroma muraria 124
Timarcha tenebricosa 269
Tinca tinca 175
Tipula maxima 254
Trichia striolata 198
Trichiosoma tibiale 262
Tringa glareola 94
  hypoleucos 94
  nebularia 96
  ochropus 95
  totanus 96
Triturus alpestris 167
  cristatus 167
  helveticus 168
  marmoratus 167
  vulgaris 167
Trivia monacha 202
Troglodytes troglodytes 125
Turdus iliacus 127
  merula 127
  philomelos 126
  pilaris 126
  torquatus 127
  viscivorus 126
Turritella communis 200
Tylopsis liliifolia 223
Tyria jacobaeae 250
Tyto alba 107

Unio pictorum 206
Upupa epops 112
Uria aalge 103
Urocerus gigas 262
Ursus arctos 41

Vanellus vanellus 92
Vanessa atalanta 234
Venerupis rhomboides 205
Vespa crabro 260
Vespula vulgaris 260
Vipera aspis 161
  berus 161
  latasti 161
Vormela peregusna 44
Vulpes vulpes 43

Xestobium rufovillosum 268
Xylocopa violacea 258
Xysticus cristatus 216

Zygaena filipendulae 249
Zygiella x-notata 215

Most of the societies and organizations given here cater for amateur as well as professional interests. Many have libraries that members can use and most run schemes to help with the identification of material. Journals or newsletters for members are produced regularly by many of the societies.

Amateur Entomologists' Society
8 Heather Close, New Haw,
Weybridge, Surrey, KT15 3PF

Covers all kinds of insects and caters especially for young members. Numerous excursions and an annual exhibition. Exchange scheme for livestock.

British Arachnological Society
c/o Dr P. Selden,
Dept of Extra-Mural Studies,
University of Manchester, Oxford Road, Manchester, M13 9PL

Devoted to the study of all British arachnids as well as those from foreign lands.

British Butterfly Conservation Society
Tudor House, Quorn,
Leicestershire, LE12 8AD

Dedicated to the conservation of British butterflies. The society holds meetings and field trips in many parts of the country.

British Herpetological Society
c/o Zoological Society of London,
Regent's Park, London, NW1 4RY

Devoted to the study of all European reptiles and amphibians.

British Trust for Ornithology
The Nunnery, Thetford,
Norfolk IP24 2PU

Devoted to the study of all branches of ornithology, with a strong emphasis on the amateur. Many field excursions all over the country.

Field Studies Council
Preston Montford,
Montford Bridge,
Shrewsbury SY4 1HW

Promotes a better understanding of our environment. Runs field courses in all branches of natural history and countryside appreciation at ten centres in England and Wales.

Freshwater Biological Association
The Ferry House, Far Sawrey,
Ambleside, Cumbria, LA22 0LP

Devoted to the study of all life in freshwater. Publications include numerous keys for the identification of aquatic creatures.

Mammal Society (Youth Group)
c/o The Linnean Society,
Burlington House, Piccadilly,
London, W1V 0LQ

Encourages the study and conservation of all British mammals.

Marine Biological Association
The Laboratory, Citadel Hill,
Plymouth, Devon, PL1 2PB

Aims to promote knowledge and understanding of marine organisms.

Royal Society for Nature Conservation
The Green, Nettleham,
Lincs. LN2 2NR

Co-ordinates all the County Naturalists Trusts, of which there are more than 4 in Britain. Manages many reserves.

Royal Society for the Protection of Birds
The Lodge, Sandy,
Beds. SG19 2DL

Devoted to the conservation of wild birds, through education, scientific research, and the management of numerous bird reserves.

Scottish Field Studies Association
Kindrogan Field Centre, Enochdhu,
Blairgowrie, Perthshire, PH10 7PG

Encourages the study and conservation of wildlife and the countryside in Scotland. Organises numerous courses on a wide variety of wildlife topics.